INSTRUCTOR'S MANUAL
AND TEST BANK
TO ACCOMPANY

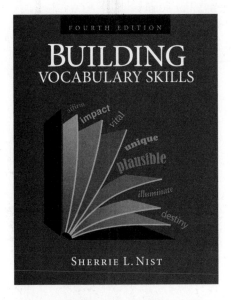

BUILDING VOCABULARY SKILLS, 4/e

IMPROVING VOCABULARY SKILLS, 4/e

ADVANCING VOCABULARY SKILLS, 4/e

JANET M. GOLDSTEIN

THE TOWNSEND PRESS VOCABULARY SERIES

Vocabulary Basics (reading level 4–6)
Groundwork for a Better Vocabulary (reading level 5–8)
Building Vocabulary Skills (reading level 7–9)
Improving Vocabulary Skills (reading level 9–11)
Advancing Vocabulary Skills (reading level 11–13)
*Building Vocabulary Skills, Short Version**
*Improving Vocabulary Skills, Short Version**
*Advancing Vocabulary Skills, Short Version**
Advanced Word Power (reading level 12–14)

*The short versions of the three books are limited to 200 words, in contrast to the 260 words and 40 word parts in each of the long versions. For some students and classes, the short versions of the books will provide an easier, more manageable approach to vocabulary development.

Copyright © 2010 by Townsend Press, Inc.
Printed in the United States of America
9 8 7 6 5 4 3 2 1

ISBN-13: 978-1-59194-205-4
ISBN-10: 1-59194-205-5

For book orders and requests for desk copies or supplements, contact us in any of the following ways:
By telephone: 1-800-772-6410
By fax: 1-800-225-8894
By e-mail: cs@townsendpress.com
Through our website: www.townsendpress.com

Contents

BUILDING VOCABULARY SKILLS: Additional Unit Tests　　**71**

IMPROVING VOCABULARY SKILLS: Pretests and Posttests　　**81**

IMPROVING VOCABULARY SKILLS: Answers to the Activities in the Book　　**113**

IMPROVING VOCABULARY SKILLS: Additional Mastery Tests　　**117**

IMPROVING VOCABULARY SKILLS: Additional Unit Tests　　**145**

Introduction

BRIEF GUIDELINES FOR USING THE VOCABULARY BOOKS

1. As you probably know, each of the three vocabulary books has a recommended reading level:

Building Vocabulary Skills: reading grade level 7–9
Improving Vocabulary Skills: reading grade level 9–11
Advancing Vocabulary Skills: reading grade level 11–13

Be careful not to choose a book on too high an instructional level. Ideally, most of your students should have a sense of *some* of the words in the book you choose. As they work through the chapters, they can then strengthen their knowledge of the words they already know, as well as master the words they're only half sure of, or don't know at all. To help you choose the appropriate book, you can give students the TP Vocabulary Placement Test, offered online or reprinted on pages 229–234 of this *Instructor's Manual.*

A given level is likely to be too difficult if students know almost none of the words. You run the risk of operating on a level of frustration rather than instruction. *To repeat, then: Please take very special care that you choose a book that will not be too difficult for the majority of your students.*

2. Don't feel you must cover every single chapter in a book. Each book is packed with activities—ones that will take a fair amount of time for students to work on at home, or for you to cover with them in class. The activities are necessary, for the simple truth is that the more students work with words, the better they will understand them. *It is better to cover fewer words more thoroughly than to try to cover too many too lightly.*

3. The "Final Check" passage in each chapter poses a more difficult challenge for students than the sentence-level activities that precede it. To handle the passages, students must have done their homework with the earlier activities. The passage will be an excellent final opportunity for them to deepen their knowledge of the words in the chapter.

Because the final check is such a challenge, as well as an opportunity to solidify learning, you should *not* use it as a mastery test. Instead, use the appropriate mastery test in this manual.

4. The pages in the student book (though not in the instructor's edition) are perforated and so can be easily torn out and removed. In particular, you may want students to hand in the unit tests, which are on the front and back sides of a page.

5. Pretests are available for each book as well as each vocabulary unit in each book. The pretests start on page 7 of this *Instructor's Manual.* You have permission to make as many copies as you want of these pretests (and the other materials in this book) if you are currently using one of the vocabulary texts in a course. The pretests can be used at the start of a unit, and the posttests at the end of a unit, as an accurate way to measure vocabulary progress and mastery.

A SUGGESTED INSTRUCTIONAL APPROACH

Here is a suggested classroom approach that will maintain interest and keep students active in learning the words. You may want to use all or part of it—or you may find that it helps you decide the special way you want to teach the words to your students.

First of all, have students work through the introduction to the book (on pages 1 to 6). Don't teach it; have them *read* it (they need the reading practice!), follow directions, and insert all the answers needed. Then spend a few minutes reviewing their answers and checking their understanding of the material.

Next, give students the pretest for the unit you will be covering. Explain that at the end of the unit, they will be given a posttest on the same words, so you and they will be able to measure what they have learned. Then proceed as follows:

1. Preview each of the ten words in a chapter by printing the words, one at a time, on the board. Ask students if they can pronounce each word. As needed, write some of the pronunciations on the board. You may also want to use, or ask students to use, some of the words in sentences. And it's OK to ask for or to give short meanings of some of the words. Don't go into a lot of detail, but make this a good general introduction to the words.

Then, based on the verbal preview, ask students to turn to the first page of the chapter. Explain that in each case the two sentences in "Ten Words in Context" will give clues to the meaning of the boldfaced word. You can say, "OK, take five minutes or so and read the sentences in "Ten Words in Context." Or you can proceed immediately to Step 2.

2. Put students in groups of two or three. (It is hard to overstate the value that small-group work can have: if managed successfully, it uses peer pressure to keep everyone involved in the work of the class.) Explain, "Here's what I want you to do. One of you read the first word and the two sentences that contain the word. Make sure the word is being pronounced correctly. Always help each other out with the pronunciation. Then think about the context very carefully. The context will give you very strong clues as to what the word means. Your ability to use the context surrounding an unfamiliar word is an excellent skill to have whenever you're reading something and you come upon a word you don't know. Then I'd like all of you to see if you can pick out the right meaning from the three answer choices that follow that first word.

"After you do that, have someone else in your group pronounce the second word and read the two sentences for that word. Then work together again and pick out the right answer choice. And so on, until you've done all ten words. Look up at me when you've done all the words."

3. Of course, not every group will finish the words at exactly the same time. Therefore, you should take a middle-ground approach to the challenging fact that every group will move at a different speed. When a couple of the groups are finished (and starting to get restless), and others are still working, say, "OK—even if you're not quite finished yet, we're going to go over the ten words as a class. Somebody please volunteer to pronounce the first word and give us its meaning."

4. After reviewing the pronunciations and meanings of the words, ask your students to complete the "Matching Words with Definitions" activity. They'll need these definitions to complete the remaining activities in the chapter, so be sure that students have the correct definition for each word.

5. Once you have checked their answers to the matching activity, say, "Now I want you to work as a group in adding the words needed in Sentence Check 1 and Sentence Check 2. Again, you want to practice *looking at context* very carefully. Context will give you clues you need to figure out the meanings of words."

6. When several groups are finished, say, "OK, not everyone is quite finished, but we're going to go over the sentences you've been working with. Will someone volunteer to read the first sentence and insert the word needed?"

7. Next, say, "The last activity here is the most challenging. Why don't you all work on this individually. Read over the passage once. Then go back and start reading more carefully and slowly, and try to put in some of the words. Then go back a third time to get the remaining words. You may not be able to get all the words at first. Try to get some of them. That will help you do the rest. Pay close attention to the context. Remember you're building up your skill at using context to figure out the meaning of a word."

8. When some people are finished, say, "All right—let's review the passage. Would someone read the first couple of sentences and insert the missing words?"

9. Finally, tell students to review and study the ten words at home. Then, at the beginning of the next class, say, "Spend about two minutes reviewing the words. I'll then pass out a mastery test for the ten words. I will grade this test, so you want to do your best to remember the words." (Knowing that a grade is going to be involved always provides students with an extra boost of incentive.)

An alternative instructional approach is to proceed as described above for steps 1 to 4. Then, instead of having students work in small groups, ask them to work individually on Sentence Check 1 and Sentence Check 2. After they are finished, have them come individually to your desk so that you can quickly check their answers, clarify any confusion, and move them on to the Final Check. In this individualized scenario, everyone is working at his or her own pace, and you are working at a *very* steady pace. When students finish the Final Check, you can either have them work with people who are not done, or get a head start on another chapter that you plan to assign for homework.

ADDITIONAL ACTIVITIES

To repeat a point stated earlier: *The more students work with words, the more they can learn.* Here are other activities you can use, in addition to the many in the book. Choose whichever combination of activities goes best with your teaching style and the learning styles of your students.

1. Word cards. Students can use 3 × 5 or 4 × 6 index cards to create a bank of words. Word cards can help students master words in the book; the cards are also a helpful tool for learning unknown words that students come across in reading. Students simply jot down an unfamiliar word on the front of the card. Then, when they have finished their reading, they can complete the front and back of a card. Here is a suggested format:

Front of Card

p. 21, IVS	Adjective
succinct	
Synonym: concise	Antonym: lengthy

Back of Card

1) Expressed clearly in a few words.

2) A classified ad in a newspaper should be <u>succinct</u> so that you get your message across clearly without paying for more words than necessary.

3) In the workshop for office employees, the speaker explained how to write <u>succinct</u>, yet informative memos.

Note that the front of the card has the target word, the page number and source where the word can be located, the part of speech, a synonym, and an antonym. The back of the card has three entries: 1) the *definition*, based on the way the word is used in context; 2) a *phrase or sentence* showing the word in context (this can be taken from the source where the student has come upon the word); and 3) a *student-created sentence* which shows an understanding of the word. Students can use this same format when they encounter unfamiliar words in their textbooks and other reading.

2. Identifying words. Present lists of words written with diacritical marks and ask students to identify the words. For example:

tăk′tĭk _____

rĭ-kûr′ _____

ĭ-kwāt′ _____

mă-lĭsh′əs _____

rĭ-sĭp′rə-kāt _____

3. Analogies. Using analogies is another way to encourage students to think about words. Students should first be taught the format of analogies, and instructors should begin with the simpler types of analogies: synonyms and antonyms. For example:

Choose the italicized word needed to complete each analogy:

acknowledge : admit = avert : *cure, prevent, accept*

candid : dishonest = concise : *wordy, brief, funny*

precise : methodical = stop : *terminate, speculate, nurture*

modern : obsolete = pacify : *mediate, hamper, infuriate*

Keep in mind that analogies are difficult for students, especially at-risk students. But if instructor guidance is provided, analogies can help even at-risk students think about words conceptually.

Note that pages 5 and 6 in the introduction to the book explain how analogies work. Also, Unit Test 3 in each unit contains twenty word analogies.

4. Imaging. The use of imagery as a way of remembering vocabulary words has been researched rather extensively. Results typically indicate that students who are trained to use imagery techniques—or in simple terms, told to "form pictures in their minds"—remember the meanings of words better than those who do not employ such techniques.

Here's an example: Think of a mugger facing you, his hands clutching a long, heavy piece of gray pipe. On the pipe are written in dripping red paint the letters C-O-M-P-L-Y. You are handing over your wallet.

It's a good idea to take five or ten minutes every once in a while for students to get a piece of paper and write up their images—the more vivid the better—for remembering a given word in a chapter. Then ask students to hand in the paper (signing their names to the paper is optional). Quickly flip through the papers, reading the most effective ones aloud to the class.

5. Generating sentences. Have students generate their own sentences using the words, or as a more advanced activity, have them write a story using five of the words. (You may want to have a paraprofessional working with you for these activities, which require individual checking and detailed feedback.)

6. Group-Label. This more abstract activity is best used after students have a larger word bank from which to work. It might be used at the end of a unit of five vocabulary chapters. Students are asked to classify words into groups and to give each group a label that would be common somehow to all words in that group. Here are examples:

Words related to honesty	*Words relating to conflict*
(BVS, Unit One)	*(IVS, Unit One)*
acknowledge	antagonist
candid	animosity
impartial	sabotage
integrity	exploit
legitimate	assail

SUGGESTED SYLLABI

Suggested Syllabus for Using the Book as a Core Text

Since each book consists of 30 chapters packed with activities, it can easily serve as a core text for a vocabulary course—especially when supplemented by the test bank and the online exercises. In a 15-week class that meets three hours a week, you can cover two lessons in two class hours. The third class hour can be used for the unit tests that close each of the five units in each book, as well as for the pretests, posttests, mastery tests, and the additional material available online.

It is important that students be encouraged to do a lot of reading at the same time that they are learning vocabulary words. For students who need to develop vocabulary skills, widespread reading, in addition to continuing, intensive work on vocabulary, is the best way to achieve this purpose.

Suggested Syllabus for Using the Book as a Supplement in a Reading Course

In many courses, the vocabulary book will serve as a supplementary text. In such cases, and assuming a 15-week term with three hours of class a week, either of two approaches is suggested:

Approach 1: Limit your coverage to 15 vocabulary chapters in the term, one a week. Exclude the word parts chapters (which may require more time to be of benefit to students than you have to spend), and cover Chapters 1–5 of Unit One, Chapters 7–11 of Unit Two, and Chapters 13–17 of Unit Three.

In part of the one class hour you spend on vocabulary, go over the first three pages in class, using a method similar to the one described on pages 2–3 of this manual. Assign the last part of the chapter (Sentence Check 2 and the Final Check) for homework. Then, as the first item of business in the next class, review that page. Follow up the review with the appropriate mastery test from the manual.

If only 15 chapters are covered, and there is a second course in the reading sequence at your school, the book can be continued and completed in that second course.

Approach 2: Cover 15 vocabulary chapters in class, and assign the 11 remaining vocabulary chapters as homework. Then, at the end of each unit of five vocabulary chapters, give students one of the three vocabulary unit tests in the book. The unit test will enable you to hold students responsible for the outside-of-class vocabulary chapters as well.

You might want to tell students in advance that you will give them one of the unit tests. However, don't tell them *which* of the three tests you will give. Encourage them, in other words, to review all of the words in the unit test materials.

If there is not enough time in class to give the unit tests, you can ask students to do all three of the unit tests at home. Then, in class, collect and grade *one* of the three. (Again, students should not know which of the three you will collect. That way, they will have to assume responsibility for learning all of the words.)

ABOUT THE ONLINE EXERCISES

After students complete a vocabulary chapter in the book, they can deepen their learning by going to **www.townsendpress.com** and clicking on "Online Learning Center." Here, they will find two additional tests for each chapter in each Townsend Press vocabulary book: one testing *words in context*, the other (more advanced) testing the *meanings of the words without context*.

These online tests contain a number of user- and instructor-friendly features, including actual, audible pronunciations of each word; brief explanations of the answers; a sound option; a running score at the bottom of the screen; and a record-keeping file. Students can access their scores at any time; instructors can access student scores and print score reports for individuals or entire classes.

The advanced features of the Online Learning Center allow instructors to assign additional online tests based on exercises and tests in the books, drop students from and add students to a class roster, choose which explanations a student may view, and scramble the items in a particular test.

Here are more details about the features of this powerful online program:

- Frequent use is made of the user's first name—a highly motivational word to any student!

- Every answer is followed by a brief explanation of that answer. Such explanations help ensure learning. Thus the software *teaches* as well as tests.

- A running score appears at the bottom of each screen, so the user always knows how well he or she is doing.

- A score file, available to each student and to the instructor, shows or prints out the user's final scores.

POWERPOINT PRESENTATIONS

PowerPoint presentations are available for each book and may be downloaded from the "Supplements" area for instructors at **www.townsendpress.com**.

ABOUT THE WORD LISTS

As stated in the preface, word frequency lists were consulted in selecting the vocabulary words used in each book in the TP Vocabulary Series. Two sources in particular should be noted:

Word Frequency Book—John B. Carroll, Peter Davies, and Barry Richman
The American Heritage Publishing Company, Inc.

The Living Word Vocabulary—Edgar Dale and Joseph O'Rourke
World Book–Childcraft International, Inc.

Also consulted were lists in a wide number of vocabulary books as well as words in standardized reading tests. In addition, the authors and editors prepared their own lists. A computer was used to help in the consolidation of the many word lists. Group discussion then led to final decisions about the words that would be most appropriate for students on each reading level.

RESEARCH AND VOCABULARY INSTRUCTION

Sherrie Nist has prepared an article offering suggestions on vocabulary instruction in the context of current research on vocabulary development. Some of the article has been incorporated into this introduction. The article, which includes an extensive bibliography, is available at no charge by writing to Townsend Press.

A FINAL NOTE

The authors and editors invite you to share with us your experiences in using the Townsend Press vocabulary books. This series is not a static project; it will continue to be revised on a regular basis, and we welcome your suggestions as well as details about your ongoing classroom experiences with the texts. Send your comments to the Vocabulary Series Editor, Townsend Press, 439 Kelley Drive, West Berlin, NJ 08091; or email us at **cs@townsendpress.com**. By learning your reactions and your students' reactions, we can work at making what we feel are very good books even better.

Pretest

This test contains 100 items. In the space provided, write the letter of the choice that is closest in meaning to the **boldfaced** word.

Important: Keep in mind that this test is for diagnostic purposes only. **If you do not know a word, leave the space blank rather than guess at it.**

_____ 1. **compel**   **a)** avoid   **b)** delight   **c)** force   **d)** finish

_____ 2. **drastic**   **a)** dirty   **b)** suitable   **c)** extreme   **d)** sticky

_____ 3. **comply**   **a)** choose   **b)** forget   **c)** run into   **d)** do as asked

_____ 4. **acknowledge**   **a)** prevent   **b)** admit   **c)** study   **d)** deny

_____ 5. **concise**   **a)** peaceful   **b)** clear and brief   **c)** proper   **d)** wordy

_____ 6. **isolate**   **a)** combine   **b)** heat up   **c)** separate   **d)** freeze

_____ 7. **fortify**   **a)** suggest   **b)** strengthen   **c)** avoid   **d)** approve of

_____ 8. **extensive**   **a)** bold   **b)** separated   **c)** outside   **d)** large in space or amount

_____ 9. **refuge**   **a)** shelter   **b)** rejection   **c)** building   **d)** garbage

_____ 10. **erratic**   **a)** inconsistent   **b)** mistaken   **c)** in a city   **d)** noisy

_____ 11. **morale**   **a)** spirit   **b)** principle   **c)** threat   **d)** majority

_____ 12. **lenient**   **a)** heavy   **b)** not strict   **c)** delayed   **d)** not biased

_____ 13. **undermine**   **a)** weaken   **b)** cross out   **c)** reach   **d)** dig up

_____ 14. **menace**   **a)** character   **b)** threat   **c)** assistance   **d)** puzzle

_____ 15. **impartial**   **a)** without prejudice   **b)** not whole   **c)** hidden   **d)** strict

_____ 16. **endorse**   **a)** suggest   **b)** stop   **c)** support   **d)** start

_____ 17. **imply**   **a)** approve of   **b)** interfere   **c)** do mischief   **d)** suggest

_____ 18. **obstacle**   **a)** barrier   **b)** remedy   **c)** list   **d)** answer

_____ 19. **novice**   **a)** book   **b)** false impression   **c)** beginner   **d)** servant

_____ 20. **hypocrite**   **a)** interference   **b)** insincere person   **c)** injection   **d)** threat

_____ 21. **superficial**   **a)** lacking depth   **b)** perfect   **c)** very deep   **d)** faulty

_____ 22. **denounce**   **a)** introduce   **b)** condemn   **c)** change   **d)** compliment

_____ 23. **transition**   **a)** purchase   **b)** invention   **c)** repetition   **d)** change

_____ 24. **sustain**   **a)** keep going   **b)** approve of   **c)** avoid   **d)** wait for

_____ 25. **conservative**   **a)** not definite   **b)** opinionated   **c)** resisting change   **d)** understanding

(Continues on next page)

____ 26. **compensate**   a) change   b) win out   c) receive   d) repay

____ 27. **verify**   a) imagine   b) prove   c) keep going   d) cancel

____ 28. **surpass**   a) go beyond   b) reverse   c) take   d) prove wrong

____ 29. **tentative**   a) suitable   b) not final   c) outside   d) definite

____ 30. **diversity**   a) separation   b) conclusion   c) enthusiasm   d) variety

____ 31. **prudent**   a) rudely brief   b) careful   c) obvious   d) delicate

____ 32. **apprehensive**   a) uneasy   b) thoughtful   c) relaxed   d) opinionated

____ 33. **acute**   a) mild   b) dull   c) severe   d) nervous

____ 34. **prominent**   a) clean   b) obvious   c) dangerous   d) reasonable

____ 35. **arrogant**   a) wealthy   b) ridiculous   c) average   d) overly proud

____ 36. **cite**   a) repeat   b) mention in support   c) look for   d) read

____ 37. **retort**   a) great respect   b) sharp reply   c) false idea   d) court order

____ 38. **exempt**   a) needed badly   b) attacked   c) unconcerned   d) free of a duty

____ 39. **accessible**   a) easily reached   b) itchy   c) difficult   d) folded

____ 40. **prevail**   a) climb   b) win out   c) lose   d) enroll early

____ 41. **evasive**   a) talkative   b) deliberately unclear   c) friendly   d) overly forceful

____ 42. **elapse**   a) flow   b) pass by   c) measure   d) record

____ 43. **lethal**   a) sweet-smelling   b) ancient   c) deadly   d) healthy

____ 44. **ordeal**   a) change   b) painful experience   c) good time   d) office

____ 45. **infer**   a) offer   b) conclude   c) reject   d) answer

____ 46. **unique**   a) common   b) pure   c) one-of-a-kind   d) well-known

____ 47. **subtle**   a) early   b) direct   c) not obvious   d) surprising

____ 48. **devise**   a) steal   b) escape   c) think up   d) redo

____ 49. **stimulate**   a) arouse   b) anger   c) make tired   d) confuse

____ 50. **convey**   a) communicate   b) allow   c) invent   d) approve

(Continues on next page)

____ 51. **inevitable**   a) unavoidable   b) dangerous   c) spiteful   d) doubtful

____ 52. **equate**   a) adjust   b) consider equal   c) attack   d) overcome

____ 53. **patron**   a) father   b) enemy   c) steady customer   d) one with a hopeless view

____ 54. **option**   a) problem   b) requirement   c) attitude   d) choice

____ 55. **endeavor**   a) meet   b) state   c) try   d) avoid

____ 56. **refute**   a) prove wrong   b) replay   c) appeal   d) walk

____ 57. **dismay**   a) thrill   b) lift   c) return   d) discourage

____ 58. **reciprocate**   a) pay back   b) frown   c) slip   d) step

____ 59. **retain**   a) return   b) keep   c) redo   d) come forth

____ 60. **adapt**   a) stick to something   b) adjust to a situation   c) avoid   d) strike

____ 61. **indifferent**   a) similar   b) calm   c) well-adjusted   d) unconcerned

____ 62. **elaborate**   a) large   b) complex   c) expensive   d) boring

____ 63. **liberal**   a) generous   b) thrifty   c) famous   d) short

____ 64. **mediocre**   a) outstanding   b) ordinary   c) bad-tasting   d) believable

____ 65. **emerge**   a) go under water   b) come forth   c) lie   d) draw back

____ 66. **elite**   a) free   b) underprivileged   c) superior   d) proud

____ 67. **essence**   a) fundamental characteristic   b) tiny part   c) much later   d) rule

____ 68. **allude**   a) refer indirectly   b) damage   c) protest   d) pay back

____ 69. **impair**   a) fix   b) write down   c) employ   d) damage

____ 70. **coerce**   a) attract   b) refuse   c) remove   d) force

____ 71. **plausible**   a) boring   b) unbearable   c) believable   d) misspelled

____ 72. **recur**   a) prevent   b) remember   c) forget   d) occur again

____ 73. **revoke**   a) annoy   b) protest   c) cancel   d) adjust

____ 74. **stereotype**   a) oversimplified image   b) two channels   c) plan   d) photograph

____ 75. **reprimand**   a) harsh criticism   b) business deal   c) ruling   d) answer

(Continues on next page)

____	76. **destiny**	**a)** freedom	**b)** fate	**c)** generosity	**d)** boredom
____	77. **tedious**	**a)** difficult	**b)** heavy	**c)** ridiculous	**d)** boring
____	78. **detain**	**a)** care for	**b)** attract	**c)** delay	**d)** describe
____	79. **consequence**	**a)** falsehood	**b)** result	**c)** method	**d)** series
____	80. **diminish**	**a)** lessen	**b)** make darker	**c)** enlarge	**d)** move upward
____	81. **site**	**a)** silence	**b)** location	**c)** time	**d)** vision
____	82. **discriminate**	**a)** arrest	**b)** delay	**c)** distinguish	**d)** discuss
____	83. **profound**	**a)** kind	**b)** deeply felt	**c)** cautious	**d)** logical
____	84. **vocation**	**a)** hobby	**b)** trip	**c)** report	**d)** profession
____	85. **subside**	**a)** calm down	**b)** insult	**c)** arouse	**d)** tire easily
____	86. **intervene**	**a)** come between	**b)** arrest	**c)** resist	**d)** send for
____	87. **sedate**	**a)** bold	**b)** plain	**c)** calm	**d)** pure
____	88. **perceptive**	**a)** brave	**b)** available	**c)** aware	**d)** careless
____	89. **innate**	**a)** learned	**b)** underneath	**c)** inborn	**d)** clever
____	90. **obstinate**	**a)** friendly	**b)** frightful	**c)** stubborn	**d)** cautious
____	91. **susceptible**	**a)** easily affected	**b)** greedy	**c)** lazy	**d)** easily noticed
____	92. **defy**	**a)** send for	**b)** approve	**c)** improve	**d)** resist
____	93. **valid**	**a)** logical	**b)** pure	**c)** clever	**d)** gloomy
____	94. **confirm**	**a)** follow	**b)** reject	**c)** support the truth of something	**d)** speed up
____	95. **vigorous**	**a)** harsh	**b)** energetic	**c)** kind	**d)** rushed
____	96. **adverse**	**a)** strict	**b)** profitable	**c)** rhyming	**d)** harmful
____	97. **coherent**	**a)** necessary	**b)** lively	**c)** wordy	**d)** logical and orderly
____	98. **deteriorate**	**a)** worsen	**b)** speed up	**c)** age	**d)** take advantage of
____	99. **comparable**	**a)** odd	**b)** similar	**c)** unavoidable	**d)** lacking
____	100. **audible**	**a)** nearby	**b)** believable	**c)** willing	**d)** able to be heard

---

STOP. This is the end of the test. If there is time remaining, you may go back and recheck your answers. When the time is up, hand in both your answer sheet and this test booklet to your instructor.

Posttest

> This test contains 100 items. In the space provided, write the letter of the choice that is closest in meaning to the **boldfaced** word.

_____ 1. **compel**　　**a)** finish　**b)** delight　**c)** force　**d)** avoid

_____ 2. **isolate**　　**a)** separate　**b)** heat up　**c)** combine　**d)** freeze

_____ 3. **endorse**　　**a)** suggest　**b)** stop　**c)** support　**d)** start

_____ 4. **refuge**　　**a)** garbage　**b)** building　**c)** rejection　**d)** shelter

_____ 5. **menace**　　**a)** character　**b)** threat　**c)** assistance　**d)** puzzle

_____ 6. **transition**　　**a)** invention　**b)** purchase　**c)** repetition　**d)** change

_____ 7. **acknowledge**　　**a)** prevent　**b)** study　**c)** admit　**d)** deny

_____ 8. **superficial**　　**a)** lacking depth　**b)** perfect　**c)** very deep　**d)** faulty

_____ 9. **extensive**　　**a)** outside　**b)** large in space or amount　**c)** bold　**d)** separated

_____ 10. **denounce**　　**a)** introduce　**b)** condemn　**c)** change　**d)** compliment

_____ 11. **morale**　　**a)** spirit　**b)** majority　**c)** threat　**d)** principle

_____ 12. **undermine**　　**a)** cross out　**b)** weaken　**c)** reach　**d)** dig up

_____ 13. **drastic**　　**a)** dirty　**b)** extreme　**c)** suitable　**d)** sticky

_____ 14. **impartial**　　**a)** strict　**b)** not whole　**c)** hidden　**d)** without prejudice

_____ 15. **imply**　　**a)** approve of　**b)** interfere　**c)** do mischief　**d)** suggest

_____ 16. **fortify**　　**a)** avoid　**b)** strengthen　**c)** approve of　**d)** suggest

_____ 17. **concise**　　**a)** wordy　**b)** clear and brief　**c)** peaceful　**d)** proper

_____ 18. **conservative**　　**a)** not definite　**b)** opinionated　**c)** resisting change　**d)** understanding

_____ 19. **novice**　　**a)** false impression　**b)** book　**c)** beginner　**d)** servant

_____ 20. **erratic**　　**a)** inconsistent　**b)** mistaken　**c)** in a city　**d)** noisy

_____ 21. **hypocrite**　　**a)** injection　**b)** insincere person　**c)** interference　**d)** threat

_____ 22. **lenient**　　**a)** not biased　**b)** not strict　**c)** delayed　**d)** heavy

_____ 23. **sustain**　　**a)** avoid　**b)** approve of　**c)** wait for　**d)** keep going

_____ 24. **obstacle**　　**a)** remedy　**b)** list　**c)** answer　**d)** barrier

_____ 25. **comply**　　**a)** choose　**b)** run into　**c)** forget　**d)** do as asked

(Continues on next page)

____ 26. **arrogant**   a) average   b) wealthy   c) ridiculous   d) overly proud

____ 27. **infer**   a) offer   b) conclude   c) reject   d) answer

____ 28. **verify**   a) cancel   b) prove   c) keep going   d) improve

____ 29. **prudent**   a) rudely brief   b) careful   c) obvious   d) delicate

____ 30. **evasive**   a) talkative   b) deliberately unclear   c) friendly   d) overly forceful

____ 31. **apprehensive**   a) relaxed   b) thoughtful   c) opinionated   d) uneasy

____ 32. **accessible**   a) easily reached   b) folded   c) difficult   d) itchy

____ 33. **unique**   a) pure   b) common   c) one-of-a-kind   d) well-known

____ 34. **acute**   a) dull   b) mild   c) nervous   d) severe

____ 35. **subtle**   a) surprising   b) direct   c) not obvious   d) early

____ 36. **retort**   a) great respect   b) sharp reply   c) false idea   d) court order

____ 37. **diversity**   a) variety   b) enthusiasm   c) conclusion   d) separation

____ 38. **exempt**   a) needed badly   b) attacked   c) unconcerned   d) free of a duty

____ 39. **devise**   a) escape   b) think up   c) steal   d) redo

____ 40. **compensate**   a) receive   b) win out   c) change   d) repay

____ 41. **cite**   a) read   b) mention in support   c) look for   d) repeat

____ 42. **convey**   a) invent   b) allow   c) communicate   d) approve

____ 43. **lethal**   a) sweet-smelling   b) healthy   c) ancient   d) deadly

____ 44. **surpass**   a) go beyond   b) reverse   c) take   d) prove wrong

____ 45. **ordeal**   a) office   b) painful experience   c) good time   d) change

____ 46. **prevail**   a) lose   b) enroll early   c) climb   d) win out

____ 47. **stimulate**   a) arouse   b) anger   c) make tired   d) confuse

____ 48. **tentative**   a) definite   b) not final   c) outside   d) suitable

____ 49. **elapse**   a) pass by   b) record   c) measure   d) flow

____ 50. **prominent**   a) dangerous   b) clean   c) obvious   d) reasonable

(Continues on next page)

_____ 51. **option**   a) attitude   b) requirement   c) problem   d) choice

_____ 52. **reprimand**   a) business deal   b) harsh criticism   c) answer   d) ruling

_____ 53. **adapt**   a) adjust to a situation   b) stick to something   c) avoid   d) strike

_____ 54. **refute**   a) prove wrong   b) replay   c) appeal   d) walk

_____ 55. **plausible**   a) boring   b) unbearable   c) believable   d) misspelled

_____ 56. **reciprocate**   a) pay back   b) step   c) frown   d) slip

_____ 57. **essence**   a) rule   b) tiny part   c) much later   d) fundamental characteristic

_____ 58. **revoke**   a) adjust   b) annoy   c) protect   d) cancel

_____ 59. **retain**   a) redo   b) keep   c) return   d) come forth

_____ 60. **inevitable**   a) unavoidable   b) dangerous   c) spiteful   d) doubtful

_____ 61. **emerge**   a) draw back   b) come forth   c) lie   d) go under water

_____ 62. **impair**   a) damage   b) employ   c) write down   d) fix

_____ 63. **equate**   a) overcome   b) consider equal   c) attack   d) adjust

_____ 64. **coerce**   a) attract   b) refuse   c) remove   d) force

_____ 65. **patron**   a) steady customer   b) enemy   c) father   d) one with a hopeless view

_____ 66. **liberal**   a) thrifty   b) generous   c) short   d) famous

_____ 67. **dismay**   a) thrill   b) lift   c) return   d) discourage

_____ 68. **elite**   a) underprivileged   b) free   c) proud   d) superior

_____ 69. **endeavor**   a) state   b) meet   c) avoid   d) try

_____ 70. **allude**   a) pay back   b) damage   c) protest   d) refer indirectly

_____ 71. **recur**   a) occur again   b) remember   c) forget   d) prevent

_____ 72. **indifferent**   a) similar   b) calm   c) well-adjusted   d) unconcerned

_____ 73. **mediocre**   a) believable   b) outstanding   c) bad-tasting   d) ordinary

_____ 74. **stereotype**   a) photograph   b) oversimplified image   c) plan   d) two channels

_____ 75. **elaborate**   a) large   b) complex   c) expensive   d) boring

(Continues on next page)

____	76. **destiny**	a) fate	b) freedom	c) generosity	d) boredom
____	77. **deteriorate**	a) worsen	b) speed up	c) age	d) take advantage of
____	78. **perceptive**	a) careless	b) available	c) aware	d) brave
____	79. **sedate**	a) plain	b) bold	c) pure	d) calm
____	80. **vocation**	a) profession	b) hobby	c) trip	d) report
____	81. **innate**	a) learned	b) underneath	c) inborn	d) clever
____	82. **detain**	a) care for	b) delay	c) describe	d) attract
____	83. **diminish**	a) move upward	b) make darker	c) enlarge	d) lessen
____	84. **coherent**	a) necessary	b) lively	c) wordy	d) logical and orderly
____	85. **intervene**	a) send for	b) come between	c) arrest	d) resist
____	86. **profound**	a) cautious	b) deeply felt	c) kind	d) logical
____	87. **obstinate**	a) frightful	b) stubborn	c) friendly	d) cautious
____	88. **comparable**	a) similar	b) odd	c) unavoidable	d) lacking
____	89. **susceptible**	a) easily affected	b) greedy	c) lazy	d) easily noticed
____	90. **consequence**	a) series	b) falsehood	c) result	d) method
____	91. **valid**	a) clever	b) pure	c) logical	d) gloomy
____	92. **confirm**	a) follow	b) reject	c) support the truth of something	d) speed up
____	93. **site**	a) silence	b) time	c) location	d) vision
____	94. **vigorous**	a) kind	b) rushed	c) harsh	d) energetic
____	95. **discriminate**	a) arrest	b) delay	c) distinguish	d) harm
____	96. **tedious**	a) difficult	b) boring	c) ridiculous	d) heavy
____	97. **adverse**	a) harmful	b) profitable	c) rhyming	d) strict
____	98. **defy**	a) send for	b) approve	c) improve	d) resist
____	99. **subside**	a) tire easily	b) arouse	c) insult	d) calm down
____	100. **audible**	a) willing	b) believable	c) nearby	d) able to be heard

STOP. This is the end of the test. If there is time remaining, you may go back and recheck your answers. When the time is up, hand in both your answer sheet and this test booklet to your instructor.

Unit One: *Pretest*

In the space provided, write the letter of the choice that is closest in meaning to the **boldfaced** word.

_____ 1. **compel**   **a)** avoid   **b)** delight   **c)** force   **d)** finish

_____ 2. **avert**   **a)** begin   **b)** travel   **c)** prevent   **d)** do too late

_____ 3. **drastic**   **a)** dirty   **b)** suitable   **c)** extreme   **d)** sticky

_____ 4. **anecdote**   **a)** brief story   **b)** reply   **c)** cure   **d)** confession

_____ 5. **comply**   **a)** choose   **b)** forget   **c)** run into   **d)** do as asked

_____ 6. **alternative**   **a)** command   **b)** design   **c)** assignment   **d)** choice

_____ 7. **acknowledge**   **a)** prevent   **b)** admit   **c)** study   **d)** deny

_____ 8. **candid**   **a)** honest   **b)** intense   **c)** long   **d)** improper

_____ 9. **concise**   **a)** peaceful   **b)** clear and brief   **c)** proper   **d)** wordy

_____ 10. **appropriate**   **a)** illegal   **b)** proper   **c)** extreme   **d)** well-dressed

_____ 11. **illuminate**   **a)** lose   **b)** become sick   **c)** light up   **d)** desire greatly

_____ 12. **urban**   **a)** of a city   **b)** circular   **c)** not allowed   **d)** large

_____ 13. **reminisce**   **a)** gather   **b)** remember   **c)** travel   **d)** strengthen

_____ 14. **isolate**   **a)** combine   **b)** heat up   **c)** separate   **d)** freeze

_____ 15. **fortify**   **a)** suggest   **b)** strengthen   **c)** avoid   **d)** approve of

_____ 16. **extensive**   **a)** bold   **b)** separated   **c)** outside   **d)** large in space or amount

_____ 17. **forfeit**   **a)** lose   **b)** draw   **c)** give   **d)** recall

_____ 18. **refuge**   **a)** shelter   **b)** rejection   **c)** building   **d)** garbage

_____ 19. **dialog**   **a)** answer   **b)** story   **c)** a passage of conversation   **d)** belief

_____ 20. **erratic**   **a)** inconsistent   **b)** mistaken   **c)** in a city   **d)** noisy

_____ 21. **legitimate**   **a)** threatening   **b)** profitable   **c)** obvious   **d)** lawful

_____ 22. **overt**   **a)** proper   **b)** obvious   **c)** completed   **d)** fair

_____ 23. **morale**   **a)** spirit   **b)** principle   **c)** threat   **d)** majority

_____ 24. **lenient**   **a)** heavy   **b)** not strict   **c)** delayed   **d)** not biased

_____ 25. **delete**   **a)** obey   **b)** go away   **c)** erase   **d)** damage

(Continues on next page)

_____ 26. **integrity**   **a)** threat   **b)** inside   **c)** complication   **d)** honesty

_____ 27. **naive**   **a)** clever   **b)** fair   **c)** unsuspecting   **d)** merciful

_____ 28. **undermine**   **a)** weaken   **b)** cross out   **c)** reach   **d)** dig up

_____ 29. **menace**   **a)** character   **b)** threat   **c)** assistance   **d)** puzzle

_____ 30. **impartial**   **a)** without prejudice   **b)** not whole   **c)** hidden   **d)** strict

_____ 31. **apathy**   **a)** route   **b)** harm   **c)** lack of interest   **d)** pity

_____ 32. **ruthless**   **a)** private   **b)** weakened   **c)** not interesting   **d)** merciless

_____ 33. **antidote**   **a)** opposite   **b)** remedy   **c)** cause   **d)** list

_____ 34. **bland**   **a)** extreme   **b)** dull   **c)** mix   **d)** too small

_____ 35. **reinforce**   **a)** strengthen   **b)** interest   **c)** invent   **d)** reply

_____ 36. **relevant**   **a)** related   **b)** included   **c)** lacking pity   **d)** helpful

_____ 37. **propaganda**   **a)** appearance   **b)** cure   **c)** publicity   **d)** research

_____ 38. **agenda**   **a)** schedule   **b)** age   **c)** wardrobe   **d)** former times

_____ 39. **radical**   **a)** obvious   **b)** favoring extreme changes   **c)** of a nation   **d)** odd

_____ 40. **prospects**   **a)** chances   **b)** information   **c)** spirit   **d)** gold

_____ 41. **gruesome**   **a)** taller   **b)** illegal   **c)** frightful   **d)** not practical

_____ 42. **endorse**   **a)** suggest   **b)** stop   **c)** support   **d)** start

_____ 43. **illusion**   **a)** mistaken view   **b)** bad health   **c)** new idea   **d)** power

_____ 44. **imply**   **a)** approve of   **b)** interfere   **c)** do mischief   **d)** suggest

_____ 45. **obstacle**   **a)** barrier   **b)** remedy   **c)** list   **d)** answer

_____ 46. **erode**   **a)** drive   **b)** wear away   **c)** include   **d)** express indirectly

_____ 47. **novice**   **a)** book   **b)** false impression   **c)** beginner   **d)** servant

_____ 48. **impact**   **a)** force   **b)** inside   **c)** remedy   **d)** agreement

_____ 49. **hypocrite**   **a)** interference   **b)** insincere person   **c)** injection   **d)** threat

_____ 50. **idealistic**   **a)** full of ideas   **b)** searching   **c)** emphasizing ideals   **d)** necessary

**SCORE:** (Number correct) _____ × 2 = _____ %

Name: _____

Unit One: *Posttest*

In the space provided, write the letter of the choice that is closest in meaning to the **boldfaced** word.

____ 1. **novice**   **a)** book   **b)** false impression   **c)** servant   **d)** beginner

____ 2. **erratic**   **a)** noisy   **b)** inconsistent   **c)** in a city   **d)** mistaken

____ 3. **propaganda**   **a)** appearance   **b)** publicity   **c)** research   **d)** cure

____ 4. **acknowledge**   **a)** deny   **b)** prevent   **c)** study   **d)** admit

____ 5. **relevant**   **a)** helpful   **b)** related   **c)** lacking pity   **d)** included

____ 6. **forfeit**   **a)** lose   **b)** recall   **c)** give   **d)** draw

____ 7. **lenient**   **a)** heavy   **b)** not biased   **c)** not strict   **d)** delayed

____ 8. **refuge**   **a)** building   **b)** garbage   **c)** rejection   **d)** shelter

____ 9. **illuminate**   **a)** desire greatly   **b)** light up   **c)** lose   **d)** become sick

____ 10. **dialog**   **a)** a passage of conversation   **b)** short story   **c)** answer   **d)** belief

____ 11. **naive**   **a)** clever   **b)** fair   **c)** merciful   **d)** unsuspecting

____ 12. **delete**   **a)** go away   **b)** obey   **c)** damage   **d)** erase

____ 13. **anecdote**   **a)** brief story   **b)** cure   **c)** confession   **d)** reply

____ 14. **radical**   **a)** odd   **b)** favoring extreme changes   **c)** of a nation   **d)** obvious

____ 15. **impartial**   **a)** hidden   **b)** strict   **c)** without prejudice   **d)** not whole

____ 16. **reinforce**   **a)** strengthen   **b)** interest   **c)** invent   **d)** reply

____ 17. **drastic**   **a)** suitable   **b)** dirty   **c)** extreme   **d)** sticky

____ 18. **alternative**   **a)** design   **b)** assignment   **c)** choice   **d)** command

____ 19. **endorse**   **a)** support   **b)** start   **c)** suggest   **d)** stop

____ 20. **urban**   **a)** circular   **b)** not allowed   **c)** of a city   **d)** large

____ 21. **obstacle**   **a)** list   **b)** answer   **c)** barrier   **d)** remedy

____ 22. **hypocrite**   **a)** injection   **b)** insincere person   **c)** interference   **d)** sports arena

____ 23. **reminisce**   **a)** strengthen   **b)** gather   **c)** travel   **d)** remember

____ 24. **prospects**   **a)** information   **b)** gold   **c)** chances   **d)** spirit

____ 25. **apathy**   **a)** pity   **b)** lack of interest   **c)** harm   **d)** route

(Continues on next page)

_____ 26. **integrity**   a) honesty   b) threat   c) complication   d) inside

_____ 27. **avert**   a) prevent   b) begin   c) travel   d) do too late

_____ 28. **gruesome**   a) frightful   b) not practical   c) taller   d) illegal

_____ 29. **isolate**   a) freeze   b) heat up   c) separate   d) combine

_____ 30. **bland**   a) dull   b) extreme   c) mix   d) too small

_____ 31. **illusion**   a) new idea   b) bad health   c) power   d) mistaken view

_____ 32. **concise**   a) cut   b) peaceful   c) clear and brief   d) wordy

_____ 33. **legitimate**   a) profitable   b) obvious   c) threatening   d) lawful

_____ 34. **ruthless**   a) private   b) merciless   c) weakened   d) not interesting

_____ 35. **imply**   a) do much mischief   b) approve of   c) suggest   d) interfere

_____ 36. **impact**   a) inside   b) remedy   c) force   d) agreement

_____ 37. **overt**   a) proper   b) obvious   c) completed   d) fair

_____ 38. **agenda**   a) former times   b) wardrobe   c) schedule   d) age

_____ 39. **appropriate**   a) well-dressed   b) extreme   c) illegal   d) proper

_____ 40. **fortify**   a) approve of   b) suggest   c) avoid   d) strengthen

_____ 41. **candid**   a) intense   b) long   c) improper   d) honest

_____ 42. **menace**   a) threat   b) assistance   c) character   d) puzzle

_____ 43. **morale**   a) spirit   b) principle   c) majority   d) threat

_____ 44. **antidote**   a) cause   b) remedy   c) opposite   d) list

_____ 45. **undermine**   a) reach   b) cross out   c) dig up   d) weaken

_____ 46. **erode**   a) include   b) drive   c) express indirectly   d) wear away

_____ 47. **extensive**   a) separated   b) bold   c) outside   d) large in space or amount

_____ 48. **idealistic**   a) searching   b) full of ideas   c) necessary   d) emphasizing ideals

_____ 49. **comply**   a) do as asked   b) forget   c) choose   d) run into

_____ 50. **compel**   a) delight   b) finish   c) avoid   d) force

SCORE: (Number correct) _____ × 2 = _____ %

Unit Two: *Pretest*

In the space provided, write the letter of the choice that is closest in meaning to the **boldfaced** word.

_____ 1. **superficial**   a) lacking depth   b) perfect   c) very deep   d) faulty

_____ 2. **concede**   a) go beyond   b) reveal   c) dislike   d) admit

_____ 3. **deter**   a) refuse   b) make last longer   c) prevent   d) damage

_____ 4. **denounce**   a) introduce   b) condemn   c) change   d) compliment

_____ 5. **disclose**   a) reveal   b) close   c) hide   d) continue

_____ 6. **transition**   a) purchase   b) invention   c) repetition   d) change

_____ 7. **sustain**   a) keep going   b) approve of   c) avoid   d) wait for

_____ 8. **conservative**   a) not definite   b) opinionated   c) resisting change   d) understanding

_____ 9. **contrary**   a) easily reached   b) hard   c) disrespectful   d) opposite

_____ 10. **scapegoat**   a) example   b) one blamed for another's mistake   c) winner
d) one who takes

_____ 11. **derive**   a) make known   b) get   c) hold back from   d) give in

_____ 12. **supplement**   a) add to   b) prevent   c) support   d) lower

_____ 13. **compensate**   a) change   b) win out   c) receive   d) repay

_____ 14. **inhibit**   a) forbid   b) hold back   c) live in   d) provide

_____ 15. **verify**   a) imagine   b) prove   c) keep going   d) cancel

_____ 16. **surpass**   a) go beyond   b) reverse   c) take   d) prove wrong

_____ 17. **moderate**   a) generous   b) not final   c) medium   d) bright

_____ 18. **conceive of**   a) prevent   b) make last longer   c) enjoy   d) think up

_____ 19. **tentative**   a) suitable   b) not final   c) outside   d) definite

_____ 20. **diversity**   a) separation   b) conclusion   c) enthusiasm   d) variety

_____ 21. **chronological**   a) not logical   b) not extreme   c) in time order
d) in order of importance

_____ 22. **alter**   a) prevent   b) gather   c) remove   d) change

_____ 23. **refrain**   a) cancel   b) hold back   c) evaluate   d) bother

_____ 24. **ample**   a) cautious   b) plenty   c) wealthy   d) doubtful

_____ 25. **pretense**   a) false show   b) fault   c) disrespect   d) regret

(Continues on next page)

____ 26. **blunt**   a) angry   b) shy   c) straightforward   d) indirect

____ 27. **chronic**   a) in time order   b) constant   c) late   d) sharp

____ 28. **prolong**   a) encourage   b) gather in a pile   c) make last longer   d) reverse

____ 29. **remorse**   a) fear   b) pain   c) regret   d) happiness

____ 30. **optimist**   a) logical thinker   b) one who delays   c) one who rushes
                            d) positive thinker

____ 31. **bestow**   a) take advantage of   b) try   c) frighten   d) give

____ 32. **prudent**   a) rudely brief   b) careful   c) obvious   d) delicate

____ 33. **apprehensive**   a) uneasy   b) thoughtful   c) relaxed   d) opinionated

____ 34. **acute**   a) mild   b) dull   c) severe   d) nervous

____ 35. **prominent**   a) clean   b) obvious   c) dangerous   d) reasonable

____ 36. **donor**   a) one who gives   b) gift   c) one who receives   d) loan

____ 37. **phobia**   a) difficult experience   b) fear   c) disease   d) attraction

____ 38. **recipient**   a) one who receives   b) steady customer   c) contributor   d) list

____ 39. **anonymous**   a) famous   b) common   c) by an unknown author
                            d) more than enough

____ 40. **arrogant**   a) wealthy   b) ridiculous   c) average   d) overly proud

____ 41. **compile**   a) stick firmly   b) gather in a list   c) regret   d) admit

____ 42. **defect**   a) fault   b) false belief   c) choice   d) character

____ 43. **adhere**   a) send for   b) stick   c) go to   d) delay

____ 44. **dogmatic**   a) relaxed   b) thoughtful   c) opinionated   d) assumed to be true

____ 45. **alienate**   a) encourage   b) make unfriendly   c) attract   d) discourage

____ 46. **doctrine**   a) list   b) freedom   c) demonstration   d) principle

____ 47. **assess**   a) learn   b) plan   c) evaluate   d) search

____ 48. **affluent**   a) useless   b) slim   c) overly vain   d) wealthy

____ 49. **contempt**   a) love   b) disrespect   c) jealousy   d) courage

____ 50. **absurd**   a) logical   b) doubtful   c) spiteful   d) ridiculous

SCORE: (Number correct) _____ × 2 = _____ %

20

Unit Two: *Posttest*

In the space provided, write the letter of the choice that is closest in meaning to the **boldfaced** word.

_____ 1. **prudent**   a) obvious   b) careful   c) rudely brief   d) delicate

_____ 2. **deter**   a) refuse   b) damage   c) make last longer   d) prevent

_____ 3. **sustain**   a) wait for   b) keep going   c) avoid   d) approve of

_____ 4. **scapegoat**   a) one blamed for another's mistake   b) one who takes   c) winner
d) example

_____ 5. **compensate**   a) repay   b) win out   c) change   d) receive

_____ 6. **tentative**   a) outside   b) not final   c) definite   d) suitable

_____ 7. **chronological**   a) not logical   b) in time order   c) in order of importance
d) not extreme

_____ 8. **denounce**   a) condemn   b) compliment   c) change   d) introduce

_____ 9. **apprehensive**   a) relaxed   b) opinionated   c) uneasy   d) thoughtful

_____ 10. **conservative**   a) resisting change   b) opinionated   c) not definite   d) understanding

_____ 11. **donor**   a) one who gives   b) gift   c) one who receives   d) loan

_____ 12. **pretense**   a) fault   b) disrespect   c) regret   d) false show

_____ 13. **blunt**   a) shy   b) indirect   c) straightforward   d) angry

_____ 14. **supplement**   a) support   b) lower   c) prevent   d) add to

_____ 15. **inhibit**   a) provide   b) hold back   c) live in   d) forbid

_____ 16. **chronic**   a) constant   b) sharp   c) late   d) in time order

_____ 17. **transition**   a) invention   b) repetition   c) change   d) purchase

_____ 18. **remorse**   a) fear   b) pain   c) regret   d) happiness

_____ 19. **alter**   a) gather   b) change   c) remove   d) prevent

_____ 20. **prominent**   a) obvious   b) reasonable   c) dangerous   d) clean

_____ 21. **conceive of**   a) prevent   b) think up   c) enjoy   d) make last longer

_____ 22. **prolong**   a) gather in a pile   b) make last longer   c) encourage   d) reverse

_____ 23. **recipient**   a) list   b) one who receives   c) contributor   d) steady customer

_____ 24. **verify**   a) keep going   b) cancel   c) imagine   d) prove

_____ 25. **arrogant**   a) ridiculous   b) overly proud   c) wealthy   d) average

(Continues on next page)

_____ 26. **absurd**   a) doubtful   b) spiteful   c) logical   d) ridiculous

_____ 27. **acute**   a) dull   b) severe   c) nervous   d) mild

_____ 28. **ample**   a) plenty   b) doubtful   c) wealthy   d) cautious

_____ 29. **assess**   a) search   b) plan   c) learn   d) evaluate

_____ 30. **bestow**   a) try   b) frighten   c) give   d) take advantage of

_____ 31. **compile**   a) regret   b) admit   c) gather in a list   d) stick firmly

_____ 32. **superficial**   a) faulty   b) lacking depth   c) very deep   d) perfect

_____ 33. **defect**   a) fault   b) character   c) choice   d) false belief

_____ 34. **contrary**   a) hard   b) disrespectful   c) opposite   d) easily reached

_____ 35. **adhere**   a) send for   b) delay   c) stick   d) go to

_____ 36. **moderate**   a) not final   b) medium   c) bright   d) generous

_____ 37. **dogmatic**   a) relaxed   b) assumed to be true   c) opinionated   d) thoughtful

_____ 38. **diversity**   a) conclusion   b) enthusiasm   c) separation   d) variety

_____ 39. **alienate**   a) make unfriendly   b) discourage   c) attract   d) encourage

_____ 40. **concede**   a) reveal   b) admit   c) dislike   d) go beyond

_____ 41. **surpass**   a) reverse   b) prove wrong   c) go beyond   d) take

_____ 42. **phobia**   a) attraction   b) fear   c) difficult experience   d) disease

_____ 43. **doctrine**   a) freedom   b) demonstration   c) list   d) principle

_____ 44. **anonymous**   a) by an unknown author   b) famous   c) common   d) more than enough

_____ 45. **disclose**   a) continue   b) close   c) reveal   d) hide

_____ 46. **optimist**   a) one who delays   b) positive thinker   c) one who rushes
                              d) logical thinker

_____ 47. **affluent**   a) wealthy   b) useless   c) overly vain   d) slim

_____ 48. **derive**   a) get   b) hold back   c) make known   d) give in

_____ 49. **contempt**   a) disrespect   b) jealousy   c) courage   d) love

_____ 50. **refrain**   a) evaluate   b) cancel   c) bother   d) hold back

---

SCORE: (Number correct) _____ × 2 = _____ %

Unit Three: *Pretest*

In the space provided, write the letter of the choice that is closest in meaning to the **boldfaced** word.

_____ 1. **cite**   a) repeat   b) mention in support   c) look for   d) read

_____ 2. **rational**   a) limited   b) of poor quality   c) logical   d) patriotic

_____ 3. **retort**   a) great respect   b) sharp reply   c) false idea   d) court order

_____ 4. **exempt**   a) needed badly   b) attacked   c) unconcerned   d) free of a duty

_____ 5. **propel**   a) discourage   b) attract   c) push   d) reject

_____ 6. **accessible**   a) easily reached   b) itchy   c) difficult   d) folded

_____ 7. **prevail**   a) climb   b) win out   c) lose   d) enroll early

_____ 8. **compatible**   a) capable   b) able to get along well   c) proud   d) friendly

_____ 9. **awe**   a) jealousy   b) great respect   c) pride   d) great courage

_____ 10. **retrieve**   a) get back   b) lose   c) distribute   d) announce

_____ 11. **fallacy**   a) fact   b) theory   c) false idea   d) suggestion

_____ 12. **miserly**   a) bored   b) thoughtful   c) thorough   d) stingy

_____ 13. **ecstatic**   a) unmoving   b) joyful   c) hungry   d) powerful

_____ 14. **evolve**   a) turn around   b) change gradually   c) take one's place
                            d) think about

_____ 15. **liable**   a) famous   b) likely   c) guilty   d) dangerous

_____ 16. **fictitious**   a) truthful   b) likely   c) mindful   d) imaginary

_____ 17. **pessimist**   a) courageous person   b) one with a hopeless view   c) speaker
                            d) politician

_____ 18. **dubious**   a) doubtful   b) weak   c) small   d) lacking confidence

_____ 19. **encounter**   a) add up   b) meet   c) falsify   d) confess

_____ 20. **gullible**   a) needy   b) easily fooled   c) shy   d) bad tempered

_____ 21. **obsession**   a) possession   b) something pleasant
                            c) something one is overly concerned about   d) guilt

_____ 22. **evasive**   a) talkative   b) deliberately unclear   c) friendly   d) overly forceful

_____ 23. **harass**   a) compliment   b) bother   c) stock up   d) encourage

_____ 24. **fluent**   a) speaking smoothly   b) full   c) overflowing   d) polluted

_____ 25. **elapse**   a) flow   b) pass by   c) measure   d) record

(Continues on next page)

_____ 26. **lethal**   a) sweet smelling   b) ancient   c) deadly   d) healthy

_____ 27. **ordeal**   a) change   b) painful experience   c) good time   d) office

_____ 28. **futile**   a) without prejudice   b) useless   c) old-fashioned   d) kind

_____ 29. **infer**   a) offer   b) conclude   c) reject   d) answer

_____ 30. **persistent**   a) not brave   b) rude   c) stubbornly continuing   d) bad-smelling

_____ 31. **unique**   a) common   b) pure   c) one of a kind   d) well-known

_____ 32. **delusion**   a) escape   b) announcement   c) false belief   d) example

_____ 33. **savor**   a) enjoy   b) disapprove   c) dread   d) approve

_____ 34. **vivid**   a) brightly colored   b) loud   c) large   d) very talkative

_____ 35. **subtle**   a) early   b) direct   c) not obvious   d) surprising

_____ 36. **devise**   a) steal   b) escape   c) think up   d) redo

_____ 37. **universal**   a) doubting   b) easily understood   c) including everyone   d) local

_____ 38. **stimulate**   a) arouse   b) anger   c) make tired   d) confuse

_____ 39. **versatile**   a) rich   b) unclear   c) lucky   d) able to do many things well

_____ 40. **convey**   a) communicate   b) allow   c) invent   d) approve

_____ 41. **inevitable**   a) unavoidable   b) dangerous   c) spiteful   d) doubtful

_____ 42. **equate**   a) adjust   b) consider equal   c) attack   d) overcome

_____ 43. **passive**   a) not active but acted upon   b) joyful   c) quiet   d) moody

_____ 44. **patron**   a) father   b) enemy   c) steady customer   d) one with a hopeless view

_____ 45. **defer**   a) entertain   b) intrude   c) yield   d) annoy

_____ 46. **option**   a) problem   b) requirement   c) attitude   d) choice

_____ 47. **indignant**   a) impressed   b) angry   c) curious   d) afraid

_____ 48. **endeavor**   a) meet   b) state   c) try   d) avoid

_____ 49. **impose on**   a) arrest   b) confuse   c) disguise as   d) take advantage of

_____ 50. **malicious**   a) bright   b) mean   c) sweet   d) clever

---

SCORE: (Number correct) _____ × 2 = _____ %

Unit Three: *Posttest*

In the space provided, write the letter of the choice that is closest in meaning to the **boldfaced** word.

_____ 1. **equate**   **a)** attack   **b)** consider equal   **c)** overcome   **d)** adjust

_____ 2. **fallacy**   **a)** fact   **b)** suggestion   **c)** theory   **d)** false idea

_____ 3. **awe**   **a)** great respect   **b)** jealousy   **c)** pride   **d)** great courage

_____ 4. **evolve**   **a)** change gradually   **b)** take one's place   **c)** think about   **d)** turn around

_____ 5. **rational**   **a)** logical   **b)** limited   **c)** of poor quality   **d)** patriotic

_____ 6. **patron**   **a)** generous person   **b)** steady customer   **c)** father   **d)** enemy

_____ 7. **liable**   **a)** famous   **b)** likely   **c)** dangerous   **d)** guilty

_____ 8. **dubious**   **a)** small   **b)** lacking confidence   **c)** weak   **d)** doubtful

_____ 9. **endeavor**   **a)** state   **b)** avoid   **c)** try   **d)** meet

_____ 10. **harass**   **a)** bother   **b)** stock up   **c)** encourage   **d)** compliment

_____ 11. **exempt**   **a)** unconcerned   **b)** needed badly   **c)** free of a duty   **d)** attacked

_____ 12. **cite**   **a)** look for   **b)** read   **c)** repeat   **d)** mention in support

_____ 13. **elapse**   **a)** pass by   **b)** measure   **c)** record   **d)** flow

_____ 14. **passive**   **a)** quiet   **b)** joyful   **c)** moody   **d)** not active but acted upon

_____ 15. **gullible**   **a)** shy   **b)** easily fooled   **c)** needy   **d)** bad tempered

_____ 16. **lethal**   **a)** ancient   **b)** deadly   **c)** healthy   **d)** sweet smelling

_____ 17. **propel**   **a)** discourage   **b)** attract   **c)** reject   **d)** push

_____ 18. **ordeal**   **a)** office   **b)** change   **c)** good time   **d)** painful experience

_____ 19. **malicious**   **a)** clever   **b)** mean   **c)** sweet   **d)** bright

_____ 20. **defer**   **a)** annoy   **b)** intrude   **c)** yield   **d)** entertain

_____ 21. **impose on**   **a)** arrest   **b)** take advantage of   **c)** disguise as   **d)** confuse

_____ 22. **evasive**   **a)** overly forceful   **b)** talkative   **c)** friendly   **d)** deliberately unclear

_____ 23. **pessimist**   **a)** speaker   **b)** politician   **c)** one with a hopeless view
d) courageous person

_____ 24. **infer**   **a)** reject   **b)** answer   **c)** conclude   **d)** offer

_____ 25. **retrieve**   **a)** announce   **b)** get back   **c)** distribute   **d)** lose

(Continues on next page)

_____ 26. **miserly** a) thorough b) bored c) thoughtful d) stingy

_____ 27. **persistent** a) bad smelling b) not brave c) stubbornly continuing d) rude

_____ 28. **devise** a) think up b) redo c) escape d) steal

_____ 29. **fictitious** a) mindful b) likely c) imaginary d) truthful

_____ 30. **indignant** a) angry b) curious c) afraid d) impressed

_____ 31. **versatile** a) rich b) able to do many things well c) lucky d) unclear

_____ 32. **delusion** a) announcement b) example c) false belief d) escape

_____ 33. **accessible** a) itchy b) folded c) difficult d) easily reached

_____ 34. **compatible** a) friendly b) proud c) able to get along well d) capable

_____ 35. **option** a) attitude b) choice c) requirement d) problem

_____ 36. **savor** a) disapprove b) approve c) dread d) enjoy

_____ 37. **ecstatic** a) unmoving b) powerful c) hungry d) joyful

_____ 38. **vivid** a) very talkative b) brightly colored c) large d) loud

_____ 39. **prevail** a) lose b) win out c) enroll early d) climb

_____ 40. **subtle** a) direct b) early c) not obvious d) surprising

_____ 41. **encounter** a) meet b) add up c) confess d) falsify

_____ 42. **universal** a) including everyone b) easily understood c) local d) doubting

_____ 43. **retort** a) false idea b) sharp reply c) great respect d) court order

_____ 44. **stimulate** a) anger b) confuse c) make tired d) arouse

_____ 45. **unique** a) one of a kind b) pure c) well-known d) common

_____ 46. **obsession** a) something pleasant b) guilt c) something one is overly concerned about d) possession

_____ 47. **fluent** a) speaking smoothly b) full c) overflowing d) polluted

_____ 48. **convey** a) approve b) allow c) communicate d) invent

_____ 49. **futile** a) old-fashioned b) useless c) old d) without prejudice

_____ 50. **inevitable** a) dangerous b) doubtful c) spiteful d) unavoidable

SCORE: (Number correct) _____ × 2 = _____ %

26

Name: _____

Unit Four: *Pretest*

In the space provided, write the letter of the choice that is closest in meaning to the **boldfaced** word.

_____ 1. **refute**
a) prove wrong   b) replay   c) appeal   d) walk

_____ 2. **dismay**
a) thrill   b) lift   c) return   d) discourage

_____ 3. **gesture**
a) guess   b) thunder   c) sign   d) meal

_____ 4. **reciprocate**
a) pay back   b) frown   c) slip   d) step

_____ 5. **revert**
a) claim   b) return to former condition   c) pay back   d) answer

_____ 6. **exile**
a) formal criticism   b) exit   c) axe   d) separation from native country

_____ 7. **recede**
a) remove   b) move back   c) hide   d) flow over

_____ 8. **ritual**
a) business deal   b) war   c) ceremony   d) show

_____ 9. **retain**
a) return   b) keep   c) redo   d) come forth

_____ 10. **adapt**
a) stick to something   b) adjust to a situation   c) avoid   d) strike

_____ 11. **indifferent**
a) similar   b) calm   c) well-adjusted   d) unconcerned

_____ 12. **exotic**
a) out   b) infected   c) local   d) foreign

_____ 13. **notable**
a) well-known   b) written   c) unable   d) odd

_____ 14. **elaborate**
a) large   b) complex   c) expensive   d) boring

_____ 15. **liberal**
a) generous   b) thrifty   c) famous   d) short

_____ 16. **frugal**
a) appealing   b) illegal   c) thrifty   d) hasty

_____ 17. **mediocre**
a) outstanding   b) ordinary   c) bad tasting   d) believable

_____ 18. **indulgent**
a) interesting   b) giving in to someone's wishes   c) poor   d) uninteresting

_____ 19. **impulsive**
a) ugly   b) prompt   c) acting on sudden urges   d) important

_____ 20. **emerge**
a) go under water   b) come forth   c) lie   d) draw back

_____ 21. **elite**
a) free   b) underprivileged   c) superior   d) proud

_____ 22. **query**
a) answer   b) argue   c) question   d) make strange

_____ 23. **immunity**
a) freedom from something required   b) infection   c) plenty   d) thrift

_____ 24. **affirm**
a) support   b) reverse   c) indicate to be true   d) exercise

_____ 25. **essence**
a) fundamental characteristic   b) tiny part   c) much later   d) rule

(Continues on next page)

_____ 26. **allude**   **a)** refer indirectly   **b)** damage   **c)** protest   **d)** pay back

_____ 27. **impair**   **a)** fix   **b)** write down   **c)** employ   **d)** damage

_____ 28. **sadistic**   **a)** depressed   **b)** infected   **c)** taking pleasure in cruelty   **d)** clever

_____ 29. **alleged**   **a)** supposed to be true   **b)** factual   **c)** trustworthy   **d)** logical

_____ 30. **coerce**   **a)** attract   **b)** refuse   **c)** remove   **d)** force

_____ 31. **ridicule**   **a)** pay back   **b)** compliment   **c)** mock   **d)** shrink

_____ 32. **plausible**   **a)** boring   **b)** unbearable   **c)** believable   **d)** misspelled

_____ 33. **recur**   **a)** prevent   **b)** remember   **c)** forget   **d)** occur again

_____ 34. **shrewd**   **a)** kind   **b)** annoying   **c)** tricky   **d)** mad

_____ 35. **tactic**   **a)** result   **b)** surrender   **c)** method   **d)** ceremony

_____ 36. **revoke**   **a)** annoy   **b)** protest   **c)** cancel   **d)** adjust

_____ 37. **stereotype**   **a)** oversimplified image   **b)** two channels   **c)** plan   **d)** photograph

_____ 38. **reprimand**   **a)** harsh criticism   **b)** business deal   **c)** ruling   **d)** answer

_____ 39. **skeptical**   **a)** stubborn   **b)** forceful   **c)** generous   **d)** doubting

_____ 40. **provoke**   **a)** make angry   **b)** take back   **c)** rise up   **d)** prove wrong

_____ 41. **strategy**   **a)** plan   **b)** purpose   **c)** discipline   **d)** foundation

_____ 42. **vital**   **a)** weak   **b)** stiff   **c)** necessary   **d)** unimportant

_____ 43. **destiny**   **a)** freedom   **b)** fate   **c)** generosity   **d)** boredom

_____ 44. **tedious**   **a)** difficult   **b)** heavy   **c)** ridiculous   **d)** boring

_____ 45. **detain**   **a)** care for   **b)** attract   **c)** delay   **d)** describe

_____ 46. **simultaneous**   **a)** done at the same time   **b)** recorded   **c)** very important   **d)** fast

_____ 47. **transaction**   **a)** trip   **b)** business deal   **c)** detour   **d)** ceremony

_____ 48. **procrastinate**   **a)** remember   **b)** put off doing something   **c)** misbehave   **d)** make angry

_____ 49. **consequence**   **a)** falsehood   **b)** result   **c)** method   **d)** series

_____ 50. **diminish**   **a)** lessen   **b)** make darker   **c)** enlarge   **d)** move upward

SCORE: (Number correct) _____ × 2 = _____ %

Unit Four: *Posttest*

In the space provided, write the letter of the choice that is closest in meaning to the **boldfaced** word.

_____ 1. **refute**   **a)** prove wrong   **b)** replay   **c)** appeal   **d)** walk

_____ 2. **dismay**   **a)** return   **b)** lift   **c)** discourage   **d)** thrill

_____ 3. **gesture**   **a)** guess   **b)** meal   **c)** sign   **d)** thunder

_____ 4. **reciprocate**   **a)** slip   **b)** frown   **c)** step   **d)** pay back

_____ 5. **revert**   **a)** claim   **b)** answer   **c)** pay back   **d)** return to former condition

_____ 6. **exile**   **a)** separation from native country   **b)** formal criticism   **c)** axe   **d)** exit

_____ 7. **recede**   **a)** move back   **b)** flow over   **c)** hide   **d)** remove

_____ 8. **ritual**   **a)** show   **b)** business deal   **c)** ceremony   **d)** war

_____ 9. **retain**   **a)** come forth   **b)** keep   **c)** return   **d)** redo

_____ 10. **adapt**   **a)** adjust to a situation   **b)** strike   **c)** avoid   **d)** stick to something

_____ 11. **indifferent**   **a)** well-adjusted   **b)** calm   **c)** unconcerned   **d)** similar

_____ 12. **exotic**   **a)** foreign   **b)** infected   **c)** local   **d)** out

_____ 13. **notable**   **a)** written   **b)** not able   **c)** well-known   **d)** odd

_____ 14. **elaborate**   **a)** large   **b)** boring   **c)** expensive   **d)** complex

_____ 15. **liberal**   **a)** thrifty   **b)** famous   **c)** short   **d)** generous

_____ 16. **frugal**   **a)** thrifty   **b)** illegal   **c)** hasty   **d)** appealing

_____ 17. **mediocre**   **a)** bad tasting   **b)** believable   **c)** ordinary   **d)** outstanding

_____ 18. **indulgent**   **a)** interesting   **b)** uninteresting   **c)** poor   **d)** giving in to someone's wishes

_____ 19. **impulsive**   **a)** prompt   **b)** important   **c)** acting on sudden urges   **d)** ugly

_____ 20. **emerge**   **a)** lie   **b)** come forth   **c)** go under water   **d)** draw back

_____ 21. **elite**   **a)** superior   **b)** proud   **c)** underprivileged   **d)** free

_____ 22. **query**   **a)** make strange   **b)** argue   **c)** question   **d)** answer

_____ 23. **immunity**   **a)** infection   **b)** plenty   **c)** freedom from something required   **d)** thrift

_____ 24. **affirm**   **a)** indicate to be true   **b)** exercise   **c)** reverse   **d)** support

_____ 25. **essence**   **a)** fundamental characteristic   **b)** rule   **c)** much later   **d)** tiny part

(Continues on next page)

_____ 26. **allude**　　**a)** protest　　**b)** pay back　　**c)** damage　　**d)** refer indirectly

_____ 27. **impair**　　**a)** write down　　**b)** damage　　**c)** employ　　**d)** fix

_____ 28. **sadistic**　　**a)** clever　　**b)** infected　　**c)** depressed　　**d)** taking pleasure in cruelty

_____ 29. **alleged**　　**a)** logical　　**b)** factual　　**c)** supposed to be true　　**d)** trustworthy

_____ 30. **coerce**　　**a)** force　　**b)** remove　　**c)** attract　　**d)** refuse

_____ 31. **ridicule**　　**a)** shrink　　**b)** mock　　**c)** compliment　　**d)** pay back

_____ 32. **plausible**　　**a)** boring　　**b)** misspelled　　**c)** believable　　**d)** unbearable

_____ 33. **recur**　　**a)** remember　　**b)** occur again　　**c)** forget　　**d)** prevent

_____ 34. **shrewd**　　**a)** tricky　　**b)** annoying　　**c)** mad　　**d)** kind

_____ 35. **tactic**　　**a)** surrender　　**b)** ceremony　　**c)** method　　**d)** result

_____ 36. **revoke**　　**a)** annoy　　**b)** adjust　　**c)** cancel　　**d)** protest

_____ 37. **stereotype**　　**a)** two channels　　**b)** photograph　　**c)** plan　　**d)** oversimplified image

_____ 38. **reprimand**　　**a)** ruling　　**b)** business deal　　**c)** harsh criticism　　**d)** answer

_____ 39. **skeptical**　　**a)** forceful　　**b)** doubting　　**c)** generous　　**d)** stubborn

_____ 40. **provoke**　　**a)** take back　　**b)** prove wrong　　**c)** rise up　　**d)** make angry

_____ 41. **strategy**　　**a)** plan　　**b)** foundation　　**c)** purpose　　**d)** discipline

_____ 42. **vital**　　**a)** weak　　**b)** necessary　　**c)** unimportant　　**d)** stiff

_____ 43. **destiny**　　**a)** fate　　**b)** boredom　　**c)** generosity　　**d)** freedom

_____ 44. **tedious**　　**a)** heavy　　**b)** boring　　**c)** difficult　　**d)** ridiculous

_____ 45. **detain**　　**a)** attract　　**b)** describe　　**c)** delay　　**d)** care for

_____ 46. **simultaneous**　　**a)** recorded　　**b)** fast　　**c)** very important　　**d)** done at the same time

_____ 47. **transaction**　　**a)** ceremony　　**b)** business deal　　**c)** detour　　**d)** trip

_____ 48. **procrastinate**　　**a)** put off doing something　　**b)** remember　　**c)** misbehave
d) make angry

_____ 49. **consequence**　　**a)** result　　**b)** method　　**c)** series　　**d)** falsehood

_____ 50. **diminish**　　**a)** enlarge　　**b)** make darker　　**c)** move upward　　**d)** lessen

SCORE: (Number correct) _____ × 2 = _____ %

Unit Five: *Pretest*

In the space provided, write the letter of the choice that is closest in meaning to the **boldfaced** word.

_____   1. **severity**   a) rudeness   b) generosity   c) harshness   d) calm

_____   2. **site**   a) silence   b) location   c) time   d) vision

_____   3. **theoretical**   a) gloomy   b) based on theory   c) practical   d) pretty

_____   4. **discriminate**   a) arrest   b) delay   c) distinguish   d) discuss

_____   5. **summon**   a) add up   b) send for   c) delay   d) insult

_____   6. **profound**   a) kind   b) deeply felt   c) cautious   d) logical

_____   7. **vocation**   a) hobby   b) trip   c) report   d) profession

_____   8. **dispense**   a) stop   b) delay   c) encourage   d) distribute

_____   9. **dismal**   a) unknown   b) round   c) tired   d) gloomy

_____ 10. **subside**   a) calm down   b) insult   c) arouse   d) tire easily

_____ 11. **ingenious**   a) false   b) able to be heard   c) clever   d) tricky

_____ 12. **ascend**   a) go into   b) go down   c) go under   d) go up

_____ 13. **finite**   a) perfect   b) absent   c) limited   d) endless

_____ 14. **mania**   a) contempt   b) glow   c) rejection   d) extreme enthusiasm

_____ 15. **literally**   a) by letter   b) successfully   c) word for word   d) deeply

_____ 16. **inflict**   a) cause something painful   b) study   c) prepare   d) go down in quality

_____ 17. **nostalgia**   a) desire for the past   b) sadness   c) disease   d) olden days

_____ 18. **infinite**   a) indoors   b) inborn   c) limited   d) endless

_____ 19. **lure**   a) tempt   b) ignore   c) equal   d) dislike

_____ 20. **initiate**   a) complete   b) continue   c) start   d) become smaller

_____ 21. **lament**   a) delay   b) rush   c) struggle   d) mourn

_____ 22. **data**   a) test   b) information   c) rumors   d) conversation

_____ 23. **intervene**   a) come between   b) arrest   c) resist   d) send for

_____ 24. **sedate**   a) bold   b) plain   c) calm   d) pure

_____ 25. **morbid**   a) limited   b) causing horror   c) causing respect   d) pleasurable

(Continues on next page)

_____ 26. **parallel**   **a)** at a constant distance apart   **b)** nearsighted   **c)** farsighted   **d)** far

_____ 27. **inept**   **a)** guilty   **b)** tired   **c)** clumsy   **d)** stubborn

_____ 28. **perceptive**   **a)** brave   **b)** available   **c)** aware   **d)** careless

_____ 29. **innate**   **a)** learned   **b)** underneath   **c)** inborn   **d)** clever

_____ 30. **obstinate**   **a)** friendly   **b)** frightful   **c)** stubborn   **d)** cautious

_____ 31. **trivial**   **a)** unimportant   **b)** inexact   **c)** accurate   **d)** clear

_____ 32. **deduction**   **a)** conclusion   **b)** statement   **c)** lie   **d)** fact

_____ 33. **distort**   **a)** stick to the facts   **b)** misrepresent   **c)** resist   **d)** mourn

_____ 34. **treacherous**   **a)** rude   **b)** disloyal   **c)** unkind   **d)** proud

_____ 35. **sequence**   **a)** information   **b)** separation   **c)** order   **d)** circle

_____ 36. **dominant**   **a)** in control   **b)** expressing sorrow   **c)** clumsy   **d)** lively

_____ 37. **dimensions**   **a)** information   **b)** measurements   **c)** grade   **d)** view

_____ 38. **sophisticated**   **a)** disloyal   **b)** pure   **c)** well-groomed   **d)** knowledgeable

_____ 39. **controversy**   **a)** agreement   **b)** chat   **c)** debate   **d)** celebration

_____ 40. **disperse**   **a)** spread out   **b)** give away   **c)** throw out   **d)** decrease

_____ 41. **susceptible**   **a)** sensitive   **b)** greedy   **c)** lazy   **d)** easily noticed

_____ 42. **defy**   **a)** send for   **b)** approve   **c)** improve   **d)** resist

_____ 43. **valid**   **a)** logical   **b)** pure   **c)** clever   **d)** gloomy

_____ 44. **seclusion**   **a)** punishment   **b)** pride   **c)** stubbornness   **d)** separation

_____ 45. **deceptive**   **a)** constant   **b)** well-spoken   **c)** misleading   **d)** changing

_____ 46. **confirm**   **a)** follow   **b)** reject   **c)** support the truth of something   **d)** speed up

_____ 47. **vigorous**   **a)** harsh   **b)** energetic   **c)** kind   **d)** rushed

_____ 48. **submit**   **a)** make fun of   **b)** arrest   **c)** give in   **d)** refuse

_____ 49. **transmit**   **a)** spread   **b)** hold   **c)** sleep   **d)** grow

_____ 50. **restrain**   **a)** struggle   **b)** hold back   **c)** refuse   **d)** order to come

SCORE: (Number correct) _____ × 2 = _____ %

Unit Five: *Posttest*

In the space provided, write the letter of the choice that is closest in meaning to the **boldfaced** word.

_____ 1. **vigorous**   a) kind   b) energetic   c) rushed   d) harsh

_____ 2. **discriminate**   a) distinguish   b) delay   c) arrest   d) discuss

_____ 3. **deceptive**   a) well-spoken   b) changing   c) misleading   d) constant

_____ 4. **susceptible**   a) greedy   b) easily noticed   c) lazy   d) sensitive

_____ 5. **profound**   a) cautious   b) logical   c) deeply felt   d) kind

_____ 6. **dispense**   a) delay   b) distribute   c) encourage   d) stop

_____ 7. **distort**   a) misrepresent   b) mourn   c) resist   d) stick to the facts

_____ 8. **subside**   a) tire easily   b) calm down   c) insult   d) arouse

_____ 9. **dismal**   a) round   b) gloomy   c) tired   d) unknown

_____ 10. **mania**   a) glow   b) extreme enthusiasm   c) rejection   d) contempt

_____ 11. **inflict**   a) study   b) go down in quality   c) prepare   d) cause something painful

_____ 12. **treacherous**   a) unkind   b) proud   c) rude   d) disloyal

_____ 13. **infinite**   a) endless   b) limited   c) indoors   d) inborn

_____ 14. **initiate**   a) become smaller   b) complete   c) start   d) continue

_____ 15. **data**   a) rumors   b) information   c) test   d) conversation

_____ 16. **sedate**   a) plain   b) pure   c) calm   d) bold

_____ 17. **parallel**   a) nearsighted   b) far   c) farsighted   d) at a constant distance apart

_____ 18. **nostalgia**   a) sadness   b) desire for the past   c) disease   d) olden days

_____ 19. **transmit**   a) sleep   b) hold   c) grow   d) spread

_____ 20. **disperse**   a) throw out   b) give away   c) decrease   d) spread out

_____ 21. **perceptive**   a) careless   b) available   c) brave   d) aware

_____ 22. **dismal**   a) tired   b) round   c) unknown   d) gloomy

_____ 23. **obstinate**   a) friendly   b) cautious   c) stubborn   d) frightful

_____ 24. **dominant**   a) expressing sorrow   b) in control   c) clumsy   d) lively

_____ 25. **finite**   a) endless   b) absent   c) limited   d) perfect

(Continues on next page)

_____ 26. **dimensions** **a)** measurements **b)** grade **c)** view **d)** information

_____ 27. **lament** **a)** rush **b)** mourn **c)** struggle **d)** delay

_____ 28. **sophisticated** **a)** well-groomed **b)** pure **c)** knowledgeable **d)** disloyal

_____ 29. **submit** **a)** refuse **b)** arrest **c)** make fun of **d)** give in

_____ 30. **morbid** **a)** causing horror **b)** causing respect **c)** limited **d)** pleasurable

_____ 31. **controversy** **a)** debate **b)** chat **c)** agreement **d)** celebration

_____ 32. **lure** **a)** ignore **b)** dislike **c)** equal **d)** tempt

_____ 33. **defy** **a)** improve **b)** resist **c)** send for **d)** approve

_____ 34. **summon** **a)** delay **b)** send for **c)** insult **d)** add up

_____ 35. **vocation** **a)** report **b)** trip **c)** profession **d)** hobby

_____ 36. **deduction** **a)** conclusion **b)** statement **c)** lie **d)** fact

_____ 37. **site** **a)** location **b)** vision **c)** time **d)** silence

_____ 38. **restrain** **a)** refuse **b)** hold back **c)** order to come **d)** struggle

_____ 39. **innate** **a)** underneath **b)** clever **c)** inborn **d)** learned

_____ 40. **valid** **a)** pure **b)** clever **c)** logical **d)** gloomy

_____ 41. **severity** **a)** generosity **b)** harshness **c)** calm **d)** rudeness

_____ 42. **intervene** **a)** arrest **b)** send for **c)** resist **d)** come between

_____ 43. **confirm** **a)** follow **b)** speed up **c)** support the truth of something **d)** reject

_____ 44. **sequence** **a)** separation **b)** circle **c)** order **d)** information

_____ 45. **theoretical** **a)** gloomy **b)** pretty **c)** practical **d)** based on theory

_____ 46. **inept** **a)** tired **b)** clumsy **c)** guilty **d)** stubborn

_____ 47. **seclusion** **a)** pride **b)** separation **c)** stubbornness **d)** punishment

_____ 48. **ascend** **a)** go up **b)** go under **c)** go into **d)** go down

_____ 49. **trivial** **a)** unimportant **b)** accurate **c)** inexact **d)** clear

_____ 50. **literally** **a)** by letter **b)** deeply **c)** successfully **d)** word for word

SCORE: (Number correct) _____ × 2 = _____ %

Pretest / Posttest

ANSWER SHEET

1. ____	26. ____	51. ____	76. ____
2. ____	27. ____	52. ____	77. ____
3. ____	28. ____	53. ____	78. ____
4. ____	29. ____	54. ____	79. ____
5. ____	30. ____	55. ____	80. ____
6. ____	31. ____	56. ____	81. ____
7. ____	32. ____	57. ____	82. ____
8. ____	33. ____	58. ____	83. ____
9. ____	34. ____	59. ____	84. ____
10. ____	35. ____	60. ____	85. ____
11. ____	36. ____	61. ____	86. ____
12. ____	37. ____	62. ____	87. ____
13. ____	38. ____	63. ____	88. ____
14. ____	39. ____	64. ____	89. ____
15. ____	40. ____	65. ____	90. ____
16. ____	41. ____	66. ____	91. ____
17. ____	42. ____	67. ____	92. ____
18. ____	43. ____	68. ____	93. ____
19. ____	44. ____	69. ____	94. ____
20. ____	45. ____	70. ____	95. ____
21. ____	46. ____	71. ____	96. ____
22. ____	47. ____	72. ____	97. ____
23. ____	48. ____	73. ____	98. ____
24. ____	49. ____	74. ____	99. ____
25. ____	50. ____	75. ____	100. ____

ANSWER KEY

1. c	26. d	51. a	76. b
2. c	27. b	52. b	77. d
3. d	28. a	53. c	78. c
4. b	29. b	54. d	79. b
5. b	30. d	55. c	80. a
6. c	31. b	56. a	81. b
7. b	32. a	57. d	82. c
8. d	33. c	58. a	83. b
9. a	34. b	59. b	84. d
10. a	35. d	60. b	85. a
11. a	36. b	61. d	86. a
12. b	37. b	62. b	87. c
13. a	38. d	63. a	88. c
14. b	39. a	64. b	89. c
15. a	40. b	65. b	90. c
16. c	41. b	66. c	91. a
17. d	42. b	67. a	92. d
18. a	43. c	68. a	93. a
19. c	44. b	69. d	94. c
20. b	45. b	70. d	95. b
21. a	46. c	71. c	96. d
22. b	47. c	72. d	97. d
23. d	48. c	73. c	98. a
24. a	49. a	74. a	99. b
25. c	50. a	75. a	100. d

ANSWER KEY

1. c	26. d	51. d	76. a
2. a	27. b	52. b	77. a
3. c	28. b	53. a	78. c
4. d	29. b	54. a	79. d
5. b	30. b	55. c	80. a
6. d	31. d	56. a	81. c
7. c	32. a	57. d	82. b
8. a	33. c	58. d	83. d
9. b	34. d	59. b	84. d
10. b	35. c	60. a	85. b
11. a	36. b	61. b	86. b
12. b	37. a	62. a	87. b
13. b	38. d	63. b	88. a
14. d	39. b	64. d	89. a
15. d	40. d	65. a	90. c
16. b	41. b	66. b	91. c
17. b	42. c	67. d	92. c
18. c	43. d	68. d	93. c
19. c	44. a	69. d	94. d
20. a	45. b	70. d	95. c
21. b	46. d	71. a	96. b
22. b	47. a	72. d	97. a
23. d	48. b	73. d	98. d
24. d	49. a	74. b	99. d
25. d	50. c	75. b	100. d

Answers to the Pretests and Posttests: BUILDING VOCABULARY SKILLS

	Unit One		Unit Two		Unit Three		Unit Four		Unit Five	
	Pretest	*Posttest*	*Pretest*	*Posttest*	*Pretest*	*Posttest*	*Pretest*	*Posttest*	*Pretest*	*Posttest*
1.	c	d	a	b	b	b	a	a	c	b
2.	c	b	d	d	c	d	d	c	b	a
3.	c	b	c	b	b	a	c	c	b	c
4.	a	d	b	a	d	a	a	d	c	d
5.	d	b	a	a	c	a	b	d	b	c
6.	d	a	d	b	a	b	d	a	b	b
7.	b	c	a	b	b	b	b	a	d	a
8.	a	d	c	a	b	d	c	c	d	b
9.	b	b	d	c	b	c	b	b	d	b
10.	b	a	b	a	a	a	b	a	a	b
11.	c	d	b	a	c	c	d	c	c	d
12.	a	d	a	d	d	d	d	a	d	d
13.	b	a	d	c	b	a	a	c	c	a
14.	c	b	b	d	b	d	b	d	d	c
15.	d	c	b	b	b	b	a	d	c	b
16.	d	a	a	a	d	b	c	a	a	c
17.	a	c	c	c	b	d	b	c	a	d
18.	a	c	d	c	a	d	b	d	d	b
19.	c	a	b	b	b	b	c	c	a	d
20.	a	c	d	a	b	c	b	b	c	d
21.	d	c	c	b	c	b	c	a	d	d
22.	b	b	d	b	b	d	c	c	b	d
23.	a	d	b	b	b	c	a	c	a	c
24.	b	c	b	d	a	c	c	a	c	b
25.	c	b	a	b	b	b	a	a	b	c
26.	d	a	c	d	c	d	a	d	a	a
27.	c	a	b	b	b	c	d	b	c	b
28.	a	a	c	a	b	a	c	d	c	c
29.	b	c	c	d	b	c	a	c	c	d
30.	a	a	d	c	c	a	d	a	c	a
31.	c	d	d	c	c	b	c	b	a	a
32.	d	c	b	b	c	c	c	c	a	d
33.	b	d	a	a	a	d	d	b	b	b
34.	b	b	c	c	a	c	c	a	b	b
35.	a	c	b	c	c	b	c	c	c	c
36.	a	c	a	b	c	d	c	c	a	a
37.	c	b	b	c	c	d	a	d	b	a
38.	a	c	a	d	a	b	a	c	d	b
39.	b	d	c	b	d	b	d	b	c	c
40.	a	d	d	b	a	c	a	d	a	c
41.	c	d	b	c	a	a	a	a	a	b
42.	c	a	a	b	b	a	c	b	d	d
43.	a	a	b	d	a	b	b	a	a	c
44.	d	b	c	a	c	d	d	b	d	c
45.	a	d	d	c	c	a	c	c	c	d
46.	b	d	d	b	d	c	a	d	c	b
47.	c	d	c	a	b	a	b	b	b	b
48.	a	d	d	a	c	c	b	a	c	a
49.	b	a	b	a	d	b	b	a	a	a
50.	c	d	d	d	b	d	a	d	b	d

Answers to the Chapter Activities: BUILDING VOCABULARY SKILLS

Chapter 1 (Taking Exams)

Ten Words in Context	Matching Words/Defs	Sentence Check 1	Sentence Check 2	Final Check
1. B 6. A	1. 8 6. 7	1. F 6. H	1–2. A, F	1. I 6. C
2. A 7. C	2. 4 7. 6	2. C 7. G	3–4. D, H	2. G 7. A
3. B 8. B	3. 2 8. 3	3. J 8. B	5–6. B, G	3. J 8. E
4. C 9. C	4. 10 9. 9	4. E 9. A	7–8. C, E	4. D 9. B
5. B 10. B	5. 1 10. 5	5. I 10. D	9–10. I, J	5. F 10. H

Chapter 2 (Nate the Woodsman)

Ten Words in Context	Matching Words/Defs	Sentence Check 1	Sentence Check 2	Final Check
1. B 6. C	1. 6 6. 7	1. B 6. I	1–2. C, H	1. J 6. B
2. C 7. B	2. 4 7. 3	2. H 7. F	3–4. I, B	2. G 7. I
3. C 8. A	3. 8 8. 5	3. E 8. A	5–6. J, F	3. H 8. C
4. A 9. A	4. 10 9. 9	4. D 9. C	7–8. G, E	4. D 9. A
5. B 10. B	5. 1 10. 2	5. G 10. J	9–10. A, D	5. F 10. E

Chapter 3 (Who's on Trial?)

Ten Words in Context	Matching Words/Defs	Sentence Check 1	Sentence Check 2	Final Check
1. C 6. C	1. 2 6. 10	1. B 6. H	1–2. I, H	1. B 6. F
2. B 7. A	2. 6 7. 9	2. J 7. A	3–4. G, D	2. H 7. G
3. A 8. A	3. 4 8. 5	3. F 8. I	5–6. C, A	3. D 8. I
4. B 9. A	4. 7 9. 8	4. G 9. E	7–8. F, J	4. C 9. E
5. B 10. C	5. 1 10. 3	5. D 10. C	9–10. B, E	5. J 10. A

Chapter 4 (Students and Politics)

Ten Words in Context	Matching Words/Defs	Sentence Check 1	Sentence Check 2	Final Check
1. A 6. B	1. 6 6. 4	1. J 6. B	1–2. B, C	1. G 6. H
2. C 7. A	2. 3 7. 9	2. D 7. A	3–4. A, J	2. A 7. C
3. C 8. B	3. 8 8. 7	3. I 8. G	5–6. D, I	3. I 8. D
4. B 9. B	4. 1 9. 2	4. H 9. C	7–8. E, G	4. B 9. J
5. C 10. C	5. 10 10. 5	5. F 10. E	9–10. F, H	5. E 10. F

Chapter 5 (Night Nurse)

Ten Words in Context	Matching Words/Defs	Sentence Check 1	Sentence Check 2	Final Check
1. B 6. C	1. 8 6. 3	1. C 6. D	1–2. H, A	1. D 6. H
2. A 7. A	2. 10 7. 9	2. B 7. A	3–4. F, G	2. A 7. I
3. C 8. C	3. 4 8. 7	3. H 8. G	5–6. E, J	3. F 8. B
4. A 9. B	4. 6 9. 2	4. I 9. J	7–8. I, D	4. J 9. C
5. B 10. C	5. 1 10. 5	5. E 10. F	9–10. B, C	5. E 10. G

Chapter 6 (Theo's Perfect Car)

Ten Word Pts in Context	Matching Word Pts/Defs	Sentence Check 1	Sentence Check 2	Final Check
1. B 6. A	1. 4 6. 6	1. F 6. I	1–2. H, C	1. A 6. B
2. B 7. C	2. 8 7. 10	2. J 7. B	3–4. B, A	2. E 7. D
3. B 8. B	3. 9 8. 5	3. G 8. A	5–6. J, I	3. G 8. I
4. A 9. A	4. 1 9. 7	4. E 9. D	7–8. G, F	4. J 9. F
5. C 10. C	5. 2 10. 3	5. C 10. H	9–10. E, D	5. C 10. H

Chapter 7 (Relating to Parents)

Ten Words in Context	Matching Words/Defs	Sentence Check 1	Sentence Check 2	Final Check
1. B 6. A	1. 8 6. 5	1. G 6. H	1–2. J, I	1. C 6. J
2. C 7. C	2. 3 7. 6	2. I 7. F	3–4. H, E	2. B 7. A
3. A 8. A	3. 10 8. 4	3. D 8. J	5–6. G, D	3. H 8. G
4. C 9. C	4. 7 9. 9	4. A 9. C	7–8. B, A	4. I 9. F
5. A 10. C	5. 1 10. 2	5. E 10. B	9–10. F, C	5. D 10. E

Chapter 8 (Job Choices)

Ten Words in Context	Matching Words/Defs	Sentence Check 1	Sentence Check 2	Final Check
1. B 6. B	1. 4 6. 3	1. C 6. G	1–2. B, E	1. I 6. G
2. A 7. B	2. 1 7. 9	2. J 7. E	3–4. I, J	2. J 7. E
3. B 8. A	3. 8 8. 6	3. F 8. B	5–6. A, H	3. D 8. H
4. C 9. B	4. 10 9. 2	4. I 9. D	7–8. C, G	4. A 9. B
5. A 10. C	5. 7 10. 5	5. H 10. A	9–10. D, F	5. F 10. C

Chapter 9 (No Joking)

Ten Words in Context	Matching Words/Defs	Sentence Check 1	Sentence Check 2	Final Check
1. B 6. B	1. 4 6. 2	1. I 6. J	1–2. H, F	1. D 6. G
2. C 7. A	2. 7 7. 10	2. F 7. C	3–4. I, D	2. E 7. C
3. B 8. C	3. 6 8. 5	3. A 8. E	5–6. J, E	3. H 8. J
4. A 9. A	4. 1 9. 3	4. H 9. D	7–8. C, A	4. I 9. A
5. C 10. C	5. 9 10. 8	5. B 10. G	9–10. G, B	5. B 10. F

Chapter 10 (Museum Pet)

Ten Words in Context	Matching Words/Defs	Sentence Check 1	Sentence Check 2	Final Check
1. A 6. B	1. 6 6. 4	1. G 6. E	1–2. D, F	1. E 6. H
2. B 7. B	2. 3 7. 8	2. B 7. I	3–4. I, A	2. B 7. J
3. A 8. C	3. 7 8. 10	3. A 8. C	5–6. C, H	3. C 8. A
4. C 9. C	4. 9 9. 2	4. D 9. F	7–8. J, B	4. F 9. I
5. C 10. B	5. 1 10. 5	5. J 10. H	9–10. E, G	5. G 10. D

Chapter 11 (Unacceptable Boyfriends)

Ten Words in Context	Matching Words/Defs	Sentence Check 1	Sentence Check 2	Final Check
1. C 6. C	1. 7 6. 4	1. E 6. I	1–2. E, F	1. B 6. C
2. C 7. A	2. 5 7. 3	2. C 7. B	3–4. G, I	2. F 7. I
3. C 8. A	3. 10 8. 1	3. D 8. H	5–6. J, D	3. D 8. H
4. A 9. B	4. 2 9. 6	4. G 9. J	7–8. H, B	4. A 9. G
5. A 10. C	5. 8 10. 9	5. F 10. A	9–10. A, C	5. E 10. J

Chapter 12 (Coping with Snow)

Ten Word Pts in Context	Matching Word Pts/Defs	Sentence Check 1	Sentence Check 2	Final Check
1. B 6. A	1. 8 6. 2	1. I 6. A	1–2. A, F	1. C 6. I
2. A 7. B	2. 4 7. 5	2. G 7. B	3–4. C, G	2. E 7. D
3. C 8. C	3. 1 8. 9	3. E 8. F	5–6. D, I	3. A 8. J
4. B 9. B	4. 3 9. 6	4. C 9. H	7–8. E, J	4. G 9. H
5. B 10. A	5. 10 10. 7	5. D 10. J	9–10. B, H	5. B 10. F

Chapter 13 (Our Headstrong Baby)

Ten Words in Context	Matching Words/Defs	Sentence Check 1	Sentence Check 2	Final Check
1. B 6. A	1. 8 6. 10	1. F 6. B	1–2. B, F	1. E 6. G
2. B 7. B	2. 3 7. 4	2. G 7. D	3–4. C, E	2. D 7. C
3. B 8. C	3. 9 8. 6	3. J 8. C	5–6. D, G	3. H 8. A
4. C 9. B	4. 7 9. 2	4. E 9. H	7–8. H, J	4. B 9. J
5. A 10. C	5. 1 10. 5	5. A 10. I	9–10. A, I	5. F 10. I

Chapter 14 (Mr. Perfect?)

Ten Words in Context	Matching Words/Defs	Sentence Check 1	Sentence Check 2	Final Check
1. B 6. A	1. 6 6. 10	1. I 6. B	1–2. C, B	1. B 6. J
2. C 7. C	2. 4 7. 1	2. H 7. J	3–4. G, F	2. C 7. I
3. B 8. A	3. 3 8. 9	3. F 8. E	5–6. I, H	3. A 8. D
4. A 9. A	4. 2 9. 5	4. A 9. G	7–8. J, E	4. E 9. F
5. B 10. B	5. 8 10. 7	5. C 10. D	9–10. A, D	5. H 10. G

Chapter 15 (A Narrow Escape)

	Ten Words in Context	Matching Words/Defs	Sentence Check 1	Final Check
1	C	6	C	H
2	B	8	E	C
3	C	9	H	F
4	A	2	B	A
5	B	4	A	J
6	A	7	G	B
7	B	10	I	D
8	C	1	D	G
9	C	3	J	E
10	A	5	F	I

Sentence Check 2: 1–2. H, G 3–4. B, F 5–6. A, I 7–8. J, C 9–10. E, D

Chapter 16 (The Power of Advertising)

	Ten Words in Context	Matching Words/Defs	Sentence Check 1	Final Check
1	C	7	C	J
2	B	3	H	F
3	A	10	D	E
4	B	6	F	D
5	A	1	J	A
6	C	5	E	I
7	C	8	A	H
8	B	4	B	B
9	A	2	G	G
10	B	9	I	C

Sentence Check 2: 1–2. A, I 3–4. D, G 5–6. C, E 7–8. J, F 9–10. H, B

Chapter 17 (Waiter)

	Ten Words in Context	Matching Words/Defs	Sentence Check 1	Final Check
1	B	8	F	E
2	A	4	H	I
3	B	9	C	J
4	A	6	I	B
5	A	3	J	D
6	C	2	G	C
7	A	5	D	F
8	C	10	E	H
9	B	7	A	G
10	C	1	B	A

Sentence Check 2: 1–2. E, C 3–4. J, B 5–6. I, D 7–8. F, H 9–10. G, A

Chapter 18 (Black Widow Spiders)

	Ten Word Pts in Context	Word Pts/Defs	Sentence Check 1	Final Check
1	B	7	B	E
2	A	10	E	I
3	C	1	J	H
4	B	8	I	A
5	C	2	G	F
6	B	9	A	J
7	A	3	C	B
8	C	6	D	D
9	B	4	F	C
10	B	5	H	G

Sentence Check 2: 1–2. C, H 3–4. I, F 5–6. E, J 7–8. B, A 9–10. G, D

Chapter 19 (Adjusting to a New Culture)

	Ten Words in Context	Matching Words/Defs	Sentence Check 1	Final Check
1	B	9	B	B
2	A	4	E	C
3	C	6	G	A
4	A	3	D	F
5	B	10	H	D
6	B	7	I	E
7	C	1	A	H
8	A	5	C	G
9	A	8	F	J
10	B	2	J	I

Sentence Check 2: 1–2. B, G 3–4. F, D 5–6. E, I 7–8. J, H 9–10. A, C

Chapter 20 (A Dream About Wealth)

	Ten Words in Context	Matching Words/Defs	Sentence Check 1	Final Check
1	B	2	I	J
2	A	10	G	C
3	B	6	B	A
4	C	8	J	I
5	C	1	H	E
6	B	9	A	G
7	C	5	F	H
8	C	3	D	F
9	A	4	E	B
10	B	7	C	D

Sentence Check 2: 1–2. J, I 3–4. B, D 5–6. C, A 7–8. F, H 9–10. E, G

Chapter 21 (Children and Drugs)

	Ten Words in Context	Matching Words/Defs	Sentence Check 1	Final Check
1	B	8	D	J
2	A	3	J	I
3	B	10	H	D
4	C	6	F	C
5	B	7	G	E
6	A	1	A	B
7	B	5	B	G
8	C	4	E	A
9	A	2	I	H
10	B	9	C	F

Sentence Check 2: 1–2. A, E 3–4. I, F 5–6. D, C 7–8. J, H 9–10. B, G

Chapter 22 (Party House)

	Ten Words in Context	Matching Words/Defs	Sentence Check 1	Final Check
1	B	8	F	B
2	C	7	I	G
3	B	1	A	A
4	B	2	G	C
5	A	5	C	D
6	C	10	J	H
7	B	4	H	I
8	B	6	D	J
9	A	3	B	F
10	C	9	E	E

Sentence Check 2: 1–2. G, J 3–4. I, C 5–6. H, A 7–8. D, E 9–10. F, B

Chapter 23 (Procrastinator)

	Ten Words in Context	Matching Words/Defs	Sentence Check 1	Final Check
1	A	6	I	E
2	B	4	D	C
3	A	7	E	G
4	C	1	A	J
5	C	9	F	H
6	B	10	G	A
7	C	8	B	D
8	A	3	J	I
9	B	5	C	F
10	B	2	H	B

Sentence Check 2: 1–2. G, F 3–4. C, I 5–6. A, J 7–8. E, D 9–10. H, B

Chapter 24 (King of Cats)

	Ten Word Pts in Context	Word Pts/Defs	Sentence Check 1	Final Check
1	B	3	E	C
2	B	4	B	J
3	A	2	D	H
4	C	10	H	I
5	B	6	G	E
6	C	8	F	D
7	C	5	C	F
8	A	9	A	A
9	C	7	J	G
10	C	1	I	B

Sentence Check 2: 1–2. H, I 3–4. B, G 5–6. A, E 7–8. F, C 9–10. A, E

Chapter 25 (A Change in View)

	Ten Words in Context	Matching Words/Defs	Sentence Check 1	Final Check
1	A	4	A	J
2	C	1	D	I
3	B	6	G	B
4	A	10	H	H
5	B	9	J	D
6	C	2	B	F
7	B	8	C	E
8	A	3	E	A
9	B	5	I	C
10	C	7	F	G

Sentence Check 2: 1–2. D, J 3–4. F, G 5–6. B, A 7–8. H, I 9–10. E, C

Chapter 26 (Balloon Flight)

	Ten Words in Context	Matching Words/Defs	Sentence Check 1	Final Check
1	C	6	F	F
2	A	3	B	E
3	B	7	D	B
4	B	4	J	A
5	C	1	H	D
6	B	2	I	H
7	A	5	A	C
8	A	10	C	J
9	A	9	E	I
10	C	8	G	G

Sentence Check 2: 1–2. B, C 3–4. H, J 5–6. I, D 7–8. A, F 9–10. E, G

Chapter 27 (Family Differences)

	Ten Words in Context	Matching Words/Defs	Sentence Check 1	Final Check
1	B	4	A	B
2	B	10	B	D
3	A	8	F	J
4	C	9	J	G
5	A	1	H	C
6	A	3	I	I
7	C	5	D	F
8	B	6	G	E
9	B	2	E	H
10	C	7	C	A

Sentence Check 2: 1–2. J, G 3–4. F, A 5–6. C, H 7–8. E, B 9–10. I, D

Chapter 28 (Murder Mystery)

	Ten Words in Context	Matching Words/Defs	Sentence Check 1	Final Check
1	B	4	D	A
2	B	9	B	H
3	A	2	A	F
4	C	10	F	D
5	C	1	E	C
6	C	6	J	J
7	A	8	C	G
8	C	3	I	E
9	A	5	H	I
10	C	7	G	B

Sentence Check 2: 1–2. C, J 3–4. I, D 5–6. E, F 7–8. B, H 9–10. A, G

Chapter 29 (Chicken Pox)

	Ten Words in Context	Matching Words/Defs	Sentence Check 1	Final Check
1	B	5	J	J
2	C	7	I	E
3	A	2	G	F
4	B	3	A	B
5	A	1	F	A
6	C	9	E	H
7	B	10	D	I
8	A	6	B	C
9	B	8	H	D
10	C	4	C	G

Sentence Check 2: 1–2. J, D 3–4. F, C 5–6. G, A 7–8. E, H 9–10. B, I

Chapter 30 (Walking)

	Ten Words in Context	Matching Words/Defs	Sentence Check 1	Final Check
1	B	4	I	C
2	B	8	G	F
3	C	6	B	B
4	C	2	C	G
5	C	1	A	J
6	B	9	D	H
7	C	5	J	I
8	C	3	F	A
9	A	10	E	E
10	C	7	H	D

Sentence Check 2: 1–2. J, G 3–4. H, D 5–6. B, A 7–8. E, F 9–10. C, I

Answers to the Unit Reviews: BUILDING VOCABULARY SKILLS

Unit One

Unit Two

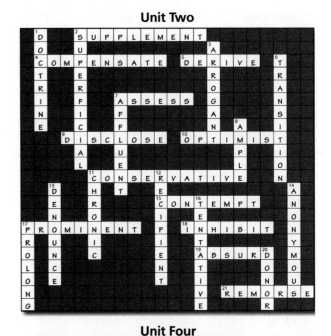

Unit Three

Unit Four

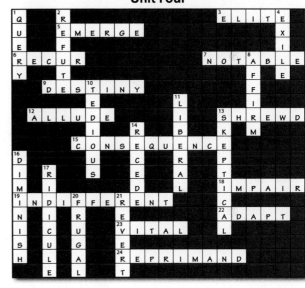

Unit Five

Answers to the Unit Tests: BUILDING VOCABULARY SKILLS

Unit One	Unit Two	Unit Three	Unit Four	Unit Five

Unit One, Test 1
1. antidote
2. undermine
3. avert
4. extensive
5. endorse
6. alternative
7. gruesome
8. novice
9. urban
10. agenda

11. A	16. B
12. C	17. D
13. C	18. A
14. B	19. D
15. D	20. A

Unit Two, Test 1
1. phobia
2. defect
3. absurd
4. chronic
5. surpassed
6. alienate
7. derived
8. altered
9. verify
10. transition

11. A	16. B
12. C	17. A
13. C	18. A
14. D	19. D
15. B	20. D

Unit Three, Test 1
1. propelled
2. retrieve
3. passive
4. accessible
5. ordeal
6. elapse
7. convey
8. vivid
9. miserly
10. unique

11. A	16. A
12. B	17. D
13. C	18. C
14. C	19. A
15. B	20. B

Unit Four, Test 1
1. plausible
2. simultaneous
3. provoke
4. frugal
5. mediocre
6. alleged
7. strategy
8. query
9. transaction
10. refuted

11. B	16. D
12. A	17. A
13. B	18. C
14. C	19. A
15. D	20. A

Unit Five, Test 1
1. susceptible
2. site
3. inflict
4. data
5. transmitted
6. infinite
7. competent
8. comparable
9. discriminate
10. sophisticated

11. A	16. A
12. B	17. C
13. C	18. D
14. A	19. A
15. B	20. D

Unit One, Test 2

1. E	14. C
2. K	15. I
3. D	16. C
4. A	17. I
5. L	18. I
6. J	19. C
7. I	20. B
8. B	21. C
9. H	22. A
10. C	23. C
11. G	24. C
12. F	25. B
13. M	

Unit Two, Test 2

1. C	14. C
2. B	15. C
3. D	16. I
4. A	17. C
5. G	18. I
6. E	19. I
7. H	20. B
8. J	21. C
9. F	22. A
10. M	23. C
11. L	24. A
12. I	25. B
13. K	

Unit Three, Test 2

1. G	14. C
2. A	15. C
3. I	16. I
4. C	17. I
5. E	18. C
6. D	19. I
7. H	20. B
8. F	21. C
9. L	22. A
10. M	23. C
11. J	24. C
12. K	25. A
13. B	

Unit Four, Test 2

1. H	14. I
2. C	15. I
3. D	16. C
4. I	17. C
5. G	18. C
6. L	19. C
7. E	20. A
8. K	21. C
9. A	22. B
10. M	23. C
11. F	24. A
12. J	25. C
13. B	

Unit Five, Test 2

1. G	14. I
2. F	15. C
3. K	16. I
4. H	17. C
5. M	18. I
6. A	19. I
7. D	20. A
8. B	21. B
9. L	22. C
10. J	23. C
11. E	24. B
12. C	25. C
13. I	

Unit One, Test 3

1. C	11. C
2. D	12. A
3. B	13. D
4. A	14. B
5. D	15. A
6. D	16. D
7. C	17. C
8. A	18. A
9. D	19. B
10. A	20. D

Unit Two, Test 3

1. A	11. A
2. C	12. D
3. A	13. D
4. C	14. C
5. D	15. D
6. B	16. B
7. A	17. A
8. A	18. D
9. A	19. A
10. B	20. C

Unit Three, Test 3

1. D	11. B
2. A	12. D
3. B	13. A
4. C	14. B
5. A	15. D
6. B	16. A
7. C	17. C
8. B	18. A
9. C	19. D
10. B	20. A

Unit Four, Test 3

1. C	11. A
2. C	12. D
3. D	13. D
4. A	14. D
5. D	15. C
6. B	16. B
7. A	17. C
8. B	18. D
9. B	19. C
10. C	20. D

Unit Five, Test 3

1. B	11. B
2. A	12. D
3. D	13. A
4. B	14. B
5. B	15. D
6. C	16. D
7. A	17. B
8. D	18. B
9. B	19. A
10. B	20. B

Unit One, Test 4 (Word Parts)

1. I	11. F
2. J	12. J
3. C	13. I
4. D	14. D
5. A	15. B
6. H	16. B
7. G	17. A
8. F	18. C
9. E	19. C
10. B	20. A

Unit Two, Test 4 (Word Parts)

1. A	11. H
2. H	12. I
3. J	13. J
4. D	14. F
5. I	15. E
6. B	16. B
7. F	17. A
8. G	18. C
9. C	19. B
10. E	20. B

Unit Three, Test 4 (Word Parts)

1. J	11. A
2. C	12. J
3. I	13. G
4. G	14. I
5. D	15. F
6. B	16. C
7. A	17. A
8. F	18. C
9. H	19. A
10. E	20. A

Unit Four, Test 4 (Word Parts)

1. C	11. A
2. D	12. D
3. E	13. G
4. G	14. I
5. I	15. C
6. B	16. B
7. J	17. B
8. H	18. A
9. A	19. C
10. F	20. C

Mastery Test: *Chapter 1 (Taking Exams)*

In the space provided, write the word from the box needed to complete each sentence. Then put the **letter** of that word in the column at the left. Use each word once.

A. **acknowledge**	B. **alternative**	C. **anecdote**	D. **appropriate**	E. **avert**
F. **candid**	G. **compel**	H. **comply**	I. **concise**	J. **drastic**

_____ 1. Fred thinks it's funny to do the opposite of what everyone else considers _____.
For instance, he likes to send sympathy cards for weddings and birthdays.

_____ 2. We keep a flashlight in every room to _____ being left in the dark in the event
of a power failure.

_____ 3. According to a(n) _____ a friend told me, someone once asked boxer
Muhammed Ali if he were the "greatest" at golf. "Yes," Ali answered. "I just haven't played yet."

_____ 4. A really successful commercial _____s viewers to leap from their chairs and rush
out to buy the advertised item.

_____ 5. All of the restaurant's desserts were fattening, so I chose another _____. I had a
frozen fruit bar at home instead.

_____ 6. To get me to _____ with her demands, my sister threatens to tell my boyfriend
what I said after our first date: "Bo-ring!"

_____ 7. Because they're not eager to _____ that cockroaches are among their residents,
Germans refer to the "German cockroach" as the "Russian roach."

_____ 8. Most newspapers have limited space for letters to the editor, so yours will have a better chance of
being published if it's _____.

_____ 9. Every day, polluters get away with dumping thousands of pounds of plastic into the sea. Clearly, we
need more _____ penalties to make them stop.

_____ 10. When Flora asked Rob to be really truthful in his opinion of her new dress, he told her, "To be
perfectly _____, I don't like the color, style, or material, but it fits you really well."

SCORE: (Number correct) _____ × 10 = _____ %

Mastery Test: *Chapter 2 (Nate the Woodsman)*

In the space provided, write the word from the box needed to complete each sentence. Then put the **letter** of that word in the column at the left. Use each word once.

A. **dialog**	B. **erratic**	C. **extensive**	D. **forfeit**	E. **fortify**
F. **illuminate**	G. **isolate**	H. **refuge**	I. **reminisce**	J. **urban**

_____ 1. Job opportunities are most numerous in _____ areas. Thus many people have no choice but to live surrounded by the concrete, metal, and glass of the city.

_____ 2. In the movie, the characters' British accents were so thick that I had trouble understanding some of the _____.

_____ 3. To _____ their stores against the coming hurricane, beachfront shopkeepers nailed boards over the windows.

_____ 4. The zoo had to _____ one baboon who was attacking the others. He was put in his own cage in another building.

_____ 5. At my class reunion, we _____(e)d about our years at school, including the time I broke my arm in gym and the day a piece of scenery fell during a play and hit the principal.

_____ 6. Lately the weather has been wildly _____ . This morning, for example, it was raining and 90 degrees; by the late afternoon, it was dry and in the 50's, and it rained again at night.

_____ 7. These days, candles are mainly used for decoration since most people have electric lights to _____ their homes.

_____ 8. Many homeless people cannot find a place of _____ from wintry weather.

_____ 9. The magazine printed only one paragraph on the "Save the Earth" meeting, but the local newspaper provided _____ coverage of the event—with photos and a full-page story.

_____ 10. The Olympic swimmer had to _____ his gold medal when officials discovered that he had taken illegal muscle-building drugs.

SCORE: (Number correct) _____ × 10 = _____ %

Mastery Test: *Chapter 3 (Who's on Trial?)*

In the space provided, write the word from the box needed to complete each sentence. Then put the **letter** of that word in the column at the left. Use each word once.

A. **delete**	B. **impartial**	C. **integrity**	D. **legitimate**	E. **lenient**
F. **menace**	G. **morale**	H. **naive**	I. **overt**	J. **undermine**

_____ 1. Abraham Lincoln is sometimes called "Honest Abe" because of his reputation for _____.

_____ 2. The paperback version of the novel was a shortened one—two chapters had been _____(e)d.

_____ 3. Violent crime is a(n) _____ to us all. In this century, nearly twice as many Americans have been murdered as have died in wars.

_____ 4. The Smiths' pleasure in their son's engagement was certainly _____. They walked around with big smiles on their faces all night.

_____ 5. When the cake collapsed, my _____ as a baker did too. I now don't even have enough confidence or desire to bake a cake from a mix.

_____ 6. After Joe smashed the headlights of the family car, he hoped his parents would be _____. Instead, they grounded him until he paid for the damage.

_____ 7. During the piano contest, the players were hidden behind a curtain so that the judges would cast _____ votes.

_____ 8. For years, termites _____(e)d the house's wooden frame until it became dangerously damaged.

_____ 9. When Lily started her job, she was _____ enough to think the other salespeople would be cooperative. However, she soon learned some people would stab her in the back for a sale.

_____ 10. In most states, a marriage is not _____ unless the bride and groom applied for a license and got blood tests before the wedding.

SCORE: (Number correct) _____ × 10 = _____ %

Mastery Test: *Chapter 4 (Students and Politics)*

In the space provided, write the word from the box needed to complete each sentence. Then put the **letter** of that word in the column at the left. Use each word once.

A. **agenda**	B. **antidote**	C. **apathy**	D. **bland**	E. **propaganda**
F. **prospects**	G. **radical**	H. **reinforce**	I. **relevant**	J. **ruthless**

_____ 1. Never eat toadstools. Not only are they poisonous, but there is also no _____ for their poison.

_____ 2. The _____ politician would have sold his own mother if the result would have been more votes for him.

_____ 3. The last item on the meeting's _____ was to schedule the date of the next meeting.

_____ 4. All ads for political candidates contain _____. Which political candidates would pay to spread information that did not support their campaign?

_____ 5. John didn't want to paint his house a _____ color, like pale grey or beige. Still, I think pink and purple are a little more interesting and exciting than necessary.

_____ 6. My uncle's _____ goals include getting rid of the income tax, giving the vote to fifteen-year-olds, and ending the army.

_____ 7. Because the city has a great housing shortage, the _____(s) of finding an affordable apartment are not good.

_____ 8. When you argue, be sure all your statements are _____. It's unfair to bring up points that are not related to the argument.

_____ 9. The comedian expected either cheers or boos from the bar crowd. Instead, he got the silence of _____.

_____ 10. Football players wrap strong tape around their ankles to _____ this weak part of the body.

SCORE: (Number correct) _____ × 10 = _____ %

Mastery Test: *Chapter 5 (Night Nurse)*

In the space provided, write the word from the box needed to complete each sentence. Then put the **letter** of that word in the column at the left. Use each word once.

A. **endorse**	B. **erode**	C. **gruesome**	D. **hypocrite**	E. **idealistic**
F. **illusion**	G. **impact**	H. **imply**	I. **novice**	J. **obstacle**

_____ 1. The baseball struck the batter with such _____ that it broke his jaw.

_____ 2. Although a majority of people in the state support the death penalty, the governor does not _____ it.

_____ 3. If you blink two lights on and off in an otherwise dark room, you create the _____ that a single light is moving back and forth.

_____ 4. Cliff's question to Judy—"Wouldn't you rather grab a hamburger than bother going to a fancy restaurant?"—was meant to _____ that he was low on cash.

_____ 5. A(n) _____ at ice-skating, I can only manage to remain upright, while my experienced friends leap and twirl around me.

_____ 6. The bodies taken out of the burned car were so _____ that even the medical examiner found the sight shocking.

_____ 7. In the movie *Mr. Smith Goes to Washington*, Jimmy Stewart plays a(n) _____ senator who values honesty and public service more than riches.

_____ 8. In the fairy tale "Rapunzel," there is one great _____ to the hero and heroine's happiness: she is locked in a tall tower with no door.

_____ 9. The centuries had caused the Greek statue's colorful layer of paint to _____, leaving only the underlying white marble.

_____ 10. Roy is such a(n) _____. He disapproves of handguns for other people, but he keeps one on his night table.

SCORE: (Number correct) _____ × 10 = _____ %	

Mastery Test: *Chapter 7 (Relating to Parents)*

In the space provided, write the word from the box needed to complete each sentence. Then put the **letter** of that word in the column at the left. Use each word once.

A. **concede**	B. **conservative**	C. **contrary**	D. **denounce**	E. **deter**
F. **disclose**	G. **scapegoat**	H. **superficial**	I. **sustain**	J. **transition**

_____ 1. There was too little time to make the _____ from bright sunlight to the dark movie theater. So I blindly felt my way down the aisle and then sat in the lap of a total stranger.

_____ 2. Alex and Joe have _____ views of life. To Alex "life is a bowl of cherries," but to Joe "it's the pits."

_____ 3. Gordon used to favor major changes in the company's treatment of workers. As soon as he became president, however, he turned _____.

_____ 4. The car's patches of rust, lumpy seats, and moldy odor were enough to _____ me from buying it.

_____ 5. When Max cheated on the test, the teacher _____(e)d him in front of the whole class and also expressed her disapproval of Max in a letter to his parents.

_____ 6. Josie and Kate's friendship is deep, not _____. For example, they share their innermost thoughts and offer each other support in difficult times.

_____ 7. Marilyn didn't intend to _____ the cost of the tie she gave Andy, but she revealed it down to the penny: when she wrapped the gift, she forgot to remove the price tag.

_____ 8. After bragging about his skill as a carpenter, Tony was unwilling to _____ that the crooked table was his own creation and not from a junk shop.

_____ 9. Studies show that girls are more likely than boys to accept blame for their errors. Boys are more likely to look for _____s to blame instead.

_____ 10. After the first ten minutes of weightlifting, I couldn't _____ the workout without risking muscle damage, so I stopped.

SCORE: (Number correct) _____ × 10 = _____ %

Name: _____

Mastery Test: *Chapter 8 (Job Choices)*

In the space provided, write the word from the box needed to complete each sentence. Then put the **letter** of that word in the column at the left. Use each word once.

A. **compensate**	B. **conceive**	C. **derive**	D. **diversity**	E. **inhibit**
F. **moderate**	G. **supplement**	H. **surpass**	I. **tentative**	J. **verify**

_____ 1. No one in town could _____ of Gail as a drill instructor—she seemed too gentle and sweet to give orders.

_____ 2. Bob had hoped to get a C in geometry, so the A he received certainly _____(e)d what he expected.

_____ 3. Clint calls himself a _____ TV watcher, but I feel he watches much more than just a few programs a day.

_____ 4. The _____ of products at outdoor markets is one of their attractions. Often they have baked goods, home decorations, fresh produce, and even clothing for sale.

_____ 5. David _____s his income from several part-time jobs: word processing, waiting on tables, and yard work.

_____ 6. Since mold grows most quickly in warm temperatures, refrigeration _____s its growth on food.

_____ 7. When people apply for jobs at a company, the personnel director calls their previous employers to _____ that they have reported their job experience truthfully.

_____ 8. Tyrone's supervisor gave him only _____ approval to take a day off. She had to check with her own boss to be sure.

_____ 9. Because hay doesn't give our horses full nutrition, we _____ their diet with grains.

_____ 10. Mrs. Brown promised to _____ Al for the gas he used driving her to the airport, but she hasn't paid him a penny yet.

SCORE: (Number correct) _____ × 10 = _____ %

Mastery Test: *Chapter 9 (No Joking)*

In the space provided, write the word from the box needed to complete each sentence. Then put the **letter** of that word in the column at the left. Use each word once.

A. **alter**	B. **ample**	C. **blunt**	D. **chronic**	E. **chronological**
F. **optimist**	G. **pretense**	H. **prolong**	I. **refrain**	J. **remorse**

_____   1. When successful businessmen were asked what they most regretted about their past, many expressed _____ that they hadn't spent more time with their children.

_____   2. Tonight's "study meeting" isn't really happening. It's just a _____ to get Denny over to the house for his surprise birthday party.

_____   3. A volcanic blast can dramatically _____ the appearance of a mountain, even knocking a thousand feet off its peak.

_____   4. Most children don't _____ their enjoyment of a box of candy. Rather than eat it slowly, they gulp it down by the handful.

_____   5. In this age of nuclear weapons, I'm still enough of a(n) _____ to believe that the world is headed toward peace rather than destruction.

_____   6. The restaurant offered a(n) _____ selection of meat dishes for Julio, but it had too few vegetarian ones for his wife.

_____   7. The movie doesn't present events in _____ order, but begins at the end of the story and shows what came earlier in flashbacks.

_____   8. Because of Steve's _____ lateness, I've learned always to ask him to arrive an hour earlier than I really want him to arrive.

_____   9. Please _____ from speaking loudly in the library.

_____   10. By constantly asking my opinion of his poems, Jesse has forced me to be _____ and say they're terrible.

SCORE: (Number correct) _____ × 10 = _____ %

Name: _____

Mastery Test: *Chapter 10 (Museum Pet)*

In the space provided, write the word from the box needed to complete each sentence. Then put the **letter** of that word in the column at the left. Use each word once.

A. **acute**	B. **anonymous**	C. **apprehensive**	D. **arrogant**	E. **bestow**
F. **donor**	G. **phobia**	H. **prominent**	I. **prudent**	J. **recipient**

_____ 1. Some airlines offer classes to help people overcome their _____s about air travel.

_____ 2. Because the dentist had said the root canal would hurt "only a little," Doug wasn't prepared for the _____ pain that followed.

_____ 3. It isn't _____ for a worker to insult the boss when quitting a job. The worker might need the boss later for a reference.

_____ 4. The generous parents of the young man killed on the highway _____(e)d his organs on transplant banks.

_____ 5. The "No Smoking" sign was placed in a(n) _____ spot near the restaurant's door so that customers would be sure to see it before entering.

_____ 6. As the _____ of an athletic scholarship, Brad has to keep up a B average or leave the team.

_____ 7. The caller told police about a robbery going on at Fifth and Walnut, but she wouldn't give her name. For her own protection, she wanted her tip to remain _____.

_____ 8. Knowing he was wealthier than his classmates, the new boy was at first _____, but his attitude changed when he realized he was one of the worst students in the class.

_____ 9. The landscapers were _____ about planting the bushes when the homeowner wasn't there, since he had strong opinions about the way his yard should look.

_____ 10. Peggy volunteered to be a blood _____ during the Red Cross drive, but a nurse said she weighed too little to give blood.

SCORE: (Number correct) _____ × 10 = _____ %

Mastery Test: *Chapter 11 (Unacceptable Boyfriends)*

In the space provided, write the word from the box needed to complete each sentence. Then put the **letter** of that word in the column at the left. Use each word once.

A. **absurd**	B. **adhere**	C. **affluent**	D. **alienate**	E. **assess**
F. **compile**	G. **contempt**	H. **defect**	I. **doctrine**	J. **dogmatic**

_____ 1. Many years ago, my grandmother _____(e)d a scrapbook containing all my grandfather's love letters. The collection is now a treasure in our family.

_____ 2. The stamp wouldn't _____ to the envelope until I spread a drop of glue on the stamp's back.

_____ 3. The Amish are a religious group whose _____ forbids them to use modern conveniences, such as electrical appliances.

_____ 4. Sylvia has few friends. Her critical manner and hot temper _____ people.

_____ 5. Predictions of the exact day the world will end are _____, yet people have been making such ridiculous announcements for centuries.

_____ 6. Our English teacher is _____. She allows only one interpretation of a story or poem—hers.

_____ 7. When the new refrigerator was delivered, Liza discovered it had a serious _____ —the freezer didn't get cold enough to make ice cubes.

_____ 8. People in prison for abusing children are viewed with great _____ by the other inmates. Even murderers get more respect.

_____ 9. Before their business failed, the Lopezes were _____. They were so rich, in fact, that they could buy whatever they wanted.

_____ 10. After the tornado, county officials examined property to _____ the damage.

SCORE: (Number correct) _____ × 10 = _____ %

Mastery Test: *Chapter 13 (Our Headstrong Baby)*

In the space provided, write the word from the box needed to complete each sentence. Then put the **letter** of that word in the column at the left. Use each word once.

A. **accessible**	B. **awe**	C. **cite**	D. **compatible**	E. **exempt**
F. **prevail**	G. **propel**	H. **rational**	I. **retort**	J. **retrieve**

_____ 1. I hate to say that Hank is a liar, but I could _____ many things he's told me that weren't true.

_____ 2. The wheels that used to _____ Joshua's toy train are jammed with sand, so now it just sits there going "toot toot."

_____ 3. The friendly way that Muffy and Ralph play together proves that a cat and dog can be _____ .

_____ 4. The sixth-graders looked up with _____ at the visiting professional baseball player.

_____ 5. Because the prisoner had a weak heart, he was _____ from the hard physical labor required of the others.

_____ 6. When my little nephew visited, I needed to move my supply of candy from a(n) _____ cupboard to one out of his reach.

_____ 7. The paper boy threw the newspaper onto the Smiths' front porch and then went to _____ it when he remembered that the Smiths were out of town.

_____ 8. When Lydia and Jeff discuss money, they always start out calm and _____ and end up yelling and unreasonable.

_____ 9. If their best player is back in form tonight, the basketball team is sure to _____ over their opponents.

_____ 10. When the rude customer tried to cut into the line, saying, "I don't like to be kept waiting," the clerk gave this _____: "Then I won't make you wait to hear just what I think of you."

SCORE: (Number correct) _____ × 10 = _____ %

Mastery Test: *Chapter 14 (Mr. Perfect?)*

In the space provided, write the word from the box needed to complete each sentence. Then put the **letter** of that word in the column at the left. Use each word once.

A. **dubious**	B. **ecstatic**	C. **encounter**	D. **evolve**	E. **fallacy**
F. **fictitious**	G. **gullible**	H. **liable**	I. **miserly**	J. **pessimist**

_____ 1. After dinner, Frank told a hilarious story. He'd once had the _____ privilege of being the very first patient of a nervous young dentist.

_____ 2. The idea that snakes are slimy is a common _____. Actually, their skin is dry.

_____ 3. The children's story that John wrote is set in the _____ land of Tarara-boom-de-ay.

_____ 4. When I heard how many other people had applied for the job I wanted, the _____ in me decided I didn't have a chance.

_____ 5. Vivian was _____ enough to believe that the piece of green glass was an emerald, and she paid a high price for it.

_____ 6. Ron was _____ when he realized he'd picked the winning lottery number, but his joy turned to panic when he couldn't find his ticket.

_____ 7. The flower had slowly _____(e)d from a tightly closed bud to a fully open bloom. But high-speed photography showed the change happening within seconds.

_____ 8. Standing in line for a plane ticket, Betsy was surprised to _____ a celebrity doing the same thing.

_____ 9. Mr. McDermott is wealthy but _____. He would never give a cent to charity.

_____ 10. A smart supermarket manager places new items at eye level. If they're too high or too low on the shelf, they're _____ to be overlooked.

SCORE: (Number correct) _____ × 10 = _____ %

Mastery Test: *Chapter 15 (A Narrow Escape)*

In the space provided, write the word from the box needed to complete each sentence. Then put the **letter** of that word in the column at the left. Use each word once.

A. **elapse**	B. **evasive**	C. **fluent**	D. **futile**	E. **harass**
F. **infer**	G. **lethal**	H. **obsession**	I. **ordeal**	J. **persistent**

_____ 1. Grady's efforts to start his damaged car were _____, so he had to call a tow truck.

_____ 2. The striking workers outside the factory _____(e)d people who crossed the picket line by yelling at them and calling them names.

_____ 3. At first, the college counselor refused to let Chris retake the English entrance exam. But Chris was _____ in asking and was finally allowed to retake the test.

_____ 4. When Yolanda discovered that Ben had been in prison for ten years, she understood why he had been so _____ about his past.

_____ 5. Being either extremely thin or very overweight indicates that food may be a(n) _____.

_____ 6. Tara is not speaking to her mother, so I _____ that they have had a fight.

_____ 7. People who were abused as children often suffer an emotional _____ that goes on long after the physical pain is over.

_____ 8. Dogs love chocolate, but the sweet stuff can be _____ for them. More than one family has seen its pet die after it ate chocolate candy.

_____ 9. In order to control his temper, Ira let some time _____ before scolding his daughter about the broken lamp.

_____ 10. You can learn a foreign language from books and records. But to become truly _____ in the language, you must also converse with native speakers.

SCORE: (Number correct) _____ × 10 = _____ %

Name: _____

Mastery Test: *Chapter 16 (The Power of Advertising)*

In the space provided, write the word from the box needed to complete each sentence. Then put the **letter** of that word in the column at the left. Use each word once.

A. **convey**	B. **delusion**	C. **devise**	D. **savor**	E. **stimulate**
F. **subtle**	G. **unique**	H. **universal**	I. **versatile**	J. **vivid**

_____ 1. We must _____ a way to keep Tia away from the house until we finish setting up her surprise party.

_____ 2. Although Georgia dyed her hair, the color change was so _____ that few people noticed it.

_____ 3. Because my brother's Volkswagen is _____, I would know it anywhere. It's painted in day-glo colors and has a bumper sticker that says, "Yo! I'm here!"

_____ 4. As her Alzheimer's disease worsened, my grandmother held the _____ that people on TV could see her.

_____ 5. Naomi's photo of hot-air balloons is _____—red, orange, and purple balloons are sailing through a bright blue sky.

_____ 6. A talented actor can _____ emotions through gestures and postures, as well as through words.

_____ 7. When we go to the movies, Sam fills his shirt pocket with M&Ms. Eating them one at a time, he_____s them until the picture's end.

_____ 8. "We're looking for someone really _____ for this position," said the interviewer, "someone who can write well, speak well in public, and demonstrate our new hang glider."

_____ 9. The fruit cup served before the main course was supposed to _____ my appetite. Instead, it satisfied my hunger.

_____ 10. Knowing that no movie can have _____ appeal, producers must decide what type of person they hope to reach.

SCORE: (Number correct) _____ × 10 = _____ %

Mastery Test: *Chapter 17 (Waiter)*

In the space provided, write the word from the box needed to complete each sentence. Then put the **letter** of that word in the column at the left. Use each word once.

A. **defer**	B. **endeavor**	C. **equate**	D. **impose**	E. **indignant**
F. **inevitable**	G. **malicious**	H. **option**	I. **passive**	J. **patron**

_____ 1. Donna wrote a letter of complaint to the publisher of a textbook. She was _____ that the book always referred to doctors as "he" and nurses as "she."

_____ 2. Some people believe any spanking of a child is wrong. They _____ it with child abuse.

_____ 3. If Vince continues to talk on his cell phone while he's driving, it's _____ that he'll cause an accident.

_____ 4. We've become loyal _____s of the Lebanese restaurant because we enjoy its delicious Middle Eastern food.

_____ 5. Devan's dog is the most _____ animal I've ever seen. A mouse actually ran over its paw, and it didn't even bother to raise its head.

_____ 6. I know you don't like Barry, but please _____ to be polite to him when he's here as a guest.

_____ 7. When you order a pizza here, you have the choice of usual toppings, like mushrooms and pepperoni, as well as unusual _____s such as avocado, broccoli, or pineapple.

_____ 8. My brother often _____s on my mother's generosity by asking her for money.

_____ 9. The children playing baseball broke a window by accident—it wasn't a(n) _____ act.

_____ 10. "When it comes to decorating our apartment," Jasmin said, "I _____ to my husband's judgment. He has better taste than I do."

SCORE: (Number correct) _____ × 10 = _____ %

Mastery Test: *Chapter 19 (Adjusting to a New Culture)*

In the space provided, write the word from the box needed to complete each sentence. Then put the **letter** of that word in the column at the left. Use each word once.

A. **adapt**	B. **dismay**	C. **exile**	D. **gesture**	E. **recede**
F. **reciprocate**	G. **refute**	H. **retain**	I. **revert**	J. **ritual**

_____ 1. The _____ of shaking one's head back and forth does not mean "no" in all cultures.

_____ 2. The neatness of Bill's house _____s his claim that he is lazy and sloppy.

_____ 3. Grandma sold most of her belongings when she moved to a retirement apartment, but she _____(e)d what had been Grandpa's favorite chair.

_____ 4. After Alice Weston died, her dog would at first only lie quietly in his new owner's home. But after a few weeks, he _____(e)d to the situation and became livelier.

_____ 5. The Bensons have had us over so often that we really should _____, but I don't know how we'll fit their large family into our small dining room.

_____ 6. The long line outside the box office so _____(e)d Bryan that he didn't even attempt to buy a ticket.

_____ 7. After he lost his throne, the Shah of Iran spent the rest of his life in _____, never returning to his native country.

_____ 8. The hurricane victims had to wait until the flood waters _____(e)d before they could return to their homes.

_____ 9. Mr. Byron is so fearful of germs that several times a day he goes through a(n) _____ of wiping his hands with alcohol and then rinsing them.

_____ 10. Many teenagers speak politely in the presence of adults but _____ to rough slang when talking among themselves.

SCORE: (Number correct) _____ × 10 = _____ %

Mastery Test: *Chapter 20 (A Dream About Wealth)*

In the space provided, write the word from the box needed to complete each sentence. Then put the **letter** of that word in the column at the left. Use each word once.

A. **elaborate**	B. **emerge**	C. **exotic**	D. **frugal**	E. **impulsive**
F. **indifferent**	G. **indulgent**	H. **liberal**	I. **mediocre**	J. **notable**

_____ 1. The Gilmans are _____ supporters of their local public TV station; they make a large donation every year.

_____ 2. The crowd scene in the painting was so _____ that even the buttons on people's coats were carefully painted in.

_____ 3. Aunt Mary shows how _____ she is when she carefully opens a gift so that the wrapping can be re-used.

_____ 4. Maggie is _____, but she often regrets doing whatever she feels like, such as sliding down a muddy hill in her best pants.

_____ 5. When the rock star _____(e)d from his car, screaming fans rushed forward to get his autograph.

_____ 6. Before Ronald Reagan was President, he was _____ as a film star and TV actor.

_____ 7. Kevin gets a haircut only to prevent hair from falling into his eyes. He's _____ about how stylish or well-groomed he looks.

_____ 8. Phyllis loves to browse through shops with Indian brass work, African wood carvings, and other _____ arts and crafts.

_____ 9. Eddy's _____ parents spoil him. They buy him lots of candy and toys and let his worst behavior go without even a scolding.

_____ 10. The clothes at that shop are _____. They aren't as shabby as those in some of the cheapest stores, but they aren't as well-made as clothing in the best department stores.

SCORE: (Number correct) _____ × 10 = _____ %

Mastery Test: *Chapter 21 (Children and Drugs)*

In the space provided, write the word from the box needed to complete each sentence. Then put the **letter** of that word in the column at the left. Use each word once.

A. **affirm**	B. **alleged**	C. **allude**	D. **coerce**	E. **elite**
F. **essence**	G. **immunity**	H. **impair**	I. **query**	J. **sadistic**

_____ 1. The Loch Ness Monster is _____ to live in a lake in Scotland, but there's no proof that the dinosaur-like creature even exists.

_____ 2. Aging tends to _____ people's vision. They can't see as well as they used to.

_____ 3. If a witness in a trial is uncomfortable with swearing on a Bible, he or she may simply _____ to tell the truth.

_____ 4. The teacher promised _____ from punishment to whoever had broken the classroom window—if that person confessed immediately.

_____ 5. Paul _____(e)d to his adoption when he said, "Not surprisingly, I don't look like either of my parents."

_____ 6. Russell had several questions, but he was too shy to _____ the famous speaker.

_____ 7. The _____ of Santa Claus is loving generosity.

_____ 8. Some consider Columbian to be the _____ coffee—the best in aroma and flavor.

_____ 9. When I was younger, my parents _____(e)d me into drinking eggnog every day. Not surprisingly, I still hate the taste of the stuff.

_____ 10. Before being fired, the _____ teacher enjoyed embarrassing any student who displeased him in the slightest.

SCORE: (Number correct) _____ × 10 = _____ %

Name: _____

Mastery Test: *Chapter 22 (Party House)*

In the space provided, write the word from the box needed to complete each sentence. Then put the **letter** of that word in the column at the left. Use each word once.

A. **plausible**	B. **provoke**	C. **recur**	D. **reprimand**	E. **revoke**
F. **ridicule**	G. **shrewd**	H. **skeptical**	I. **stereotype**	J. **tactic**

_____ 1. It _____s me if someone tries to step in line in front of me. I feel like shoving the person away.

_____ 2. Singer Dolly Parton laughs at the _____ of the "dumb blonde." "I know I'm not dumb," she says. "And I'm not really blonde, either."

_____ 3. "Have some of this delicious wheat-and-bean-sprouts cake," I said to Tom, whose _____ look showed he doubted it was wise to accept the offer.

_____ 4. Since Chet was wearing a neck brace, the teacher found his excuse for missing the test—an auto accident—to be entirely _____.

_____ 5. When Derrick was a teen, his parents' most effective weapon against him was the threat that they would _____ his driving privileges.

_____ 6. In children's stories, the fox is often presented as a _____ individual who outsmarts all his enemies.

_____ 7. The political cartoon _____(e)d the senator, but he found the mockery so clever that he couldn't help laughing.

_____ 8. I have a frightening dream that _____s two or three times a year. I dream I'm in an elevator that gets stuck between floors, and I have no way to let anyone know where I am.

_____ 9. My brother and I agreed on our _____ before asking to go to the fair. He would tell Mom that Dad said we could go, and I would tell Dad that Mom said we could go.

_____ 10. People were angry when the police officer who had beaten an innocent bystander received only a _____. Community members felt he should have received a greater punishment.

SCORE: (Number correct) _____ × 10 = _____ %

Mastery Test: *Chapter 23 (Procrastinator)*

In the space provided, write the word from the box needed to complete each sentence. Then put the **letter** of that word in the column at the left. Use each word once.

A. **consequence**	B. **destiny**	C. **detain**	D. **diminish**	E. **procrastinate**
F. **simultaneous**	G. **strategy**	H. **tedious**	I. **transaction**	J. **vital**

_____ 1. "If it is _____ that you marry Roger, it will happen no matter what else happens," Aunt Blanche told my sister. "No one can escape fate."

_____ 2. To celebrate the city's 200th birthday, there were several _____ parties in city parks and streets. They were all scheduled to take place from 8 p.m. to midnight.

_____ 3. When you buy something expensive, keep the receipt for a while. Then, if you return the purchase, you'll have proof the _____ took place.

_____ 4. "I need this delivered across town as quickly as possible," Will's boss told him. "Don't let anything _____ you."

_____ 5. Flo's _____ for weight loss includes a three-mile walk every morning and absolutely no snacking at night.

_____ 6. If the ivory trade is not stopped, the world's population of elephants will _____ to such a low number that they could disappear from the wild.

_____ 7. When you're involved in a _____ task like window-washing, it helps to have someone to talk to—unless, of course, the person is as boring as the window-washing.

_____ 8. Martin insulted several guests at Bea's party. As a _____, Bea won't ever invite him over again.

_____ 9. The restaurant failed because the owners overlooked one _____ fact: There were already too many seafood restaurants in the area.

_____ 10. When the brakes on Betsy's car began to make a strange sound, she took the car to a mechanic immediately. "I don't _____ when my safety is involved," she said.

SCORE: (Number correct) _____ × 10 = _____ %

Mastery Test: *Chapter 25 (A Change in View)*

In the space provided, write the word from the box needed to complete each sentence. Then put the **letter** of that word in the column at the left. Use each word once.

A. **discriminate**	B. **dismal**	C. **dispense**	D. **profound**	E. **severity**
F. **site**	G. **subside**	H. **summon**	I. **theoretical**	J. **vocation**

_____ 1. The relief workers _____(e)d bags of rice to the hungry refugees waiting in line.

_____ 2. It's no use talking to Paul until his anger _____s and he becomes more reasonable.

_____ 3. Discussions about possible life on planets around other suns are _____ since no one has ever visited there.

_____ 4. When Amy's uncle found her playing with his woodworking tools, he scolded her with such _____ that she started to cry.

_____ 5. Randy feared a long lecture when he was _____(e)d to the principal's office.

_____ 6. That rock band plays only on weekends. And you'd never guess the full-time _____ of its lead singer—he's a lawyer.

_____ 7. The _____ of the music festival had to be changed because local residents didn't want it nearby.

_____ 8. The movie was so _____—with its sad story, cheerless characters, and gray skies—that afterwards we all felt low.

_____ 9. Because he's color blind, Tom cannot _____ between blue and purple.

_____ 10. After watching a man threaten to jump off a ledge, Maggie felt _____ relief when he was persuaded to climb back inside the building.

SCORE: (Number correct) _____ × 10 = _____ %

Mastery Test: *Chapter 26 (Balloon Flight)*

In the space provided, write the word from the box needed to complete each sentence. Then put the **letter** of that word in the column at the left. Use each word once.

A. **ascend**	B. **finite**	C. **infinite**	D. **inflict**	E. **ingenious**
F. **initiate**	G. **literally**	H. **lure**	I. **mania**	J. **nostalgia**

_____ 1. For a week after our family reunion, I felt strong _____. I wanted to go back and relive all the good times of those past days.

_____ 2. The Japanese often _____ a business meeting by drinking tea. They then discuss business afterward.

_____ 3. The supply of hot water in our house is definitely _____. After two people take showers, there isn't a drop of hot water left.

_____ 4. To go down a flight of stairs is much easier than to _____ it.

_____ 5. Using clothespins, ropes, and wheels, Lauren invented a(n) _____ machine that makes her bed each morning.

_____ 6. Patrick's sharp comments _____ many wounds, but he never seems to notice the pain he causes others.

_____ 7. I've recently developed a _____ for basketball. No matter who's playing, if there's a game on TV, I'll watch it.

_____ 8. The preschool teacher's patience seemed _____. She never once raised her voice in anger, in spite of the children's constant demands.

_____ 9. Vince called the police when his little girl said a man had tried to _____ her into a car with candy and money.

_____ 10. Ron's nickname—"Tiny"—is not meant _____(ly); he's nearly seven feet tall.

SCORE: (Number correct) _____ × 10 = _____ %

Mastery Test: *Chapter 27 (Family Differences)*

In the space provided, write the word from the box needed to complete each sentence. Then put the **letter** of that word in the column at the left. Use each word once.

A. **data**	B. **inept**	C. **innate**	D. **intervene**	E. **lament**
F. **morbid**	G. **obstinate**	H. **parallel**	I. **perceptive**	J. **sedate**

_____ 1. Do most people have a(n)_____ fear of spiders, or do they gain the fear after birth, through experience?

_____ 2. The town council spent months studying _____ on the town recreation center before approving its construction.

_____ 3. Some newspapers appeal to people's curiosity about horrible events by publishing every _____ detail of accidents and crimes.

_____ 4. Rather than take a risk and _____ in the fight between two armed men, Ralph called the police to come and end the fight.

_____ 5. The children shrieked as they splashed and dived, while I, remaining _____, swam calmly around the pool.

_____ 6. Dad was such a(n) _____ handyman that when he tried to do home repairs, he usually made the problem worse.

_____ 7. Train tracks are _____ and thus never meet, but when you look down the tracks at a distance, they appear to move closer and closer together.

_____ 8. Diane, who _____s whenever she sees a dead animal on the road, keeps her own cats inside to protect them.

_____ 9. The boss thinks he's _____ enough to know when there are problems at work, but the truth is that he's not aware of half of what goes on in the office.

_____ 10. Sometimes it can be good to be _____. The author of the now-famous Dr. Seuss books stubbornly kept trying to get his first one published even though it was rejected 23 times.

SCORE: (Number correct) _____ × 10 = _____ %

Mastery Test: *Chapter 28 (Murder Mystery)*

In the space provided, write the word from the box needed to complete each sentence. Then put the **letter** of that word in the column at the left. Use each word once.

A. **controversy**	B. **deduction**	C. **dimensions**	D. **disperse**	E. **distort**
F. **dominant**	G. **sequence**	H. **sophisticated**	I. **treacherous**	J. **trivial**

_____ 1. Keith thinks everyone else's problems are _____. According to him, only his own worries are significant.

_____ 2. The company president was horrified when a _____ employee sold the secret fried chicken recipe to another company.

_____ 3. When I spotted a suitcase in the living room, I made the _____ that my sister had arrived.

_____ 4. The three-year-old _____(e)d my phone message, telling Gil I'd said, "I'll sue you for money" instead of "I'll see you Monday."

_____ 5. Being _____, the potential employer controls the pace and direction of a job interview.

_____ 6. Because I had written down the room's _____ incorrectly, the carpet I bought was too large.

_____ 7. As scientists come closer to cloning a human being, there is much _____ over whether such a procedure is morally acceptable.

_____ 8. The gang of shoplifters _____(e)d throughout the store to steal a variety of items, then met outside to share their loot. As soon as they were together again, the security guard arrested them.

_____ 9. Because Dan knows a lot about Italian culture, he seemed _____ while we traveled in Italy. In France, however, he suddenly seemed childish and uninformed.

_____ 10. After spending months saying "A B C E D," the child finally learned to say the alphabet in the correct _____.

SCORE: (Number correct) _____ × 10 = _____ %

Mastery Test: *Chapter 29 (Chicken Pox)*

In the space provided, write the word from the box needed to complete each sentence. Then put the **letter** of that word in the column at the left. Use each word once.

A. **confirm**	B. **deceptive**	C. **defy**	D. **restrain**	E. **seclusion**
F. **submit**	G. **susceptible**	H. **transmit**	I. **valid**	J. **vigorous**

_____ 1. The little girl, very frightened of Santa Claus, was so determined to run out of the mall that her parents could hardly _____ her.

_____ 2. Darryl recently went into _____ for an entire weekend. He needed to be alone in order to figure out his taxes.

_____ 3. It's good Larry called to _____ our reservations because the motel had no record of our request for a room.

_____ 4. Junk mail can be so _____. Often mail advertisements are designed to seem like announcements of wonderful prizes.

_____ 5. Crystal loses one job after another because she won't _____ to anyone's orders. She argues with her supervisors constantly.

_____ 6. It's no wonder Brad is out of shape. The most _____ exercise he gets is walking a block to the ice cream parlor.

_____ 7. Because Carlos is so _____ to poison ivy, he wears long pants and long sleeves if he thinks he might get anywhere near the pesky plant.

_____ 8. Since Mary's parents didn't approve of musicians, Mary had to _____ them if she wanted to go out with Buddy.

_____ 9. If one child in a day-care center gets measles, he or she is likely to _____ the catching illness to other children.

_____ 10. Joan has a _____ reason for not trusting Paul: she's heard him lie many times.

SCORE: (Number correct) _____ × 10 = _____ %

Mastery Test: *Chapter 30 (Walking)*

In the space provided, write the word from the box needed to complete each sentence. Then put the **letter** of that word in the column at the left. Use each word once.

A. **accelerate**	B. **adverse**	C. **advocate**	D. **audible**	E. **coherent**
F. **comparable**	G. **competent**	H. **consecutive**	I. **conspicuous**	J. **deteriorate**

_____ 1. Polly's family became frightened when she had a(n) _____ reaction to penicillin.

_____ 2. One lawyer's presentation was a model of logic and order, but the other's was far from _____.

_____ 3. Year after year, my grandfather's eyesight _____s. Every time he goes to the eye doctor, he needs stronger lenses.

_____ 4. The drugstore's own brand of lotion and shampoo seems _____ to name brands in quality. There doesn't seem to be any difference.

_____ 5. My mother opposed my sister's marrying Jim, but my father was a strong _____ of their marriage.

_____ 6. The teenagers thought that if they whispered, they would not be heard by others in the movie theater. However, their conversation was _____ to many who sat nearby.

_____ 7. Since both candidates for the job were equally _____, the employer chose the one with the more pleasant personality.

_____ 8. The test was designed to be taken in three _____ parts: first, some multiple-choice questions; next, a matching exercise; and finally, an essay question.

_____ 9. Not only is the cheetah the fastest mammal in the world; it takes this wild cat only two seconds to _____ from a standing start to a speed of 45 miles an hour.

_____ 10. To tease his wife, Vic pretended not to see the "Happy Birthday" sign strung along the living room wall, even though the sign was so big it was too _____ to miss.

SCORE: (Number correct) _____ × 10 = _____ %

Answers to the Mastery Tests: BUILDING VOCABULARY SKILLS

Chapter 1 (Taking Exams)

1. D		6. H	
2. E		7. A	
3. C		8. I	
4. G		9. J	
5. B		10. F	

Chapter 2 (Nate the Woodsman)

1. J		6. B	
2. A		7. F	
3. E		8. H	
4. G		9. C	
5. I		10. D	

Chapter 3 (Who's on Trial?)

1. C		6. E	
2. A		7. B	
3. F		8. J	
4. I		9. H	
5. G		10. D	

Chapter 4 (Students and Politics)

1. B		6. G	
2. J		7. F	
3. A		8. I	
4. E		9. C	
5. D		10. H	

Chapter 5 (Night Nurse)

1. G		6. C	
2. A		7. E	
3. F		8. J	
4. H		9. B	
5. I		10. D	

Chapter 7 (Relating to Parents)

1. J		6. H	
2. C		7. F	
3. B		8. A	
4. E		9. G	
5. D		10. I	

Chapter 8 (Job Choices)

1. B		6. E	
2. H		7. J	
3. F		8. I	
4. D		9. G	
5. C		10. A	

Chapter 9 (No Joking)

1. J		6. B	
2. G		7. E	
3. A		8. D	
4. H		9. I	
5. F		10. C	

Chapter 10 (Museum Pet)

1. G		6. J	
2. A		7. B	
3. I		8. D	
4. E		9. C	
5. H		10. F	

Chapter 11 (Unacceptable Boyfriends)

1. F		6. J	
2. B		7. H	
3. I		8. G	
4. D		9. C	
5. A		10. E	

Chapter 13 (Our Headstrong Baby)

1. C		6. A	
2. G		7. J	
3. D		8. H	
4. B		9. F	
5. E		10. I	

Chapter 14 (Mr. Perfect?)

1. A		6. B	
2. E		7. D	
3. F		8. C	
4. J		9. I	
5. G		10. H	

Chapter 15 (A Narrow Escape)

1. D		6. F	
2. E		7. I	
3. J		8. G	
4. B		9. A	
5. H		10. C	

Chapter 16 (The Power of Advertising)

1. C	6. A
2. F	7. D
3. G	8. I
4. B	9. E
5. J	10. H

Chapter 17 (Waiter)

1. E	6. B
2. C	7. H
3. F	8. D
4. J	9. G
5. I	10. A

Chapter 19 (Adjusting to a New Culture)

1. D	6. B
2. G	7. C
3. H	8. E
4. A	9. J
5. F	10. I

Chapter 20 (A Dream About Wealth)

1. H	6. J
2. A	7. F
3. D	8. C
4. E	9. G
5. B	10. I

Chapter 21 (Children and Drugs)

1. B	6. I
2. H	7. F
3. A	8. E
4. G	9. D
5. C	10. J

Chapter 22 (Party House)

1. B	6. G
2. I	7. F
3. H	8. C
4. A	9. J
5. E	10. D

Chapter 23 (Procrastinator)

1. B	6. D
2. F	7. H
3. I	8. A
4. C	9. J
5. G	10. E

Chapter 25 (A Change in View)

1. C	6. J
2. G	7. F
3. I	8. B
4. E	9. A
5. H	10. D

Chapter 26 (Balloon Flight)

1. J	6. D
2. F	7. I
3. B	8. C
4. A	9. H
5. E	10. G

Chapter 27 (Family Differences)

1. C	6. B
2. A	7. H
3. F	8. E
4. D	9. I
5. J	10. G

Chapter 28 (Murder Mystery)

1. J	6. C
2. I	7. A
3. B	8. D
4. E	9. H
5. F	10. G

Chapter 29 (Chicken Pox)

1. D	6. J
2. E	7. G
3. A	8. C
4. B	9. H
5. F	10. I

Chapter 30 (Walking)

1. B	6. D
2. E	7. G
3. J	8. H
4. F	9. A
5. C	10. I

Mastery Test: *Unit One*

PART A

Complete each sentence in a way that clearly shows you understand the meaning of the **boldfaced** word. Take a minute to plan your answer before you write.

Example: If you receive a wedding invitation, it is **appropriate** ___*to respond by the date requested*___ .

1. One well-known product **endorsed** by a well-known person is _____

    _____.

2. Two things that can **illuminate** a room are _____

    _____.

3. The driver **averted** a crash by _____

    _____.

4. One **obstacle** to winning a championship can be _____

    _____.

5. A sign of high **morale** on a team is _____

    _____.

6. The judge was so **lenient** that _____

    _____.

7. Being a **novice** as a waiter, Artie _____

    _____.

8. Although the restaurant was attractive, its success was **undermined** by _____

    _____."

9. I know that my father has **integrity** because _____

    _____.

10. When it comes to taxes, Dinah is so **radical** that she believes _____

    _____.

(Continues on next page)

PART B

Use each of the following ten words in sentences of your own. Make it clear that you know the meaning of the word you use. Feel free to use the past tense or plural form of a word.

A. **agenda**	B. **compel**	C. **drastic**	D. **erode**	E. **erratic**
F. **illusion**	G. **legitimate**	H. **menace**	I. **prospects**	J. **urban**

11. _____

_____

12. _____

_____

13. _____

_____

14. _____

_____

15. _____

_____

16. _____

_____

17. _____

_____

18. _____

_____

19. _____

_____

20. _____

_____

SCORE: (Number correct) _____ × 5 = _____ %

Mastery Test: *Unit Two*

PART A
Complete each sentence in a way that clearly shows you understand the meaning of the **boldfaced** word. Take a minute to plan your answer before you write.

Example: I **altered** my appearance for the party by _____ putting on a blond wig _____.

1. When Peter gained ten pounds, his **blunt** friend Buddy remarked, "_____

   _____"

2. People who write letters to advice columns like to be **anonymous** because _____

   _____.

3. Harold was filled with **contempt** when he saw the big, strong man _____

   _____.

4. Fran decided to **supplement** her income by _____

   _____.

5. Mrs. Carson is the most **dogmatic** teacher in our school. For example, she tells students, "_____

   _____"

6. If I suddenly discovered that I had become **affluent**, the first thing I would do is _____

   _____.

7. Pauline is so **arrogant** that when Greg told her she looked pretty, she replied, " _____

   _____"

8. While waiting for my turn for a haircut, I felt **apprehensive** because _____

   _____.

9. My friend Ted is very **prudent** about his money. For instance, _____

   _____.

10. When Stephanie served roast goose and a delicious peanut-butter pie for Thanksgiving dinner, her

    conservative brother said, " _____

    _____"

(Continues on next page)

PART B

Use each of the following ten words in sentences of your own. Make it clear that you know the meaning of the word you use. Feel free to use the past tense or plural form of a word.

A. adhere	B. assess	C. bestow	D. denounce	E. derive
F. diversity	G. phobia	H. pretense	I. remorse	J. surpass

11. _____

_____

12. _____

_____

13. _____

_____

14. _____

_____

15. _____

_____

16. _____

_____

17. _____

_____

18. _____

_____

19. _____

_____

20. _____

_____

SCORE: (Number correct) _____ × 5 = _____ %

Name: _____

Mastery Test: *Unit Three*

PART A
Complete each sentence in a way that clearly shows you understand the meaning of the **boldfaced** word. Take a minute to plan your answer before you write.

Example: Two ways a boat can be **propelled** are by _____*motor and wind*_____.

1. A **unique** color combination for a car would be _____
_____.

2. My sister is so **versatile** that _____
_____.

3. Lonnie needs to get from New York to Florida. One of his **options** is to _____
_____.

4. Because of her **obsession** with clothes, Sheila _____
_____.

5. Here's an **evasive** answer to "What did you do on your vacation?": "_____
_____."

6. Glen is so **miserly** that _____
_____.

7. A man who believes he and his date are **compatible** might say at the end of an evening, "_____
_____."

8. Wild teenagers on the street **harassed** passing cars by _____
_____.

9. An animal-lover would become **indignant** if _____
_____.

10. An obviously **fictitious** detail about my past is that I _____
_____.

(Continues on next page)

PART B

Use each of the following ten words in sentences of your own. Make it clear that you know the meaning of the word you use. Feel free to use the past tense or plural form of a word.

A. **accessible**	B. **delusion**	C. **elapse**	D. **encounter**	E. **impose**
F. **inevitable**	G. **liable**	H. **ordeal**	I. **retrieve**	J. **savor**

11. _____

_____

12. _____

_____

13. _____

_____

14. _____

_____

15. _____

_____

16. _____

_____

17. _____

_____

18. _____

_____

19. _____

_____

20. _____

_____

SCORE: (Number correct) _____ × 5 = _____ %

76

Mastery Test: *Unit Four*

PART A
Complete each sentence in a way that clearly shows you understand the meaning of the **boldfaced** word. Take a minute to plan your answer before you write.

Example: A **mediocre** essay is likely to _____ receive a grade of C _____.

1. One activity I find especially **tedious** is _____

   _____.

2. A cab driver might respond to a **liberal** tip by _____

   _____.

3. When the heater broke, we **adapted** to the sudden drop in temperature by _____

   _____.

4. One **tactic** for dieting is _____

   _____.

5. After Gina invited Daniel out for coffee, he **reciprocated** by _____

   _____.

6. One **impulsive** thing I once did was _____

   _____.

7. An **indulgent** parent might react to a child screaming for candy by _____

   _____.

8. I sometimes **procrastinate** when _____

   _____.

9. To stay healthy, it is **vital** that I _____

   _____.

10. A **skeptical** response to "I love you" is " _____

    _____."

(Continues on next page)

PART B

Use each of the following ten words in sentences of your own. Make it clear that you know the meaning of the word you use. Feel free to use the past tense or plural form of a word.

A. **coerce**	B. **diminish**	C. **emerge**	D. **gesture**	E. **indifferent**
F. **recur**	G. **ritual**	H. **sadistic**	I. **shrewd**	J. **strategy**

11. _____

_____

12. _____

_____

13. _____

_____

14. _____

_____

15. _____

_____

16. _____

_____

17. _____

_____

18. _____

_____

19. _____

_____

20. _____

_____

SCORE: (Number correct) _____ × 5 = _____ %

78

Name: _____

Mastery Test: *Unit Five*

PART A

Complete each sentence in a way that clearly shows you understand the meaning of the **boldfaced** word. Take a minute to plan your answer before you write.

Example: A child might **defy** a parent by _____*refusing to mow the lawn*_____.

1. A camper might experience such **adverse** conditions as _____

   _____.

2. One **valid** reason for missing class is _____

   _____.

3. Drivers usually **accelerate** their cars when _____

   _____.

4. Ramon felt **dismal** because _____

   _____.

5. There is a **controversy** in our country about _____

   _____.

6. If it were **literally** "raining cats and dogs," then _____

   _____.

7. Our teacher **confirmed** the rumor that the test was being postponed when she _____

   _____.

8. Babies have an **innate** ability to _____

   _____.

9. If you were to **submit** to someone's demand for a loan, you would _____

   _____.

10. One **trivial** annoyance in my life is _____

   _____.

(Continues on next page)

PART B

Use each of the following ten words in sentences of your own. Make it clear that you know the meaning of the word you use. Feel free to use the past tense or plural form of a word.

A. **audible**	B. **competent**	C. **distort**	D. **inflict**	E. **intervene**
F. **mania**	G. **severity**	H. **sophisticated**	I. **vigorous**	J. **vocation**

11. _____

_____

12. _____

_____

13. _____

_____

14. _____

_____

15. _____

_____

16. _____

_____

17. _____

_____

18. _____

_____

19. _____

_____

20. _____

_____

SCORE: (Number correct) _____ × 5 = _____ %

Pretest

This test contains 100 items. In the space provided, write the letter of the choice that is closest in meaning to the **boldfaced** word.

Important: Keep in mind that this test is for diagnostic purposes only. **If you do not know a word, leave the space blank rather than guess at it.**

_____ 1. **animosity**   **a)** approval   **b)** ill will   **c)** fear   **d)** shyness

_____ 2. **encounter**   **a)** meeting   **b)** total   **c)** departure   **d)** attack

_____ 3. **adamant**   **a)** realistic   **b)** stubborn   **c)** weak   **d)** flexible

_____ 4. **eccentric**   **a)** odd   **b)** common   **c)** active   **d)** calm

_____ 5. **malign**   **a)** depend on   **b)** speak evil of   **c)** boast   **d)** praise

_____ 6. **tangible**   **a)** more than normal   **b)** touchable   **c)** hidden   **d)** orderly

_____ 7. **acclaim**   **a)** false name   **b)** great approval   **c)** disagreement   **d)** sadness

_____ 8. **escalate**   **a)** remove   **b)** lessen   **c)** include   **d)** intensify

_____ 9. **elicit**   **a)** draw forth   **b)** approve   **c)** praise   **d)** disprove

_____ 10. **obsolete**   **a)** current   **b)** difficult to believe   **c)** out-of-date   **d)** not sold

_____ 11. **allusion**   **a)** indirect reference   **b)** physical weakness   **c)** improvement   **d)** short story

_____ 12. **altruistic**   **a)** honest   **b)** lying   **c)** proud   **d)** unselfish

_____ 13. **euphemism**   **a)** false appearance   **b)** degree   **c)** substitute for offensive term   **d)** title

_____ 14. **arbitrary**   **a)** wordy   **b)** unreasonable   **c)** demanding   **d)** believable

_____ 15. **assail**   **a)** attack   **b)** travel   **c)** defend   **d)** confuse

_____ 16. **fluctuate**   **a)** stand still   **b)** vary irregularly   **c)** float   **d)** sink

_____ 17. **calamity**   **a)** disaster   **b)** storm   **c)** conference   **d)** breeze

_____ 18. **persevere**   **a)** treat harshly   **b)** mark   **c)** continue   **d)** delay

_____ 19. **comprehensive**   **a)** accidental   **b)** including much   **c)** delicate   **d)** small

_____ 20. **venture**   **a)** turn aside   **b)** urge   **c)** risk   **d)** misrepresent

_____ 21. **enhance**   **a)** reject   **b)** get   **c)** improve   **d)** free

_____ 22. **attribute**   **a)** admiration   **b)** program   **c)** disease   **d)** quality

_____ 23. **discern**   **a)** see clearly   **b)** devise   **c)** rule out   **d)** consider

_____ 24. **exemplify**   **a)** construct   **b)** represent   **c)** plan   **d)** test

_____ 25. **attest**   **a)** bear witness   **b)** examine   **c)** tear up   **d)** dislike

(Continues on next page)

_____ 26. **concurrent**   **a)** apart   **b)** happening together   **c)** north   **d)** off-and-on

_____ 27. **constitute**   **a)** make up   **b)** eliminate   **c)** separate   **d)** remove

_____ 28. **predominant**   **a)** smallest   **b)** most noticeable   **c)** having a tendency   **d)** hidden

_____ 29. **nominal**   **a)** open to harm   **b)** large   **c)** important   **d)** slight

_____ 30. **confiscate**   **a)** deny   **b)** make difficult   **c)** desire   **d)** seize with authority

_____ 31. **suffice**   **a)** think up   **b)** be enough   **c)** prevent   **d)** pay back

_____ 32. **degenerate**   **a)** give up   **b)** improve   **c)** stay the same   **d)** worsen

_____ 33. **implausible**   **a)** possible   **b)** hard to believe   **c)** imaginary   **d)** historical

_____ 34. **sinister**   **a)** frightened   **b)** lively   **c)** generous   **d)** evil

_____ 35. **intricate**   **a)** easy   **b)** complex   **c)** workable   **d)** touching

_____ 36. **qualm**   **a)** pleasure   **b)** dead end   **c)** feeling of doubt   **d)** place of safety

_____ 37. **garble**   **a)** refuse   **b)** mix up   **c)** claim   **d)** speak clearly

_____ 38. **immaculate**   **a)** roomy   **b)** clean   **c)** empty   **d)** complete

_____ 39. **retaliate**   **a)** repair   **b)** repeat   **c)** renew   **d)** pay back

_____ 40. **blatant**   **a)** sudden   **b)** immediate   **c)** quiet   **d)** obvious

_____ 41. **intermittent**   **a)** hesitant   **b)** nervous   **c)** off-and-on   **d)** constant

_____ 42. **digress**   **a)** stray   **b)** improve   **c)** resist   **d)** repeat

_____ 43. **incentive**   **a)** fear   **b)** pride   **c)** concern   **d)** encouragement

_____ 44. **succumb**   **a)** approach   **b)** repeat   **c)** give in   **d)** cut short

_____ 45. **devastate**   **a)** spread out   **b)** begin again   **c)** reassure   **d)** upset greatly

_____ 46. **speculate**   **a)** search   **b)** think about   **c)** inspect   **d)** state to be so

_____ 47. **infamous**   **a)** not known   **b)** small   **c)** having a bad reputation   **d)** related

_____ 48. **benefactor**   **a)** landlord   **b)** one who gives aid   **c)** optimist   **d)** kindness

_____ 49. **intrinsic**   **a)** belonging by its very nature   **b)** on the surface   **c)** not noticeable
          d) careful

_____ 50. **alleviate**   **a)** make anxious   **b)** depart   **c)** infect   **d)** relieve

(Continues on next page)

_____ 51. **mandatory**   **a)** masculine   **b)** sexist   **c)** required   **d)** threatening

_____ 52. **lucrative**   **a)** silly   **b)** profitable   **c)** causing disease   **d)** attractive

_____ 53. **aspire**   **a)** dislike   **b)** strongly desire   **c)** impress   **d)** deliver

_____ 54. **benevolent**   **a)** kind   **b)** wealthy   **c)** nasty   **d)** poor

_____ 55. **dissent**   **a)** approval   **b)** defeat   **c)** winning   **d)** disagreement

_____ 56. **proponent**   **a)** foe   **b)** supporter   **c)** examiner   **d)** one part of the whole

_____ 57. **quest**   **a)** search   **b)** request   **c)** place   **d)** memory

_____ 58. **conversely**   **a)** rudely   **b)** uncooperative   **c)** in an opposite manner   **d)** unfriendly

_____ 59. **prevalent**   **a)** famous   **b)** widespread   **c)** escapable   **d)** plain

_____ 60. **traumatic**   **a)** causing painful emotions   **b)** reversed   **c)** delicate   **d)** harmless

_____ 61. **flippant**   **a)** cold   **b)** formal   **c)** disrespectful   **d)** nervous

_____ 62. **perception**   **a)** meeting   **b)** party   **c)** dead end   **d)** impression

_____ 63. **prone**   **a)** disliked   **b)** tending   **c)** active   **d)** rested

_____ 64. **rationale**   **a)** research paper   **b)** debate   **c)** logical basis   **d)** mood

_____ 65. **impasse**   **a)** exit   **b)** central point   **c)** gate   **d)** dead end

_____ 66. **divulge**   **a)** reveal   **b)** embarrass   **c)** hide   **d)** remove

_____ 67. **nullify**   **a)** harm   **b)** allow   **c)** examine   **d)** cancel

_____ 68. **elation**   **a)** trade   **b)** comparison   **c)** joy   **d)** majority opinion

_____ 69. **ominous**   **a)** happy   **b)** threatening   **c)** depressed   **d)** friendly

_____ 70. **averse**   **a)** attracted   **b)** fearful   **c)** warm   **d)** opposed

_____ 71. **transcend**   **a)** send   **b)** travel   **c)** show off   **d)** rise above

_____ 72. **deplete**   **a)** encourage   **b)** use up   **c)** delay   **d)** add to

_____ 73. **complacent**   **a)** workable   **b)** easy   **c)** self-satisfied   **d)** healthy

_____ 74. **empathy**   **a)** fear   **b)** encouragement   **c)** ability to share someone's feelings   **d)** avoidance

_____ 75. **waive**   **a)** sleep   **b)** show off   **c)** give up   **d)** fly

(Continues on next page)

_____ 76. **gape**   **a)** stare   **b)** repair   **c)** beat   **d)** hide from

_____ 77. **punitive**   **a)** inexpensive   **b)** punishing   **c)** ridiculously inadequate   **d)** possible

_____ 78. **condone**   **a)** forgive   **b)** represent   **c)** arrest   **d)** appoint

_____ 79. **precedent**   **a)** gift   **b)** example   **c)** fee   **d)** later event

_____ 80. **contemplate**   **a)** think seriously about   **b)** create   **c)** add to   **d)** reveal

_____ 81. **detrimental**   **a)** dirty   **b)** nutritious   **c)** harmful   **d)** helpful

_____ 82. **ironic**   **a)** deeply felt   **b)** meaning opposite of what is said   **c)** simple   **d)** great

_____ 83. **vindictive**   **a)** not easily understood   **b)** gentle   **c)** vengeful   **d)** temporary

_____ 84. **saturate**   **a)** break apart   **b)** put down   **c)** fully soak   **d)** describe

_____ 85. **deficient**   **a)** forgotten   **b)** lacking   **c)** complete   **d)** well-known

_____ 86. **fallible**   **a)** capable of error   **b)** complete   **c)** incomplete   **d)** simple

_____ 87. **exhaustive**   **a)** respected   **b)** nervous   **c)** complete   **d)** tired

_____ 88. **habitat**   **a)** headache   **b)** natural environment   **c)** importance   **d)** usual behavior

_____ 89. **vile**   **a)** offensive   **b)** secretive   **c)** nice   **d)** tricky

_____ 90. **pragmatic**   **a)** ordinary   **b)** slow   **c)** wise   **d)** practical

_____ 91. **pacify**   **a)** betray   **b)** calm   **c)** retreat   **d)** remove

_____ 92. **esteem**   **a)** age   **b)** doubt   **c)** respect   **d)** length of life

_____ 93. **transient**   **a)** stubborn   **b)** temporary   **c)** permanent   **d)** easy-going

_____ 94. **avid**   **a)** bored   **b)** disliked   **c)** enthusiastic   **d)** plentiful

_____ 95. **nurture**   **a)** harden   **b)** thank   **c)** nourish   **d)** starve

_____ 96. **augment**   **a)** change   **b)** cause to become   **c)** increase   **d)** describe

_____ 97. **explicit**   **a)** everyday   **b)** distant   **c)** permanent   **d)** stated exactly

_____ 98. **magnitude**   **a)** large size   **b)** attraction   **c)** respect   **d)** example

_____ 99. **ambivalent**   **a)** everyday   **b)** having mixed feelings   **c)** temporary   **d)** able to be done

_____ 100. **dispel**   **a)** assist   **b)** anger   **c)** describe   **d)** cause to vanish

---

STOP. This is the end of the test. If there is time remaining, you may go back and recheck your answers. When the time is up, hand in both your answer sheet and this test booklet to your instructor.

Posttest

> This test contains 100 items. In the space provided, write the letter of the choice that is closest in meaning to the **boldfaced** word.

____ 1. **enhance**   **a)** free   **b)** get   **c)** improve   **d)** reject

____ 2. **encounter**   **a)** departure   **b)** total   **c)** meeting   **d)** attack

____ 3. **obsolete**   **a)** current   **b)** out-of date   **c)** difficult to believe   **d)** not sold

____ 4. **eccentric**   **a)** active   **b)** common   **c)** calm   **d)** odd

____ 5. **escalate**   **a)** remove   **b)** include   **c)** lessen   **d)** intensify

____ 6. **euphemism**   **a)** degree   **b)** false appearance   **c)** substitute for offensive term   **d)** title

____ 7. **exemplify**   **a)** test   **b)** construct   **c)** represent   **d)** plan

____ 8. **adamant**   **a)** flexible   **b)** stubborn   **c)** weak   **d)** realistic

____ 9. **comprehensive**   **a)** delicate   **b)** including much   **c)** accidental   **d)** small

____ 10. **animosity**   **a)** fear   **b)** shyness   **c)** approval   **d)** ill will

____ 11. **discern**   **a)** rule out   **b)** devise   **c)** see clearly   **d)** consider

____ 12. **allusion**   **a)** indirect reference   **b)** physical weakness   **c)** improvement   **d)** short story

____ 13. **altruistic**   **a)** unselfish   **b)** honest   **c)** lying   **d)** proud

____ 14. **malign**   **a)** praise   **b)** boast   **c)** speak evil of   **d)** depend on

____ 15. **arbitrary**   **a)** unreasonable   **b)** wordy   **c)** believable   **d)** demanding

____ 16. **assail**   **a)** defend   **b)** travel   **c)** attack   **d)** confuse

____ 17. **fluctuate**   **a)** sink   **b)** vary irregularly   **c)** float   **d)** stand still

____ 18. **elicit**   **a)** praise   **b)** disprove   **c)** draw forth   **d)** approve

____ 19. **persevere**   **a)** mark   **b)** treat harshly   **c)** continue   **d)** delay

____ 20. **venture**   **a)** misrepresent   **b)** turn aside   **c)** urge   **d)** risk

____ 21. **attest**   **a)** examine   **b)** bear witness   **c)** tear up   **d)** dislike

____ 22. **acclaim**   **a)** disagreement   **b)** great approval   **c)** false name   **d)** sadness

____ 23. **calamity**   **a)** conference   **b)** breeze   **c)** disaster   **d)** storm

____ 24. **attribute**   **a)** admiration   **b)** quality   **c)** disease   **d)** program

____ 25. **tangible**   **a)** more than normal   **b)** touchable   **c)** hidden   **d)** orderly

(Continues on next page)

____ 26. **retaliate**   a) repair   b) pay back   c) renew   d) repeat

____ 27. **qualm**   a) pleasure   b) place of safety   c) feeling of doubt   d) dead end

____ 28. **intrinsic**   a) belonging by its very nature   b) not noticeable   c) on the surface   d) careful

____ 29. **confiscate**   a) make difficult   b) deny   c) seize with authority   d) desire

____ 30. **immaculate**   a) roomy   b) clean   c) empty   d) complete

____ 31. **degenerate**   a) give up   b) improve   c) stay the same   d) worsen

____ 32. **implausible**   a) possible   b) hard to believe   c) imaginary   d) historical

____ 33. **devastate**   a) reassure   b) upset greatly   c) spread out   d) begin again

____ 34. **sinister**   a) frightened   b) generous   c) lively   d) evil

____ 35. **nominal**   a) slight   b) large   c) important   d) open to harm

____ 36. **speculate**   a) inspect   b) think about   c) search   d) state to be so

____ 37. **succumb**   a) cut short   b) approach   c) give in   d) repeat

____ 38. **garble**   a) claim   b) mix up   c) refuse   d) speak clearly

____ 39. **constitute**   a) make up   b) remove   c) eliminate   d) separate

____ 40. **blatant**   a) quiet   b) sudden   c) immediate   d) obvious

____ 41. **intricate**   a) complex   b) easy   c) workable   d) touching

____ 42. **predominant**   a) hidden   b) having a tendency   c) most noticeable   d) smallest

____ 43. **incentive**   a) fear   b) concern   c) pride   d) encouragement

____ 44. **infamous**   a) having a bad reputation   b) not known   c) small   d) related

____ 45. **concurrent**   a) apart   b) north   c) happening together   d) off-and-on

____ 46. **benefactor**   a) landlord   b) one who gives aid   c) optimist   d) kindness

____ 47. **intermittent**   a) hesitant   b) nervous   c) off-and-on   d) constant

____ 48. **suffice**   a) think up   b) prevent   c) be enough   d) pay back

____ 49. **alleviate**   a) infect   b) relieve   c) make anxious   d) depart

____ 50. **digress**   a) resist   b) improve   c) stray   d) repeat

(Continues on next page)

_____ 51. **averse**   **a)** opposed   **b)** fearful   **c)** warm   **d)** attracted

_____ 52. **conversely**   **a)** unfriendly   **b)** rudely   **c)** uncooperative   **d)** in an opposite manner

_____ 53. **aspire**   **a)** dislike   **b)** strongly desire   **c)** impress   **d)** deliver

_____ 54. **elation**   **a)** comparison   **b)** trade   **c)** joy   **d)** majority opinion

_____ 55. **quest**   **a)** place   **b)** memory   **c)** search   **d)** request

_____ 56. **mandatory**   **a)** sexist   **b)** threatening   **c)** required   **d)** masculine

_____ 57. **ominous**   **a)** happy   **b)** depressed   **c)** threatening   **d)** friendly

_____ 58. **traumatic**   **a)** harmless   **b)** reversed   **c)** delicate   **d)** causing painful emotions

_____ 59. **lucrative**   **a)** causing disease   **b)** profitable   **c)** silly   **d)** attractive

_____ 60. **impasse**   **a)** gate   **b)** exit   **c)** central point   **d)** dead end

_____ 61. **transcend**   **a)** send   **b)** travel   **c)** show off   **d)** rise above

_____ 62. **complacent**   **a)** workable   **b)** self-satisfied   **c)** healthy   **d)** easy

_____ 63. **divulge**   **a)** remove   **b)** reveal   **c)** hide   **d)** embarrass

_____ 64. **benevolent**   **a)** poor   **b)** kind   **c)** wealthy   **d)** nasty

_____ 65. **rationale**   **a)** mood   **b)** debate   **c)** logical basis   **d)** research paper

_____ 66. **proponent**   **a)** supporter   **b)** examiner   **c)** foe   **d)** one part of the whole

_____ 67. **nullify**   **a)** cancel   **b)** examine   **c)** allow   **d)** harm

_____ 68. **flippant**   **a)** cold   **b)** disrespectful   **c)** formal   **d)** nervous

_____ 69. **prone**   **a)** active   **b)** tending   **c)** disliked   **d)** rested

_____ 70. **empathy**   **a)** fear   **b)** encouragement   **c)** ability to share someone's feelings
            d) avoidance

_____ 71. **waive**   **a)** fly   **b)** sleep   **c)** show off   **d)** give up

_____ 72. **prevalent**   **a)** plain   **b)** widespread   **c)** escapable   **d)** famous

_____ 73. **dissent**   **a)** disagreement   **b)** winning   **c)** defeat   **d)** approval

_____ 74. **perception**   **a)** impression   **b)** meeting   **c)** dead end   **d)** party

_____ 75. **deplete**   **a)** add to   **b)** delay   **c)** use up   **d)** encourage

(Continues on next page)

____	76. **vindictive**	a) not easily understood	b) gentle	c) vengeful	d) temporary
____	77. **precedent**	a) gift	b) fee	c) example	d) later event
____	78. **vile**	a) tricky	b) nice	c) secretive	d) offensive
____	79. **ironic**	a) simple	b) meaning opposite of what is said	c) deeply felt	d) great
____	80. **saturate**	a) fully soak	b) put down	c) break apart	d) describe
____	81. **pacify**	a) betray	b) remove	c) retreat	d) calm
____	82. **detrimental**	a) harmful	b) nutritious	c) dirty	d) helpful
____	83. **explicit**	a) everyday	b) permanent	c) distant	d) stated exactly
____	84. **exhaustive**	a) complete	b) nervous	c) respected	d) tired
____	85. **ambivalent**	a) everyday	b) temporary	c) having mixed feelings	d) able to be done
____	86. **dispel**	a) cause to vanish	b) anger	c) describe	d) assist
____	87. **pragmatic**	a) practical	b) slow	c) wise	d) ordinary
____	88. **esteem**	a) respect	b) doubt	c) age	d) length of life
____	89. **contemplate**	a) think seriously about	b) create	c) add to	d) reveal
____	90. **transient**	a) permanent	b) easy-going	c) stubborn	d) temporary
____	91. **augment**	a) cause to become	b) change	c) describe	d) increase
____	92. **fallible**	a) incomplete	b) complete	c) capable of error	d) simple
____	93. **punitive**	a) punishing	b) inexpensive	c) ridiculously inadequate	d) possible
____	94. **avid**	a) enthusiastic	b) disliked	c) bored	d) plentiful
____	95. **habitat**	a) headache	b) natural environment	c) importance	d) usual behavior
____	96. **nurture**	a) harden	b) thank	c) nourish	d) starve
____	97. **deficient**	a) forgotten	b) well-known	c) complete	d) lacking
____	98. **gape**	a) hide from	b) beat	c) stare	d) repair
____	99. **magnitude**	a) large size	b) attraction	c) respect	d) example
____	100. **condone**	a) arrest	b) represent	c) forgive	d) appoint

---

STOP. This is the end of the test. If there is time remaining, you may go back and recheck your answers. When the time is up, hand in both your answer sheet and this test booklet to your instructor.

Unit One: *Pretest*

In the space provided, write the letter of the choice that is closest in meaning to the **boldfaced** word.

_____ 1. **animosity**   a) approval   b) ill will   c) fear   d) shyness

_____ 2. **encounter**   a) meeting   b) total   c) departure   d) attack

_____ 3. **absolve**   a) make guilty   b) reject   c) clear from guilt   d) approve

_____ 4. **adamant**   a) realistic   b) stubborn   c) weak   d) flexible

_____ 5. **amiable**   a) stingy   b) rude   c) proud   d) good-natured

_____ 6. **eccentric**   a) odd   b) common   c) active   d) calm

_____ 7. **amoral**   a) honest   b) poor   c) without principles   d) generous

_____ 8. **malign**   a) depend on   b) speak evil of   c) boast   d) praise

_____ 9. **antagonist**   a) friend   b) relative   c) boss   d) opponent

_____ 10. **epitome**   a) perfect example   b) large hole   c) horrible sight   d) tallest point

_____ 11. **sabotage**   a) aid   b) follow   c) deliberately damage   d) hide from

_____ 12. **dilemma**   a) error   b) difficult choice   c) tendency   d) picture

_____ 13. **wary**   a) kind   b) unfriendly   c) tired   d) cautious

_____ 14. **curt**   a) ignorant   b) talkative   c) friendly   d) rudely brief

_____ 15. **irate**   a) very angry   b) proud   c) silly   d) very friendly

_____ 16. **demoralize**   a) encourage   b) lower the spirits of   c) set a bad example for
d) lecture

_____ 17. **zeal**   a) laziness   b) injustice   c) enthusiastic devotion   d) hatred

_____ 18. **inclination**   a) tendency   b) favor   c) lack   d) increase

_____ 19. **retort**   a) question   b) reply   c) argue   d) approve

_____ 20. **subsequent**   a) beneath   b) before   c) above   d) following

_____ 21. **tangible**   a) more than normal   b) touchable   c) hidden   d) orderly

_____ 22. **acclaim**   a) false name   b) great approval   c) disagreement   d) sadness

_____ 23. **escalate**   a) remove   b) lessen   c) include   d) intensify

_____ 24. **elicit**   a) draw forth   b) approve   c) praise   d) disprove

_____ 25. **exploit**   a) save   b) throw away   c) take advantage of   d) sell overseas

(Continues on next page)

_____ 26. **adjacent**   **a)** above   **b)** under   **c)** next to   **d)** within

_____ 27. **methodical**   **a)** religious   **b)** systematic   **c)** careless   **d)** immoral

_____ 28. **obsolete**   **a)** current   **b)** difficult to believe   **c)** out-of-date   **d)** not sold

_____ 29. **engross**   **a)** destroy   **b)** impress   **c)** disgust   **d)** hold the attention of

_____ 30. **terminate**   **a)** stop   **b)** continue   **c)** begin   **d)** approach

_____ 31. **succinct**   **a)** prepared   **b)** brief and clear   **c)** impressed   **d)** not fair

_____ 32. **infirmity**   **a)** hospital   **b)** small city   **c)** physical weakness   **d)** relationship

_____ 33. **revitalize**   **a)** renew strength   **b)** break in on   **c)** feel weak   **d)** get an idea

_____ 34. **deterrent**   **a)** ending   **b)** memory   **c)** prevention   **d)** blame

_____ 35. **implication**   **a)** word   **b)** statement   **c)** rule   **d)** something hinted at

_____ 36. **infringe**   **a)** add to   **b)** intrude   **c)** impress   **d)** encourage

_____ 37. **sparse**   **a)** spread thinly   **b)** gentle   **c)** plentiful   **d)** threatening

_____ 38. **innovation**   **a)** exercise   **b)** application   **c)** something new   **d)** test

_____ 39. **inequity**   **a)** injustice   **b)** bigger portion   **c)** small party   **d)** boring job

_____ 40. **subjective**   **a)** impressive   **b)** cruel   **c)** based on personal feelings   **d)** distantly related

_____ 41. **banal**   **a)** humid   **b)** commonplace   **c)** secret   **d)** true

_____ 42. **syndrome**   **a)** attitude   **b)** thought   **c)** something required   **d)** group of symptoms

_____ 43. **appease**   **a)** make calm   **b)** tell the truth   **c)** attack   **d)** approve

_____ 44. **taint**   **a)** surprise   **b)** dishonor   **c)** annoy   **d)** boast

_____ 45. **allusion**   **a)** indirect reference   **b)** physical weakness   **c)** improvement   **d)** short story

_____ 46. **altruistic**   **a)** honest   **b)** lying   **c)** proud   **d)** unselfish

_____ 47. **mercenary**   **a)** clean   **b)** mean   **c)** calm   **d)** greedy

_____ 48. **euphemism**   **a)** false appearance   **b)** degree   **c)** substitute for offensive term   **d)** title

_____ 49. **arbitrary**   **a)** wordy   **b)** unreasonable   **c)** demanding   **d)** believable

_____ 50. **assail**   **a)** attack   **b)** travel   **c)** defend   **d)** confuse

> _**SCORE:**_ (Number correct) _____ × 2 = _____ %

Unit One: *Posttest*

In the space provided, write the letter of the choice that is closest in meaning to the **boldfaced** word.

_____ 1. **acclaim**   a) great approval   b) sadness   c) disagreement   d) false name

_____ 2. **antagonist**   a) relative   b) opponent   c) boss   d) friend

_____ 3. **elicit**   a) approve   b) draw forth   c) praise   d) disprove

_____ 4. **allusion**   a) short story   b) indirect reference   c) improvement
                              d) physical weakness

_____ 5. **adjacent**   a) under   b) above   c) next to   d) within

_____ 6. **absolve**   a) reject   b) approve   c) clear from guilt   d) make guilty

_____ 7. **methodical**   a) careless   b) systematic   c) immoral   d) religious

_____ 8. **zeal**   a) enthusiastic devotion   b) injustice   c) laziness   d) hatred

_____ 9. **dilemma**   a) picture   b) difficult choice   c) error   d) tendency

_____ 10. **arbitrary**   a) unreasonable   b) believable   c) demanding   d) wordy

_____ 11. **obsolete**   a) out-of-date   b) not sold   c) difficult to believe   d) current

_____ 12. **euphemism**   a) substitute for offensive term   b) title   c) false appearance   d) degree

_____ 13. **terminate**   a) stop   b) begin   c) approach   d) continue

_____ 14. **amiable**   a) good-natured   b) stingy   c) proud   d) rude

_____ 15. **eccentric**   a) common   b) active   c) odd   d) calm

_____ 16. **succinct**   a) brief and clear   b) not fair   c) impressed   d) prepared

_____ 17. **curt**   a) talkative   b) rudely brief   c) friendly   d) ignorant

_____ 18. **assail**   a) travel   b) confuse   c) defend   d) attack

_____ 19. **banal**   a) secret   b) commonplace   c) true   d) humid

_____ 20. **infirmity**   a) physical weakness   b) small city   c) relationship   d) hospital

_____ 21. **wary**   a) tired   b) unfriendly   c) cautious   d) kind

_____ 22. **exploit**   a) throw away   b) sell overseas   c) take advantage of   d) save

_____ 23. **inequity**   a) bigger portion   b) boring job   c) small party   d) injustice

_____ 24. **revitalize**   a) get an idea   b) feel weak   c) renew strength   d) break in on

_____ 25. **deterrent**   a) prevention   b) memory   c) blame   d) ending

(Continues on next page)

_____ 26. **amoral**   a) generous   b) without principles   c) honest   d) poor

_____ 27. **implication**   a) statement   b) rule   c) something hinted at   d) word

_____ 28. **subsequent**   a) before   b) above   c) following   d) beneath

_____ 29. **epitome**   a) horrible sight   b) large hole   c) tallest point   d) perfect example

_____ 30. **sabotage**   a) deliberately damage   b) follow   c) hide from   d) aid

_____ 31. **infringe**   a) intrude   b) impress   c) add to   d) encourage

_____ 32. **malign**   a) praise   b) depend on   c) boast   d) speak evil of

_____ 33. **innovation**   a) test   b) exercise   c) something new   d) application

_____ 34. **taint**   a) dishonor   b) boast   c) annoy   d) surprise

_____ 35. **engross**   a) destroy   b) hold the attention of   c) disgust   d) impress

_____ 36. **demoralize**   a) lecture   b) encourage   c) set a bad example for
d) lower the spirits of

_____ 37. **subjective**   a) impressive   b) based on personal feelings   c) distantly related   d) cruel

_____ 38. **retort**   a) reply   b) approve   c) argue   d) question

_____ 39. **animosity**   a) shyness   b) ill will   c) approval   d) fear

_____ 40. **syndrome**   a) something required   b) thought   c) attitude   d) group of symptoms

_____ 41. **irate**   a) proud   b) very friendly   c) silly   d) very angry

_____ 42. **tangible**   a) touchable   b) orderly   c) hidden   d) more than normal

_____ 43. **appease**   a) tell the truth   b) approve   c) attack   d) make calm

_____ 44. **altruistic**   a) lying   b) unselfish   c) proud   d) honest

_____ 45. **encounter**   a) total   b) attack   c) departure   d) meeting

_____ 46. **escalate**   a) include   b) lessen   c) intensify   d) remove

_____ 47. **mercenary**   a) calm   b) mean   c) greedy   d) clean

_____ 48. **adamant**   a) stubborn   b) flexible   c) weak   d) realistic

_____ 49. **sparse**   a) gentle   b) threatening   c) plentiful   d) spread thinly

_____ 50. **inclination**   a) favor   b) increase   c) lack   d) tendency

SCORE: (Number correct) _____ × 2 = _____ %

Unit Two: *Pretest*

In the space provided, write the letter of the choice that is closest in meaning to the **boldfaced** word.

_____ 1. **fluctuate**   **a)** stand still   **b)** vary irregularly   **c)** float   **d)** sink

_____ 2. **rehabilitate**   **a)** restore to normal life   **b)** relax   **c)** plan in meetings   **d)** interpret

_____ 3. **flagrant**   **a)** gentle   **b)** hidden   **c)** slight   **d)** outrageous

_____ 4. **calamity**   **a)** disaster   **b)** storm   **c)** conference   **d)** breeze

_____ 5. **persevere**   **a)** treat harshly   **b)** mark   **c)** continue   **d)** delay

_____ 6. **comprehensive**   **a)** accidental   **b)** including much   **c)** delicate   **d)** small

_____ 7. **venture**   **a)** turn aside   **b)** urge   **c)** risk   **d)** misrepresent

_____ 8. **ponder**   **a)** think deeply about   **b)** allow   **c)** reduce   **d)** flatten

_____ 9. **turmoil**   **a)** workplace   **b)** quiet setting   **c)** fire   **d)** uproar

_____ 10. **conventional**   **a)** large   **b)** at a conference   **c)** outstanding   **d)** ordinary

_____ 11. **enhance**   **a)** reject   **b)** get   **c)** improve   **d)** free

_____ 12. **mobile**   **a)** firm in opinion   **b)** able to move   **c)** stationary   **d)** restricted

_____ 13. **orient**   **a)** determine the location of   **b)** lose   **c)** represent   **d)** consist of

_____ 14. **attribute**   **a)** admiration   **b)** program   **c)** disease   **d)** quality

_____ 15. **enigma**   **a)** rash   **b)** puzzle   **c)** tool   **d)** cleanser

_____ 16. **discern**   **a)** see clearly   **b)** devise   **c)** rule out   **d)** consider

_____ 17. **dispatch**   **a)** recall   **b)** remove   **c)** send   **d)** plant

_____ 18. **exemplify**   **a)** construct   **b)** represent   **c)** plan   **d)** test

_____ 19. **nocturnal**   **a)** supposed   **b)** not logical   **c)** complex   **d)** active at night

_____ 20. **attest**   **a)** bear witness   **b)** examine   **c)** tear up   **d)** dislike

_____ 21. **concurrent**   **a)** apart   **b)** happening together   **c)** north   **d)** off-and-on

_____ 22. **hypothetical**   **a)** moral   **b)** factual   **c)** avoidable   **d)** supposed

_____ 23. **constitute**   **a)** make up   **b)** eliminate   **c)** separate   **d)** remove

_____ 24. **recession**   **a)** parade   **b)** amusement   **c)** giving in   **d)** business decline

_____ 25. **predominant**   **a)** smallest   **b)** most noticeable   **c)** having a tendency   **d)** hidden

(Continues on next page)

_____ 26. **decipher**   **a)** interpret   **b)** study   **c)** improve   **d)** pay back

_____ 27. **default**   **a)** jump   **b)** do automatically   **c)** fail to do something required   **d)** seize

_____ 28. **nominal**   **a)** open to harm   **b)** large   **c)** important   **d)** slight

_____ 29. **prerequisite**   **a)** requirement beforehand   **b)** test   **c)** close inspection   **d)** extra credit

_____ 30. **confiscate**   **a)** deny   **b)** make difficult   **c)** desire   **d)** seize with authority

_____ 31. **sanctuary**   **a)** opinion   **b)** hardship   **c)** place of safety   **d)** something complicated

_____ 32. **suffice**   **a)** think up   **b)** be enough   **c)** prevent   **d)** pay back

_____ 33. **degenerate**   **a)** give up   **b)** improve   **c)** stay the same   **d)** worsen

_____ 34. **vulnerable**   **a)** kind   **b)** intelligent   **c)** wicked   **d)** sensitive

_____ 35. **implausible**   **a)** possible   **b)** hard to believe   **c)** imaginary   **d)** historical

_____ 36. **intercede**   **a)** ask for a favor   **b)** remove   **c)** isolate   **d)** come between to help solve

_____ 37. **scrutiny**   **a)** knowledge   **b)** lack of interest   **c)** close inspection   **d)** ignorance

_____ 38. **sinister**   **a)** frightened   **b)** lively   **c)** generous   **d)** evil

_____ 39. **incoherent**   **a)** not logical   **b)** well-spoken   **c)** quiet   **d)** unable to read

_____ 40. **intricate**   **a)** easy   **b)** complex   **c)** workable   **d)** touching

_____ 41. **qualm**   **a)** pleasure   **b)** dead end   **c)** feeling of doubt   **d)** place of safety

_____ 42. **blight**   **a)** something that damages   **b)** natural environment   **c)** example
d) storm

_____ 43. **garble**   **a)** refuse   **b)** mix up   **c)** claim   **d)** speak clearly

_____ 44. **contrive**   **a)** allow   **b)** inspect   **c)** think up   **d)** prepare

_____ 45. **gaunt**   **a)** large   **b)** complex   **c)** well   **d)** thin

_____ 46. **immaculate**   **a)** roomy   **b)** clean   **c)** empty   **d)** complete

_____ 47. **retaliate**   **a)** repair   **b)** repeat   **c)** renew   **d)** pay back

_____ 48. **gloat**   **a)** express spiteful pleasure   **b)** give up   **c)** eat   **d)** deny

_____ 49. **plagiarism**   **a)** support   **b)** contribution   **c)** stealing someone's writings   **d)** removal

_____ 50. **blatant**   **a)** sudden   **b)** immediate   **c)** quiet   **d)** obvious

SCORE: (Number correct) _____ × 2 = _____ %

Unit Two: *Posttest*

In the space provided, write the letter of the choice that is closest in meaning to the **boldfaced** word.

_____ 1. **vulnerable**   a) intelligent   b) sensitive   c) wicked   d) kind

_____ 2. **persevere**   a) continue   b) mark   c) delay   d) treat harshly

_____ 3. **conventional**   a) large   b) outstanding   c) at a conference   d) ordinary

_____ 4. **enigma**   a) tool   b) puzzle   c) cleanser   d) rash

_____ 5. **comprehensive**   a) including much   b) small   c) delicate   d) accidental

_____ 6. **attest**   a) examine   b) dislike   c) tear up   d) bear witness

_____ 7. **calamity**   a) storm   b) breeze   c) conference   d) disaster

_____ 8. **ponder**   a) think deeply about   b) allow   c) reduce   d) flatten

_____ 9. **blatant**   a) immediate   b) obvious   c) quiet   d) sudden

_____ 10. **constitute**   a) make up   b) separate   c) remove   d) eliminate

_____ 11. **sinister**   a) evil   b) generous   c) frightened   d) lively

_____ 12. **enhance**   a) get   b) free   c) improve   d) reject

_____ 13. **dispatch**   a) recall   b) remove   c) send   d) plant

_____ 14. **predominant**   a) most noticeable   b) having a tendency   c) hidden   d) smallest

_____ 15. **venture**   a) misrepresent   b) urge   c) turn aside   d) risk

_____ 16. **default**   a) do automatically   b) seize   c) fail to do something required   d) jump

_____ 17. **discern**   a) devise   b) consider   c) rule out   d) see clearly

_____ 18. **implausible**   a) hard to believe   b) historical   c) imaginary   d) possible

_____ 19. **hypothetical**   a) factual   b) avoidable   c) moral   d) supposed

_____ 20. **prerequisite**   a) test   b) extra credit   c) close inspection   d) requirement beforehand

_____ 21. **suffice**   a) be enough   b) pay back   c) prevent   d) think up

_____ 22. **mobile**   a) stationary   b) able to move   c) restricted   d) firm in opinion

_____ 23. **attribute**   a) admiration   b) quality   c) disease   d) program

_____ 24. **fluctuate**   a) float   b) sink   c) vary irregularly   d) stand still

_____ 25. **scrutiny**   a) lack of interest   b) ignorance   c) close inspection   d) knowledge

(Continues on next page)

_____ 26. **nocturnal**   **a)** not logical   **b)** complex   **c)** supposed   **d)** active at night

_____ 27. **nominal**   **a)** large   **b)** slight   **c)** open to harm   **d)** important

_____ 28. **incoherent**   **a)** well-spoken   **b)** unable to read   **c)** quiet   **d)** not logical

_____ 29. **intricate**   **a)** touching   **b)** workable   **c)** easy   **d)** complex

_____ 30. **rehabilitate**   **a)** relax   **b)** restore to normal life   **c)** plan in meetings   **d)** interpret

_____ 31. **qualm**   **a)** dead end   **b)** feeling of doubt   **c)** place of safety   **d)** pleasure

_____ 32. **degenerate**   **a)** improve   **b)** worsen   **c)** stay the same   **d)** give up

_____ 33. **plagiarism**   **a)** support   **b)** removal   **c)** stealing someone's writings   **d)** contribution

_____ 34. **turmoil**   **a)** quiet setting   **b)** uproar   **c)** fire   **d)** workplace

_____ 35. **confiscate**   **a)** desire   **b)** make difficult   **c)** seize with authority   **d)** deny

_____ 36. **blight**   **a)** natural environment   **b)** storm   **c)** example   **d)** something that damages

_____ 37. **exemplify**   **a)** represent   **b)** test   **c)** plan   **d)** construct

_____ 38. **garble**   **a)** mix up   **b)** claim   **c)** speak clearly   **d)** refuse

_____ 39. **recession**   **a)** parade   **b)** business decline   **c)** giving in   **d)** amusement

_____ 40. **contrive**   **a)** inspect   **b)** prepare   **c)** allow   **d)** think up

_____ 41. **intercede**   **a)** remove   **b)** come between to help solve   **c)** isolate   **d)** strike

_____ 42. **gaunt**   **a)** complex   **b)** thin   **c)** well   **d)** large

_____ 43. **flagrant**   **a)** hidden   **b)** outrageous   **c)** slight   **d)** gentle

_____ 44. **immaculate**   **a)** clean   **b)** complete   **c)** empty   **d)** roomy

_____ 45. **decipher**   **a)** study   **b)** pay back   **c)** improve   **d)** interpret

_____ 46. **retaliate**   **a)** renew   **b)** repeat   **c)** pay back   **d)** repair

_____ 47. **orient**   **a)** represent   **b)** lose   **c)** consist of   **d)** determine the location of

_____ 48. **gloat**   **a)** eat   **b)** give up   **c)** deny   **d)** express spiteful pleasure

_____ 49. **concurrent**   **a)** apart   **b)** off-and-on   **c)** north   **d)** happening together

_____ 50. **sanctuary**   **a)** hardship   **b)** something complicated   **c)** place of safety   **d)** opinion

SCORE: (Number correct) _____ × 2 = _____ %

Unit Three: *Pretest*

In the space provided, write the letter of the choice that is closest in meaning to the **boldfaced** word.

_____ 1. **incorporate**   **a)** anger   **b)** separate   **c)** combine   **d)** calm

_____ 2. **intermittent**   **a)** hesitant   **b)** nervous   **c)** off-and-on   **d)** constant

_____ 3. **digress**   **a)** stray   **b)** improve   **c)** resist   **d)** repeat

_____ 4. **incentive**   **a)** fear   **b)** pride   **c)** concern   **d)** encouragement

_____ 5. **succumb**   **a)** approach   **b)** repeat   **c)** give in   **d)** cut short

_____ 6. **rigor**   **a)** ease   **b)** hardship   **c)** slowness   **d)** meanness

_____ 7. **squander**   **a)** waste   **b)** lose   **c)** insult   **d)** strongly desire

_____ 8. **curtail**   **a)** urge   **b)** join   **c)** cut short   **d)** relieve

_____ 9. **indispensable**   **a)** necessary   **b)** not important   **c)** saved up   **d)** wasted

_____ 10. **devastate**   **a)** spread out   **b)** begin again   **c)** reassure   **d)** upset greatly

_____ 11. **speculate**   **a)** search   **b)** think about   **c)** inspect   **d)** state to be so

_____ 12. **cynic**   **a)** pessimist   **b)** serious person   **c)** single person   **d)** clown

_____ 13. **infamous**   **a)** not known   **b)** small   **c)** having a bad reputation   **d)** related

_____ 14. **benefactor**   **a)** landlord   **b)** one who gives aid   **c)** optimist   **d)** kindness

_____ 15. **covert**   **a)** distant   **b)** hidden   **c)** changed   **d)** adjusted

_____ 16. **virile**   **a)** healthy   **b)** manly   **c)** wrinkled   **d)** required

_____ 17. **intrinsic**   **a)** belonging by its very nature   **b)** on the surface   **c)** not noticeable
                d) careful

_____ 18. **alleviate**   **a)** make anxious   **b)** depart   **c)** infect   **d)** relieve

_____ 19. **demise**   **a)** trick   **b)** death   **c)** disguise   **d)** departure

_____ 20. **revulsion**   **a)** confession   **b)** great disgust   **c)** attraction   **d)** compassion

_____ 21. **deficit**   **a)** surplus   **b)** remainder   **c)** part of the whole   **d)** shortage

_____ 22. **mandatory**   **a)** masculine   **b)** sexist   **c)** required   **d)** threatening

_____ 23. **abstain**   **a)** do without   **b)** disagree   **c)** prepare   **d)** approve of

_____ 24. **lucrative**   **a)** silly   **b)** profitable   **c)** causing disease   **d)** attractive

_____ 25. **diversion**   **a)** awareness   **b)** practice   **c)** amusement   **d)** fate

(Continues on next page)

_____ 26. **affiliate**   **a)** impress   **b)** approve   **c)** reject   **d)** join

_____ 27. **agnostic**   **a)** one who is unsure there's a God   **b)** saint   **c)** believer   **d)** genius

_____ 28. **aspire**   **a)** dislike   **b)** strongly desire   **c)** impress   **d)** deliver

_____ 29. **benevolent**   **a)** kind   **b)** wealthy   **c)** nasty   **d)** poor

_____ 30. **dissent**   **a)** approval   **b)** defeat   **c)** winning   **d)** disagreement

_____ 31. **proponent**   **a)** foe   **b)** supporter   **c)** examiner   **d)** one part of the whole

_____ 32. **charisma**   **a)** friendship   **b)** kindness   **c)** obedience   **d)** charm

_____ 33. **quest**   **a)** search   **b)** request   **c)** place   **d)** memory

_____ 34. **contend**   **a)** join   **b)** claim   **c)** arouse   **d)** allow

_____ 35. **conversely**   **a)** rudely   **b)** uncooperative   **c)** in an opposite manner   **d)** unfriendly

_____ 36. **contemporary**   **a)** modern   **b)** odd   **c)** old-fashioned   **d)** futuristic

_____ 37. **extrovert**   **a)** shy person   **b)** magnetism   **c)** main point   **d)** outgoing person

_____ 38. **prevalent**   **a)** famous   **b)** widespread   **c)** escapable   **d)** plain

_____ 39. **poignant**   **a)** annoying   **b)** beautiful   **c)** careless   **d)** touching

_____ 40. **traumatic**   **a)** causing painful emotions   **b)** reversed   **c)** delicate   **d)** harmless

_____ 41. **rapport**   **a)** support   **b)** close relationship   **c)** view   **d)** report

_____ 42. **reprisal**   **a)** getting even   **b)** defeat   **c)** question   **d)** search

_____ 43. **flippant**   **a)** cold   **b)** formal   **c)** disrespectful   **d)** nervous

_____ 44. **perception**   **a)** meeting   **b)** party   **c)** dead end   **d)** impression

_____ 45. **relentless**   **a)** angry   **b)** persistent   **c)** cruel   **d)** kind

_____ 46. **congenial**   **a)** pleasant   **b)** intelligent   **c)** mixed-up   **d)** lacking

_____ 47. **prone**   **a)** disliked   **b)** tending   **c)** active   **d)** rested

_____ 48. **rationale**   **a)** research paper   **b)** debate   **c)** logical basis   **d)** mood

_____ 49. **impasse**   **a)** exit   **b)** central point   **c)** gate   **d)** dead end

_____ 50. **prompt**   **a)** urge   **b)** avoid   **c)** waste   **d)** lie

SCORE: (Number correct) _____ × 2 = _____ %

Unit Three: *Posttest*

In the space provided, write the letter of the choice that is closest in meaning to the **boldfaced** word.

_____   1. **abstain**   a) prepare   b) disagree   c) approve of   d) do without

_____   2. **agnostic**   a) believer   b) saint   c) genius   d) one who is unsure there's a God

_____   3. **impasse**   a) exit   b) dead end   c) gate   d) central point

_____   4. **benevolent**   a) kind   b) nasty   c) poor   d) wealthy

_____   5. **cynic**   a) serious person   b) clown   c) single person   d) pessimist

_____   6. **dissent**   a) defeat   b) winning   c) disagreement   d) approval

_____   7. **conversely**   a) uncooperative   b) in an opposite manner   c) rudely   d) unfriendly

_____   8. **benefactor**   a) kindness   b) one who gives aid   c) optimist   d) landlord

_____   9. **proponent**   a) supporter   b) examiner   c) one part of the whole   d) foe

_____ 10. **intrinsic**   a) not noticeable   b) on the surface   c) careful
                                d) belonging by its very nature

_____ 11. **charisma**   a) friendship   b) kindness   c) obedience   d) charm

_____ 12. **incentive**   a) concern   b) pride   c) encouragement   d) fear

_____ 13. **infamous**   a) having a bad reputation   b) small   c) related   d) not known

_____ 14. **aspire**   a) impress   b) strongly desire   c) deliver   d) dislike

_____ 15. **quest**   a) request   b) memory   c) place   d) search

_____ 16. **squander**   a) insult   b) lose   c) strongly desire   d) waste

_____ 17. **devastate**   a) begin again   b) upset greatly   c) reassure   d) spread out

_____ 18. **contend**   a) arouse   b) allow   c) claim   d) join

_____ 19. **reprisal**   a) defeat   b) search   c) question   d) getting even

_____ 20. **rigor**   a) meanness   b) ease   c) slowness   d) hardship

_____ 21. **affiliate**   a) approve   b) reject   c) impress   d) join

_____ 22. **contemporary**   a) old-fashioned   b) futuristic   c) odd   d) modern

_____ 23. **covert**   a) hidden   b) changed   c) distant   d) adjusted

_____ 24. **extrovert**   a) main point   b) magnetism   c) outgoing person   d) shy person

_____ 25. **curtail**   a) join   b) relieve   c) cut short   d) urge

(Continues on next page)

_____ 26. **revulsion**   a) great disgust   b) attraction   c) confession   d) compassion

_____ 27. **prevalent**   a) widespread   b) escapable   c) famous   d) plain

_____ 28. **indispensable**   a) necessary   b) not important   c) saved up   d) wasted

_____ 29. **poignant**   a) touching   b) annoying   c) careless   d) beautiful

_____ 30. **traumatic**   a) reversed   b) harmless   c) delicate   d) causing painful emotions

_____ 31. **succumb**   a) repeat   b) cut short   c) approach   d) give in

_____ 32. **rapport**   a) close relationship   b) view   c) support   d) report

_____ 33. **flippant**   a) cold   b) nervous   c) formal   d) disrespectful

_____ 34. **incorporate**   a) combine   b) separate   c) anger   d) calm

_____ 35. **perception**   a) party   b) dead end   c) meeting   d) impression

_____ 36. **demise**   a) disguise   b) death   c) departure   d) trick

_____ 37. **prompt**   a) waste   b) avoid   c) lie   d) urge

_____ 38. **relentless**   a) kind   b) persistent   c) cruel   d) angry

_____ 39. **alleviate**   a) depart   b) relieve   c) infect   d) make anxious

_____ 40. **diversion**   a) practice   b) fate   c) amusement   d) awareness

_____ 41. **congenial**   a) intelligent   b) lacking   c) mixed-up   d) pleasant

_____ 42. **intermittent**   a) constant   b) nervous   c) off-and-on   d) hesitant

_____ 43. **mandatory**   a) masculine   b) threatening   c) required   d) sexist

_____ 44. **prone**   a) active   b) tending   c) rested   d) disliked

_____ 45. **virile**   a) wrinkled   b) healthy   c) manly   d) required

_____ 46. **lucrative**   a) profitable   b) attractive   c) causing disease   d) silly

_____ 47. **rationale**   a) debate   b) mood   c) logical basis   d) research paper

_____ 48. **deficit**   a) remainder   b) shortage   c) part of the whole   d) surplus

_____ 49. **digress**   a) improve   b) repeat   c) resist   d) stray

_____ 50. **speculate**   a) think about   b) state to be so   c) inspect   d) search

SCORE: (Number correct) _____ × 2 = _____ %

Unit Four: *Pretest*

In the space provided, write the letter of the choice that is closest in meaning to the **boldfaced** word.

_____ 1. **facade**   **a)** false name   **b)** building front   **c)** scorn   **d)** good intention

_____ 2. **redundant**   **a)** wordy   **b)** gentle   **c)** required   **d)** not enough

_____ 3. **blase**   **a)** excited   **b)** kind   **c)** curious   **d)** bored

_____ 4. **haughty**   **a)** arrogant   **b)** alarmed   **c)** contented   **d)** thoughtful

_____ 5. **pseudonym**   **a)** false appearance   **b)** imaginary creature   **c)** false name
                    d) dishonest person

_____ 6. **comprise**   **a)** reward   **b)** consist of   **c)** award   **d)** repeat

_____ 7. **condescend**   **a)** avoid   **b)** become messy   **c)** do something beneath oneself
                    d) get bored

_____ 8. **libel**   **a)** document   **b)** publishing false information   **c)** newspaper   **d)** rumor

_____ 9. **glib**   **a)** crunchy   **b)** smooth-talking   **c)** threatening   **d)** present but inactive

_____ 10. **benign**   **a)** rude   **b)** crazy   **c)** cruel   **d)** kindly

_____ 11. **divulge**   **a)** reveal   **b)** embarrass   **c)** hide   **d)** remove

_____ 12. **endow**   **a)** name   **b)** tease   **c)** give a quality to   **d)** cancel

_____ 13. **expulsion**   **a)** promotion   **b)** dismissal   **c)** award   **d)** attack

_____ 14. **detract**   **a)** provide   **b)** compete   **c)** lessen   **d)** compliment

_____ 15. **nullify**   **a)** harm   **b)** allow   **c)** examine   **d)** cancel

_____ 16. **elation**   **a)** trade   **b)** comparison   **c)** joy   **d)** majority opinion

_____ 17. **ominous**   **a)** happy   **b)** threatening   **c)** depressed   **d)** friendly

_____ 18. **mortify**   **a)** humiliate   **b)** praise   **c)** entertain   **d)** remember

_____ 19. **disdain**   **a)** discouragement   **b)** pain   **c)** scorn   **d)** approval

_____ 20. **averse**   **a)** attracted   **b)** fearful   **c)** warm   **d)** opposed

_____ 21. **cursory**   **a)** believable   **b)** capable of error   **c)** done hastily   **d)** inactive

_____ 22. **shun**   **a)** take care of   **b)** avoid   **c)** approve of   **d)** hesitate

_____ 23. **designate**   **a)** appoint   **b)** discover   **c)** avoid   **d)** report

_____ 24. **interim**   **a)** time   **b)** noontime   **c)** mealtime   **d)** meantime

_____ 25. **latent**   **a)** plain   **b)** inactive   **c)** on the surface   **d)** confusing

(Continues on next page)

_____ 26. **improvise**   **a)** prove   **b)** do without preparation   **c)** reject   **d)** reveal

_____ 27. **secular**   **a)** not related to religion   **b)** troublesome   **c)** in a city   **d)** religious

_____ 28. **deviate**   **a)** hide   **b)** develop   **c)** follow   **d)** turn aside

_____ 29. **simulate**   **a)** enjoy   **b)** take apart   **c)** imitate   **d)** build

_____ 30. **credible**   **a)** believable   **b)** fair   **c)** affordable   **d)** careful

_____ 31. **menial**   **a)** important   **b)** unkind   **c)** lowly   **d)** odd

_____ 32. **transcend**   **a)** send   **b)** travel   **c)** show off   **d)** rise above

_____ 33. **deplete**   **a)** encourage   **b)** use up   **c)** delay   **d)** add to

_____ 34. **complacent**   **a)** workable   **b)** easy   **c)** self-satisfied   **d)** healthy

_____ 35. **niche**   **a)** memory   **b)** wild outburst   **c)** main idea   **d)** one's place

_____ 36. **diligent**   **a)** careful in work   **b)** odd   **c)** obvious   **d)** gentle

_____ 37. **empathy**   **a)** fear   **b)** encouragement   **c)** ability to share someone's feelings   **d)** avoidance

_____ 38. **consensus**   **a)** majority opinion   **b)** counting   **c)** study   **d)** approval

_____ 39. **commemorate**   **a)** forget   **b)** imitate   **c)** add new members   **d)** honor the memory of

_____ 40. **waive**   **a)** sleep   **b)** show off   **c)** give up   **d)** fly

_____ 41. **gist**   **a)** details   **b)** central idea   **c)** left overs   **d)** respect

_____ 42. **bizarre**   **a)** odd   **b)** complex   **c)** simple   **d)** common

_____ 43. **paradox**   **a)** delicate situation   **b)** problem   **c)** seemingly contradictory idea   **d)** play

_____ 44. **viable**   **a)** in view   **b)** manly   **c)** lively   **d)** workable

_____ 45. **flaunt**   **a)** scare   **b)** show off   **c)** tempt   **d)** intrude

_____ 46. **conducive**   **a)** revealing   **b)** announcing   **c)** promoting   **d)** defeating

_____ 47. **hamper**   **a)** restrict   **b)** celebrate   **c)** betray   **d)** debate

_____ 48. **frenzy**   **a)** high regard   **b)** main idea   **c)** party   **d)** wild outburst

_____ 49. **repertoire**   **a)** sample   **b)** collection of skills   **c)** demonstration   **d)** concert

_____ 50. **falter**   **a)** frighten   **b)** approve   **c)** hesitate   **d)** jump

---

SCORE: (Number correct) _____ × 2 = _____ %

Unit Four: *Posttest*

In the space provided, write the letter of the choice that is closest in meaning to the **boldfaced** word.

_____ 1. **simulate**   **a)** imitate   **b)** take apart   **c)** build   **d)** enjoy

_____ 2. **haughty**   **a)** arrogant   **b)** contented   **c)** alarmed   **d)** thoughtful

_____ 3. **glib**   **a)** smooth-talking   **b)** present but inactive   **c)** threatening   **d)** crunchy

_____ 4. **elation**   **a)** comparison   **b)** joy   **c)** majority opinion   **d)** trade

_____ 5. **bizarre**   **a)** simple   **b)** complex   **c)** common   **d)** odd

_____ 6. **disdain**   **a)** pain   **b)** approval   **c)** scorn   **d)** discouragement

_____ 7. **conducive**   **a)** announcing   **b)** defeating   **c)** promoting   **d)** revealing

_____ 8. **menial**   **a)** unkind   **b)** lowly   **c)** important   **d)** odd

_____ 9. **waive**   **a)** show off   **b)** fly   **c)** give up   **d)** sleep

_____ 10. **cursory**   **a)** done hastily   **b)** capable of error   **c)** inactive   **d)** believable

_____ 11. **pseudonym**   **a)** imaginary creature   **b)** dishonest person   **c)** false name
        d) false appearance

_____ 12. **interim**   **a)** noontime   **b)** mealtime   **c)** time   **d)** meantime

_____ 13. **improvise**   **a)** do without preparation   **b)** reveal   **c)** reject   **d)** prove

_____ 14. **divulge**   **a)** embarrass   **b)** remove   **c)** hide   **d)** reveal

_____ 15. **deviate**   **a)** develop   **b)** follow   **c)** hide   **d)** turn aside

_____ 16. **nullify**   **a)** examine   **b)** cancel   **c)** allow   **d)** harm

_____ 17. **transcend**   **a)** travel   **b)** show off   **c)** send   **d)** rise above

_____ 18. **averse**   **a)** fearful   **b)** opposed   **c)** attracted   **d)** warm

_____ 19. **deplete**   **a)** encourage   **b)** delay   **c)** add to   **d)** use up

_____ 20. **condescend**   **a)** become messy   **b)** get bored   **c)** do something beneath oneself
        d) avoid

_____ 21. **complacent**   **a)** easy   **b)** healthy   **c)** self-satisfied   **d)** workable

_____ 22. **repertoire**   **a)** collection of skills   **b)** demonstration   **c)** sample   **d)** concert

_____ 23. **niche**   **a)** memory   **b)** one's place   **c)** main idea   **d)** wild outburst

_____ 24. **libel**   **a)** rumor   **b)** document   **c)** newspaper   **d)** publishing false information

_____ 25. **diligent**   **a)** gentle   **b)** odd   **c)** careful in work   **d)** obvious

(Continues on next page)

_____ 26. **empathy**   **a)** avoidance   **b)** fear   **c)** ability to share someone's feelings   **d)** encouragement

_____ 27. **detract**   **a)** compete   **b)** compliment   **c)** lessen   **d)** provide

_____ 28. **consensus**   **a)** counting   **b)** approval   **c)** study   **d)** majority opinion

_____ 29. **mortify**   **a)** humiliate   **b)** remember   **c)** entertain   **d)** praise

_____ 30. **frenzy**   **a)** party   **b)** main idea   **c)** wild outburst   **d)** high regard

_____ 31. **designate**   **a)** avoid   **b)** report   **c)** discover   **d)** appoint

_____ 32. **commemorate**   **a)** imitate   **b)** honor the memory of   **c)** add new members   **d)** forget

_____ 33. **facade**   **a)** good intention   **b)** building front   **c)** scorn   **d)** false name

_____ 34. **falter**   **a)** hesitate   **b)** approve   **c)** jump   **d)** frighten

_____ 35. **benign**   **a)** crazy   **b)** kindly   **c)** cruel   **d)** rude

_____ 36. **gist**   **a)** left overs   **b)** central idea   **c)** respect   **d)** details

_____ 37. **credible**   **a)** fair   **b)** affordable   **c)** careful   **d)** believable

_____ 38. **paradox**   **a)** play   **b)** delicate situation   **c)** seemingly contradictory idea   **d)** problem

_____ 39. **redundant**   **a)** not enough   **b)** wordy   **c)** required   **d)** gentle

_____ 40. **viable**   **a)** lively   **b)** manly   **c)** in view   **d)** workable

_____ 41. **endow**   **a)** give a quality to   **b)** tease   **c)** cancel   **d)** name

_____ 42. **flaunt**   **a)** tempt   **b)** show off   **c)** intrude   **d)** scare

_____ 43. **blase**   **a)** curious   **b)** kind   **c)** bored   **d)** excited

_____ 44. **latent**   **a)** on the surface   **b)** inactive   **c)** plain   **d)** confusing

_____ 45. **expulsion**   **a)** award   **b)** dismissal   **c)** attack   **d)** promotion

_____ 46. **ominous**   **a)** depressed   **b)** threatening   **c)** friendly   **d)** happy

_____ 47. **secular**   **a)** troublesome   **b)** religious   **c)** in a city   **d)** not related to religion

_____ 48. **hamper**   **a)** celebrate   **b)** debate   **c)** betray   **d)** restrict

_____ 49. **shun**   **a)** avoid   **b)** hesitate   **c)** approve of   **d)** take care of

_____ 50. **comprise**   **a)** consist of   **b)** repeat   **c)** award   **d)** reward

SCORE: (Number correct) _____ × 2 = _____ %

Unit Five: *Pretest*

In the space provided, write the letter of the choice that is closest in meaning to the **boldfaced** word.

_____ 1. **sneer**   **a)** impress   **b)** endanger   **c)** ridicule   **d)** make laugh

_____ 2. **introvert**   **a)** worker   **b)** shy person   **c)** good example   **d)** attacker

_____ 3. **vivacious**   **a)** vicious   **b)** retired   **c)** conceited   **d)** lively

_____ 4. **sibling**   **a)** sister or brother   **b)** friend   **c)** relative   **d)** parent

_____ 5. **implore**   **a)** excite   **b)** attack   **c)** beg   **d)** borrow

_____ 6. **devoid**   **a)** provided   **b)** lacking   **c)** endangered   **d)** borrowed

_____ 7. **jeopardize**   **a)** risk   **b)** meet with   **c)** anger   **d)** defend

_____ 8. **intimidate**   **a)** celebrate   **b)** visit   **c)** soothe   **d)** frighten

_____ 9. **smug**   **a)** upset   **b)** calm   **c)** conceited   **d)** lively

_____ 10. **feasible**   **a)** unbelievable   **b)** possible   **c)** amazing   **d)** wild

_____ 11. **gape**   **a)** stare   **b)** repair   **c)** beat   **d)** hide from

_____ 12. **fiscal**   **a)** secretive   **b)** about government   **c)** financial   **d)** personal

_____ 13. **condone**   **a)** forgive   **b)** represent   **c)** arrest   **d)** appoint

_____ 14. **pathetic**   **a)** rich   **b)** puzzling   **c)** wonderful   **d)** pitifully lacking

_____ 15. **precedent**   **a)** gift   **b)** example   **c)** fee   **d)** later event

_____ 16. **contemplate**   **a)** think seriously about   **b)** create   **c)** add to   **d)** reveal

_____ 17. **furtive**   **a)** loud   **b)** quiet   **c)** public   **d)** secretive

_____ 18. **detrimental**   **a)** dirty   **b)** nutritious   **c)** harmful   **d)** helpful

_____ 19. **ironic**   **a)** deeply felt   **b)** meaning opposite of what is said   **c)** simple   **d)** great

_____ 20. **implicit**   **a)** lacking   **b)** attached   **c)** above   **d)** unstated but understood

_____ 21. **vindictive**   **a)** not easily understood   **b)** gentle   **c)** vengeful   **d)** temporary

_____ 22. **cryptic**   **a)** harmful   **b)** cruel   **c)** puzzling   **d)** loud

_____ 23. **inhibition**   **a)** attack   **b)** delay   **c)** holding back   **d)** exhibit

_____ 24. **deficient**   **a)** forgotten   **b)** lacking   **c)** complete   **d)** well-known

_____ 25. **depict**   **a)** describe   **b)** settle   **c)** accept   **d)** control

(Continues on next page)

_____ 26. **constrict**   **a)** control   **b)** prove   **c)** make smaller   **d)** regard

_____ 27. **pretentious**   **a)** pleasant   **b)** showy   **c)** required   **d)** practical

_____ 28. **fallible**   **a)** capable of error   **b)** complete   **c)** incomplete   **d)** simple

_____ 29. **exhaustive**   **a)** respected   **b)** nervous   **c)** complete   **d)** tired

_____ 30. **formulate**   **a)** allow   **b)** move   **c)** purchase   **d)** develop

_____ 31. **habitat**   **a)** headache   **b)** natural environment   **c)** importance   **d)** usual behavior

_____ 32. **vile**   **a)** offensive   **b)** secretive   **c)** nice   **d)** tricky

_____ 33. **reconcile**   **a)** refine   **b)** redo   **c)** accept   **d)** increase

_____ 34. **pragmatic**   **a)** ordinary   **b)** slow   **c)** wise   **d)** practical

_____ 35. **pacify**   **a)** betray   **b)** calm   **c)** retreat   **d)** remove

_____ 36. **esteem**   **a)** age   **b)** doubt   **c)** respect   **d)** length of life

_____ 37. **transient**   **a)** stubborn   **b)** temporary   **c)** permanent   **d)** easy-going

_____ 38. **evoke**   **a)** pull back   **b)** plant   **c)** vote   **d)** draw forth

_____ 39. **muted**   **a)** softened   **b)** strangled   **c)** bright   **d)** puzzling

_____ 40. **avid**   **a)** bored   **b)** disliked   **c)** enthusiastic   **d)** plentiful

_____ 41. **dwindle**   **a)** strip   **b)** shrink   **c)** weave   **d)** cut

_____ 42. **nurture**   **a)** harden   **b)** thank   **c)** nourish   **d)** starve

_____ 43. **aloof**   **a)** distant   **b)** friendly   **c)** not clearly expressed   **d)** ordinary

_____ 44. **augment**   **a)** change   **b)** cause to become   **c)** increase   **d)** describe

_____ 45. **explicit**   **a)** everyday   **b)** distant   **c)** permanent   **d)** stated exactly

_____ 46. **longevity**   **a)** size   **b)** holding back   **c)** length of life   **d)** health

_____ 47. **magnitude**   **a)** large size   **b)** attraction   **c)** respect   **d)** example

_____ 48. **mundane**   **a)** odd   **b)** ordinary   **c)** softened   **d)** loud

_____ 49. **obscure**   **a)** enthusiastic   **b)** showy   **c)** hard to understand   **d)** bored

_____ 50. **render**   **a)** win out   **b)** reveal   **c)** cause to vanish   **d)** cause to become

_____

SCORE: (Number correct) _____ × 2 = _____ %

Unit Five: *Posttest*

In the space provided, write the letter of the choice that is closest in meaning to the **boldfaced** word.

_____ 1. **precedent**   a) fee   b) example   c) later event   d) gift

_____ 2. **nurture**   a) thank   b) starve   c) nourish   d) harden

_____ 3. **feasible**   a) possible   b) wild   c) amazing   d) unbelievable

_____ 4. **vile**   a) secretive   b) tricky   c) nice   d) offensive

_____ 5. **implicit**   a) unstated but understood   b) lacking   c) above   d) attached

_____ 6. **depict**   a) accept   b) settle   c) control   d) describe

_____ 7. **fiscal**   a) about government   b) personal   c) financial   d) secretive

_____ 8. **fallible**   a) complete   b) simple   c) incomplete   d) capable of error

_____ 9. **sibling**   a) friend   b) relative   c) parent   d) sister or brother

_____ 10. **exhaustive**   a) complete   b) nervous   c) tired   d) respected

_____ 11. **formulate**   a) purchase   b) move   c) develop   d) allow

_____ 12. **pathetic**   a) pitifully lacking   b) wonderful   c) rich   d) puzzling

_____ 13. **vindictive**   a) vengeful   b) gentle   c) not easily understood   d) temporary

_____ 14. **habitat**   a) importance   b) headache   c) usual behavior   d) natural environment

_____ 15. **devoid**   a) lacking   b) borrowed   c) endangered   d) provided

_____ 16. **reconcile**   a) redo   b) increase   c) accept   d) refine

_____ 17. **furtive**   a) public   b) quiet   c) loud   d) secretive

_____ 18. **obscure**   a) hard to understand   b) showy   c) bored   d) enthusiastic

_____ 19. **gape**   a) hide from   b) repair   c) beat   d) stare

_____ 20. **pretentious**   a) pleasant   b) practical   c) required   d) showy

_____ 21. **pragmatic**   a) slow   b) wise   c) ordinary   d) practical

_____ 22. **implore**   a) borrow   b) excite   c) beg   d) attack

_____ 23. **mundane**   a) softened   b) loud   c) ordinary   d) odd

_____ 24. **intimidate**   a) visit   b) frighten   c) soothe   d) celebrate

_____ 25. **constrict**   a) prove   b) regard   c) make smaller   d) control

(Continues on next page)

_____ 26. **pacify** a) calm b) remove c) retreat d) betray

_____ 27. **cryptic** a) cruel b) puzzling c) harmful d) loud

_____ 28. **explicit** a) everyday b) stated exactly c) permanent d) distant

_____ 29. **esteem** a) respect b) doubt c) length of life d) age

_____ 30. **transient** a) temporary b) easy-going c) permanent d) stubborn

_____ 31. **evoke** a) plant b) draw forth c) vote d) pull back

_____ 32. **render** a) cause to vanish b) cause to become c) reveal d) win out

_____ 33. **muted** a) softened b) puzzling c) bright d) strangled

_____ 34. **aloof** a) friendly b) ordinary c) not clearly expressed d) distant

_____ 35. **sneer** a) endanger b) make laugh c) ridicule d) impress

_____ 36. **avid** a) disliked b) plentiful c) enthusiastic d) bored

_____ 37. **smug** a) calm b) lively c) conceited d) upset

_____ 38. **dwindle** a) shrink b) cut c) weave d) strip

_____ 39. **ironic** a) meaning opposite of what is said b) great c) simple d) deeply felt

_____ 40. **introvert** a) good example b) attacker c) shy person d) worker

_____ 41. **augment** a) increase b) cause to become c) describe d) change

_____ 42. **deficient** a) well-known b) lacking c) forgotten d) complete

_____ 43. **vivacious** a) retired b) lively c) conceited d) vicious

_____ 44. **longevity** a) health b) size c) length of life d) holding back

_____ 45. **jeopardize** a) risk b) meet with c) anger d) defend

_____ 46. **condone** a) represent b) appoint c) arrest d) forgive

_____ 47. **magnitude** a) example b) large size c) respect d) attraction

_____ 48. **detrimental** a) dirty b) nutritious c) harmful d) helpful

_____ 49. **contemplate** a) add to b) create c) reveal d) think seriously about

_____ 50. **inhibition** a) attack b) exhibit c) holding back d) delay

SCORE: (Number correct) _____ × 2 = _____ %

IMPROVING VOCABULARY SKILLS

NAME: _____

SECTION: _____ DATE: _____

Pretest / Posttest

SCORE: _____

ANSWER SHEET

1. _____	26. _____	51. _____	76. _____
2. _____	27. _____	52. _____	77. _____
3. _____	28. _____	53. _____	78. _____
4. _____	29. _____	54. _____	79. _____
5. _____	30. _____	55. _____	80. _____
6. _____	31. _____	56. _____	81. _____
7. _____	32. _____	57. _____	82. _____
8. _____	33. _____	58. _____	83. _____
9. _____	34. _____	59. _____	84. _____
10. _____	35. _____	60. _____	85. _____
11. _____	36. _____	61. _____	86. _____
12. _____	37. _____	62. _____	87. _____
13. _____	38. _____	63. _____	88. _____
14. _____	39. _____	64. _____	89. _____
15. _____	40. _____	65. _____	90. _____
16. _____	41. _____	66. _____	91. _____
17. _____	42. _____	67. _____	92. _____
18. _____	43. _____	68. _____	93. _____
19. _____	44. _____	69. _____	94. _____
20. _____	45. _____	70. _____	95. _____
21. _____	46. _____	71. _____	96. _____
22. _____	47. _____	72. _____	97. _____
23. _____	48. _____	73. _____	98. _____
24. _____	49. _____	74. _____	99. _____
25. _____	50. _____	75. _____	100. _____

ANSWER KEY

1. b	26. b	51. c	76. a
2. a	27. a	52. b	77. b
3. b	28. b	53. b	78. a
4. a	29. d	54. a	79. b
5. b	30. d	55. d	80. a
6. b	31. b	56. b	81. c
7. b	32. d	57. a	82. b
8. d	33. b	58. c	83. c
9. a	34. d	59. b	84. c
10. c	35. b	60. a	85. b
11. a	36. c	61. c	86. a
12. d	37. b	62. d	87. c
13. c	38. b	63. b	88. b
14. b	39. d	64. c	89. a
15. a	40. d	65. d	90. d
16. b	41. c	66. a	91. b
17. a	42. a	67. d	92. c
18. c	43. d	68. c	93. b
19. b	44. c	69. b	94. c
20. c	45. d	70. d	95. c
21. c	46. b	71. d	96. c
22. d	47. c	72. b	97. d
23. a	48. b	73. c	98. a
24. b	49. a	74. c	99. b
25. a	50. d	75. c	100. d

ANSWER KEY

1.	c	26.	b	51.	a	76.	c
2.	c	27.	c	52.	d	77.	c
3.	b	28.	a	53.	b	78.	d
4.	d	29.	c	54.	c	79.	b
5.	d	30.	b	55.	c	80.	a
6.	c	31.	d	56.	c	81.	d
7.	c	32.	b	57.	c	82.	a
8.	b	33.	b	58.	d	83.	d
9.	b	34.	d	59.	b	84.	a
10.	d	35.	a	60.	d	85.	c
11.	c	36.	b	61.	d	86.	a
12.	a	37.	c	62.	b	87.	a
13.	a	38.	b	63.	b	88.	a
14.	c	39.	a	64.	b	89.	a
15.	a	40.	d	65.	c	90.	d
16.	c	41.	a	66.	a	91.	d
17.	b	42.	c	67.	a	92.	c
18.	c	43.	d	68.	b	93.	a
19.	c	44.	a	69.	b	94.	a
20.	d	45.	c	70.	c	95.	b
21.	b	46.	b	71.	d	96.	c
22.	b	47.	c	72.	b	97.	d
23.	c	48.	c	73.	a	98.	c
24.	b	49.	b	74.	a	99.	a
25.	b	50.	c	75.	c	100.	c

Answers to the Pretests and Posttests: IMPROVING VOCABULARY SKILLS

	Unit One		Unit Two		Unit Three		Unit Four		Unit Five	
	Pretest	*Posttest*	*Pretest*	*Posttest*	*Pretest*	*Posttest*	*Pretest*	*Posttest*	*Pretest*	*Posttest*
1.	b	a	b	b	c	d	b	a	c	b
2.	a	b	a	a	c	d	a	a	b	c
3.	c	b	d	d	a	b	d	a	d	a
4.	b	b	a	b	d	a	a	b	a	d
5.	d	c	c	a	c	d	c	d	c	a
6.	a	c	b	d	b	c	b	c	b	d
7.	c	b	c	d	a	b	c	c	a	c
8.	b	a	a	a	c	b	b	b	c	d
9.	d	b	d	b	a	a	b	c	c	d
10.	a	a	d	a	d	d	d	a	b	a
11.	c	a	c	a	b	d	a	c	a	c
12.	b	a	b	c	a	c	c	d	c	a
13.	d	a	a	c	c	a	b	a	a	a
14.	d	a	d	a	b	b	c	d	d	a
15.	a	c	b	d	b	d	d	d	b	a
16.	b	a	a	c	b	d	c	b	a	c
17.	c	b	c	d	a	b	b	d	d	d
18.	a	d	b	a	d	c	a	b	c	a
19.	b	b	d	d	b	d	c	d	b	d
20.	d	a	a	d	b	d	d	c	d	d
21.	b	c	b	a	d	d	c	c	c	d
22.	b	c	d	b	c	a	b	a	c	c
23.	d	d	a	b	a	a	a	b	c	c
24.	a	c	d	c	b	c	d	d	b	b
25.	c	a	b	c	c	c	b	c	a	c
26.	c	b	a	d	d	a	b	c	c	a
27.	b	c	c	b	a	a	a	c	b	b
28.	c	c	d	d	b	a	d	d	a	b
29.	d	d	a	d	a	a	c	a	c	a
30.	a	a	d	b	d	d	a	c	d	a
31.	b	a	c	b	b	d	c	d	b	b
32.	c	d	b	b	c	a	d	b	a	b
33.	a	c	d	c	a	d	b	b	c	a
34.	c	a	d	b	b	a	c	a	d	d
35.	d	b	b	c	c	d	d	b	b	c
36.	b	d	d	d	a	b	a	b	c	c
37.	a	b	c	a	d	d	c	d	b	c
38.	c	a	d	a	b	b	a	c	d	a
39.	a	b	a	b	d	b	d	b	a	a
40.	c	d	b	d	a	c	c	d	c	c
41.	b	d	c	b	b	d	b	a	b	a
42.	d	a	a	b	a	c	a	b	c	b
43.	a	d	b	b	c	c	c	c	a	b
44.	b	b	c	a	d	b	d	b	c	c
45.	a	d	d	d	b	c	b	b	d	a
46.	d	c	b	c	a	a	c	b	c	d
47.	d	c	d	d	b	c	a	d	a	b
48.	c	a	a	d	c	b	d	d	b	c
49.	b	d	c	d	d	d	b	a	c	d
50.	a	d	d	c	a	a	c	a	d	c

112

Answers to the Chapter Activities: IMPROVING VOCABULARY SKILLS

Chapter 1 (Joseph Palmer)

Ten Words in Context	Matching Words/Defs	Sentence Check 1	Sentence Check 2	Final Check
1. B 6. B	1. 2 6. 9	1. B 6. I	1–2. G, H	1. D 6. F
2. A 7. B	2. 4 7. 6	2. H 7. A	3–4. E, J	2. C 7. A
3. C 8. C	3. 7 8. 5	3. J 8. F	5–6. B, F	3. I 8. E
4. C 9. A	4. 1 9. 10	4. C 9. E	7–8. D, A	4. H 9. B
5. A 10. C	5. 8 10. 3	5. D 10. G	9–10. I, C	5. J 10. G

Chapter 2 (Telephone Salespeople)

Ten Words in Context	Matching Words/Defs	Sentence Check 1	Sentence Check 2	Final Check
1. C 6. B	1. 4 6. 3	1. C 6. B	1–2. E, A	1. I 6. J
2. B 7. C	2. 1 7. 8	2. I 7. H	3–4. D, F	2. D 7. G
3. A 8. B	3. 9 8. 10	3. D 8. E	5–6. G, I	3. C 8. H
4. A 9. A	4. 6 9. 7	4. A 9. J	7–8. J, B	4. B 9. E
5. C 10. B	5. 2 10. 5	5. G 10. F	9–10. H, C	5. A 10. F

Chapter 3 (A Cruel Sport)

Ten Words in Context	Matching Words/Defs	Sentence Check 1	Sentence Check 2	Final Check
1. B 6. B	1. 3 6. 8	1. I 6. D	1–2. D, C	1. F 6. D
2. A 7. C	2. 10 7. 5	2. H 7. F	3–4. H, J	2. H 7. B
3. C 8. C	3. 7 8. 1	3. A 8. G	5–6. I, A	3. C 8. J
4. A 9. B	4. 2 9. 4	4. B 9. J	7–8. F, E	4. A 9. G
5. A 10. A	5. 9 10. 6	5. E 10. C	9–10. G, B	5. E 10. I

Chapter 4 (Bald Is Beautiful)

Ten Words in Context	Matching Words/Defs	Sentence Check 1	Sentence Check 2	Final Check
1. B 6. A	1. 3 6. 7	1. D 6. F	1–2. H, G	1. B 6. I
2. C 7. A	2. 6 7. 4	2. B 7. G	3–4. F, E	2. D 7. G
3. A 8. B	3. 9 8. 8	3. E 8. I	5–6. D, A	3. E 8. A
4. B 9. A	4. 1 9. 5	4. J 9. C	7–8. I, C	4. C 9. F
5. A 10. C	5. 10 10. 2	5. H 10. A	9–10. B, J	5. H 10. J

Chapter 5 (No Luck With Women)

Ten Words in Context	Matching Words/Defs	Sentence Check 1	Sentence Check 2	Final Check
1. B 6. B	1. 4 6. 3	1. H 6. J	1–2. B, H	1. E 6. C
2. A 7. B	2. 8 7. 6	2. A 7. C	3–4. E, C	2. F 7. D
3. C 8. C	3. 1 8. 10	3. B 8. I	5–6. I, J	3. H 8. I
4. C 9. A	4. 9 9. 5	4. E 9. D	7–8. D, G	4. A 9. B
5. A 10. B	5. 7 10. 2	5. G 10. F	9–10. F, A	5. J 10. G

Chapter 6 (A Taste of Parenthood)

Ten Word Pts in Context	Matching Words/Defs	Sentence Check 1	Sentence Check 2	Final Check
1. B 6. B	1. 10 6. 4	1. B 6. G	1–2. D, I	1. H 6. G
2. C 7. B	2. 8 7. 1	2. H 7. F	3–4. C, F	2. J 7. C
3. A 8. A	3. 6 8. 5	3. D 8. C	5–6. G, E	3. A 8. E
4. A 9. C	4. 2 9. 3	4. I 9. A	7–8. B, H	4. B 9. I
5. B 10. C	5. 9 10. 7	5. J 10. E	9–10. J, A	5. F 10. D

Chapter 7 (Accident and Recovery)

Ten Words in Context	Matching Words/Defs	Sentence Check 1	Sentence Check 2	Final Check
1. B 6. C	1. 4 6. 9	1. A 6. F	1–2. J, A	1. D 6. H
2. A 7. C	2. 10 7. 1	2. G 7. H	3–4. H, F	2. A 7. J
3. C 8. B	3. 2 8. 5	3. D 8. I	5–6. C, D	3. E 8. G
4. A 9. B	4. 8 9. 7	4. B 9. E	7–8. G, B	4. I 9. F
5. B 10. A	5. 6 10. 3	5. C 10. J	9–10. E, I	5. B 10. C

Chapter 8 (Animal Senses)

Ten Words in Context	Matching Words/Defs	Sentence Check 1	Sentence Check 2	Final Check
1. A 6. B	1. 6 6. 3	1. E 6. I	1–2. E, C	1. D 6. B
2. C 7. A	2. 4 7. 5	2. A 7. C	3–4. H, J	2. J 7. I
3. A 8. C	3. 9 8. 8	3. D 8. J	5–6. B, G	3. F 8. G
4. B 9. C	4. 1 9. 2	4. G 9. H	7–8. D, F	4. E 9. H
5. A 10. A	5. 10 10. 7	5. F 10. B	9–10. A, I	5. C 10. A

Chapter 9 (Money Problems)

Ten Words in Context	Matching Words/Defs	Sentence Check 1	Sentence Check 2	Final Check
1. A 6. C	1. 3 6. 4	1. H 6. D	1–2. G, A	1. H 6. J
2. B 7. B	2. 5 7. 7	2. A 7. J	3–4. C, H	2. E 7. I
3. C 8. B	3. 8 8. 1	3. C 8. E	5–6. I, D	3. B 8. C
4. A 9. A	4. 9 9. 10	4. I 9. B	7–8. E, B	4. D 9. G
5. B 10. C	5. 2 10. 6	5. G 10. F	9–10. F, J	5. A 10. F

Chapter 10 (The New French Employee)

Ten Words in Context	Matching Words/Defs	Sentence Check 1	Sentence Check 2	Final Check
1. C 6. B	1. 5 6. 10	1. I 6. F	1–2. J, F	1. I 6. A
2. A 7. A	2. 9 7. 2	2. H 7. C	3–4. B, I	2. H 7. D
3. B 8. B	3. 1 8. 8	3. J 8. G	5–6. E, A	3. E 8. F
4. B 9. B	4. 6 9. 7	4. E 9. A	7–8. H, C	4. C 9. J
5. C 10. A	5. 4 10. 3	5. B 10. D	9–10. G, D	5. B 10. G

Chapter 11 (A Cruel Teacher)

Ten Words in Context	Matching Words/Defs	Sentence Check 1	Sentence Check 2	Final Check
1. A 6. B	1. 9 6. 3	1. G 6. D	1–2. G, A	1. E 6. G
2. C 7. B	2. 4 7. 10	2. B 7. J	3–4. J, I	2. A 7. H
3. A 8. B	3. 6 8. 1	3. F 8. E	5–6. E, C	3. D 8. I
4. C 9. A	4. 2 9. 7	4. A 9. I	7–8. H, D	4. F 9. J
5. A 10. B	5. 8 10. 5	5. C 10. H	9–10. B, F	5. C 10. B

Chapter 12 (It's Never Too Late)

Ten Word Pts in Context	Matching Words/Defs	Sentence Check 1	Sentence Check 2	Final Check
1. A 6. C	1. 5 6. 10	1. C 6. F	1–2. J, E	1. C 6. F
2. B 7. B	2. 9 7. 3	2. B 7. I	3–4. H, F	2. I 7. G
3. A 8. C	3. 2 8. 6	3. H 8. D	5–6. I, D	3. H 8. E
4. C 9. A	4. 8 9. 7	4. J 9. G	7–8. B, G	4. A 9. J
5. A 10. B	5. 1 10. 4	5. E 10. A	9–10. C, A	5. B 10. D

Chapter 13 (Learning to Study)

Ten Words in Context	Matching Words/Defs	Sentence Check 1	Sentence Check 2	Final Check
1. B 6. B	1. 9 6. 2	1. G 6. H	1–2. I, H	1. H 6. A
2. C 7. A	2. 1 7. 10	2. B 7. I	3–4. A, E	2. I 7. F
3. B 8. C	3. 4 8. 6	3. E 8. A	5–6. G, J	3. B 8. J
4. A 9. B	4. 3 9. 5	4. F 9. C	7–8. B, C	4. D 9. G
5. B 10. A	5. 8 10. 7	5. D 10. J	9–10. D, F	5. C 10. E

Chapter 14 (The Mad Monk)

Ten Words in Context	Matching Words/Defs	Sentence Check 1	Sentence Check 2	Final Check
1. C 6. A	1. 3 6. 10	1. G 6. C	1–2. G, A	1. F 6. D
2. A 7. B	2. 4 7. 5	2. A 7. H	3–4. H, C	2. H 7. I
3. B 8. B	3. 7 8. 9	3. J 8. I	5–6. D, E	3. G 8. J
4. A 9. C	4. 6 9. 1	4. D 9. B	7–8. J, B	4. B 9. C
5. C 10. A	5. 2 10. 8	5. F 10. E	9–10. F, I	5. A 10. E

Chapter 15 (Conflict Over Holidays)

Ten Words in Context	Matching Words/Defs	Sentence Check 1	Sentence Check 2	Final Check
1. C 6. A	1. 4 6. 3	1. D 6. F	1–2. B, H	1. G 6. A
2. A 7. B	2. 9 7. 10	2. E 7. G	3–4. A, J	2. I 7. E
3. B 8. A	3. 6 8. 8	3. H 8. B	5–6. C, E	3. F 8. C
4. B 9. B	4. 1 9. 2	4. J 9. C	7–8. F, G	4. J 9. B
5. C 10. C	5. 5 10. 7	5. A 10. I	9–10. D, I	5. D 10. H

Chapter 16 (Dr. Martin Luther King, Jr.)

Ten Words in Context	Matching Words/Defs	Sentence Check 1	Sentence Check 2	Final Check
1. B 6. A	1. 4 6. 2	1. D 6. H	1–2. G, B	1. B 6. E
2. C 7. B	2. 1 7. 8	2. E 7. A	3–4. E, D	2. H 7. F
3. C 8. C	3. 9 8. 6	3. F 8. B	5–6. J, H	3. G 8. D
4. A 9. A	4. 7 9. 10	4. G 9. J	7–8. C, F	4. C 9. I
5. C 10. C	5. 3 10. 5	5. C 10. I	9–10. A, I	5. A 10. J

Chapter 17 (Relating to Parents)

Ten Words in Context	Matching Words/Defs	Sentence Check 1	Sentence Check 2	Final Check
1. C 6. A	1. 4 6. 1	1. F 6. C	1–2. A, G	1. J 6. I
2. A 7. B	2. 6 7. 5	2. A 7. I	3–4. H, E	2. H 7. A
3. A 8. B	3. 9 8. 10	3. B 8. D	5–6. F, B	3. C 8. G
4. B 9. C	4. 8 9. 3	4. E 9. J	7–8. D, C	4. B 9. F
5. C 10. B	5. 2 10. 7	5. G 10. H	9–10. I, J	5. D 10. E

Chapter 18 (Held Back by Fears)

Ten Word Pts in Context	Matching Words/Defs	Sentence Check 1	Sentence Check 2	Final Check
1. C 6. B	1. 7 6. 6	1. F 6. G	1–2. G, E	1. B 6. G
2. B 7. C	2. 4 7. 1	2. C 7. B	3–4. H, C	2. H 7. F
3. B 8. C	3. 9 8. 10	3. A 8. J	5–6. J, I	3. E 8. A
4. A 9. A	4. 8 9. 3	4. E 9. D	7–8. F, B	4. D 9. I
5. A 10. A	5. 2 10. 5	5. I 10. H	9–10. A, D	5. J 10. C

Chapter 19 (Interview with a Rude Star)

Ten Words in Context	Matching Words/Defs	Sentence Check 1	Sentence Check 2	Final Check
1. B 6. C	1. 9 6. 1	1. C 6. A	1–2. G, D	1. B 6. J
2. A 7. A	2. 4 7. 8	2. J 7. B	3–4. H, I	2. D 7. F
3. C 8. B	3. 2 8. 7	3. G 8. E	5–6. F, A	3. E 8. G
4. A 9. C	4. 5 9. 3	4. H 9. D	7–8. C, E	4. C 9. H
5. C 10. C	5. 10 10. 6	5. F 10. I	9–10. B, J	5. A 10. I

Chapter 20 (The Nightmare of Gym)

Ten Words in Context	Matching Words/Defs	Sentence Check 1	Sentence Check 2	Final Check
1. A 6. A	1. 6 6. 1	1. B 6. F	1–2. A, I	1. F 6. C
2. C 7. B	2. 3 7. 8	2. J 7. G	3–4. F, B	2. G 7. A
3. B 8. A	3. 7 8. 2	3. A 8. C	5–6. D, G	3. B 8. E
4. C 9. C	4. 10 9. 5	4. E 9. D	7–8. H, C	4. H 9. D
5. C 10. B	5. 4 10. 9	5. I 10. H	9–10. J, E	5. J 10. I

Chapter 21 (Skipping Church)

Ten Words in Context	Matching Words/Defs	Sentence Check 1	Sentence Check 2	Final Check
1. C 6. A	1. 5 6. 8	1. G 6. B	1–2. F, G	1. H 6. A
2. C 7. B	2. 1 7. 2	2. C 7. H	3–4. B, H	2. I 7. E
3. B 8. C	3. 6 8. 9	3. D 8. E	5–6. A, J	3. J 8. B
4. B 9. A	4. 3 9. 7	4. A 9. I	7–8. D, C	4. F 9. G
5. C 10. B	5. 10 10. 4	5. F 10. J	9–10. I, E	5. C 10. D

Chapter 22 (A Model Teacher)

Ten Words in Context	Matching Words/Defs	Sentence Check 1	Sentence Check 2	Final Check
1. B 6. B	1. 7 6. 3	1. J 6. H	1–2. J, D	1. C 6. E
2. C 7. A	2. 6 7. 2	2. A 7. G	3–4. C, F	2. H 7. F
3. A 8. B	3. 9 8. 5	3. D 8. E	5–6. H, I	3. I 8. J
4. A 9. C	4. 1 9. 8	4. I 9. C	7–8. A, G	4. D 9. G
5. C 10. C	5. 10 10. 4	5. B 10. F	9–10. E, B	5. B 10. A

Chapter 23 (My Talented Roommate)

Ten Words in Context	Matching Words/Defs	Sentence Check 1	Sentence Check 2	Final Check
1. C 6. B	1. 6 6. 8	1. A 6. G	1–2. I, C	1. D 6. G
2. A 7. A	2. 3 7. 9	2. I 7. J	3–4. F, G	2. F 7. B
3. B 8. C	3. 7 8. 1	3. C 8. H	5–6. B, J	3. A 8. C
4. C 9. A	4. 5 9. 2	4. B 9. E	7–8. E, H	4. I 9. E
5. C 10. A	5. 10 10. 4	5. F 10. D	9–10. A, D	5. H 10. J

Chapter 24 (Fascinating Courses)

Ten Word Pts in Context	Matching Words/Defs	Sentence Check 1	Sentence Check 2	Final Check
1. B 6. C	1. 6 6. 5	1. C 6. J	1–2. I, F	1. E 6. F
2. C 7. B	2. 9 7. 10	2. E 7. F	3–4. J, G	2. A 7. C
3. C 8. A	3. 1 8. 7	3. G 8. B	5–6. C, H	3. B 8. D
4. A 9. B	4. 8 9. 4	4. A 9. D	7–8. B, A	4. J 9. H
5. A 10. A	5. 3 10. 2	5. I 10. H	9–10. E, D	5. G 10. I

Chapter 25 (Cal and His Sisters)

Ten Words in Context	Matching Words/Defs	Sentence Check 1	Sentence Check 2	Final Check
1. A 6. C	1. 5 6. 2	1. J 6. G	1–2. C, G	1. G 6. J
2. C 7. A	2. 1 7. 9	2. B 7. C	3–4. B, A	2. I 7. D
3. A 8. C	3. 7 8. 4	3. A 8. I	5–6. I, D	3. H 8. E
4. B 9. B	4. 3 9. 8	4. E 9. D	7–8. J, E	4. F 9. C
5. B 10. B	5. 10 10. 6	5. F 10. H	9–10. F, H	5. A 10. B

Chapter 26 (Shoplifter)

Ten Words in Context	Matching Words/Defs	Sentence Check 1	Sentence Check 2	Final Check
1. A 6. A	1. 3 6. 10	1. G 6. E	1–2. C, E	1. F 6. A
2. A 7. C	2. 6 7. 5	2. B 7. F	3–4. J, B	2. B 7. E
3. C 8. B	3. 7 8. 2	3. I 8. H	5–6. G, H	3. D 8. C
4. C 9. C	4. 9 9. 8	4. C 9. D	7–8. A, F	4. H 9. J
5. B 10. A	5. 1 10. 4	5. A 10. J	9–10. I, D	5. I 10. G

Chapter 27 (A Nutty Newspaper Office)

Ten Words in Context	Matching Words/Defs	Sentence Check 1	Sentence Check 2	Final Check
1. B 6. A	1. 6 6. 8	1. B 6. C	1–2. H, I	1. D 6. I
2. A 7. A	2. 1 7. 2	2. H 7. J	3–4. A, C	2. F 7. C
3. B 8. C	3. 5 8. 9	3. G 8. A	5–6. J, D	3. G 8. B
4. C 9. C	4. 10 9. 1	4. D 9. I	7–8. G, E	4. A 9. J
5. C 10. B	5. 3 10. 7	5. F 10. E	9–10. F, B	5. E 10. H

Chapter 28 (Roughing It)

Ten Words in Context	Matching Words/Defs	Sentence Check 1	Sentence Check 2	Final Check
1. C 6. C	1. 9 6. 2	1. J 6. B	1–2. I, C	1. J 6. G
2. B 7. A	2. 6 7. 5	2. E 7. H	3–4. D, F	2. H 7. B
3. C 8. B	3. 8 8. 10	3. I 8. F	5–6. G, J	3. C 8. D
4. A 9. A	4. 3 9. 4	4. A 9. G	7–8. B, A	4. A 9. E
5. C 10. C	5. 1 10. 7	5. D 10. C	9–10. E, H	5. F 10. I

Chapter 29 (Getting Scared)

Ten Words in Context	Matching Words/Defs	Sentence Check 1	Sentence Check 2	Final Check
1. B 6. B	1. 7 6. 2	1. I 6. J	1–2. C, J	1. A 6. G
2. C 7. A	2. 10 7. 6	2. D 7. C	3–4. A, B	2. I 7. C
3. B 8. C	3. 1 8. 3	3. B 8. A	5–6. G, I	3. J 8. D
4. A 9. C	4. 9 9. 8	4. G 9. E	7–8. H, E	4. F 9. B
5. C 10. B	5. 4 10. 5	5. H 10. F	9–10. F, D	5. H 10. E

Chapter 30 (My Sister's Date)

Ten Words in Context	Matching Words/Defs	Sentence Check 1	Sentence Check 2	Final Check
1. C 6. B	1. 4 6. 10	1. H 6. I	1–2. F, E	1. J 6. D
2. B 7. A	2. 7 7. 9	2. C 7. J	3–4. C, G	2. I 7. A
3. A 8. C	3. 8 8. 1	3. B 8. D	5–6. B, J	3. C 8. E
4. B 9. B	4. 5 9. 3	4. F 9. E	7–8. A, D	4. F 9. H
5. C 10. B	5. 2 10. 6	5. A 10. G	9–10. I, H	5. G 10. B

Answers to the Unit Reviews: IMPROVING VOCABULARY SKILLS

Unit One

Unit Two

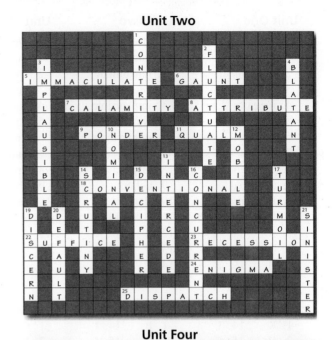

Unit Three

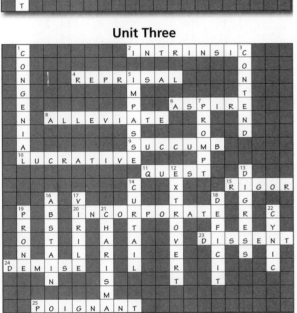

Unit Four

Unit Five

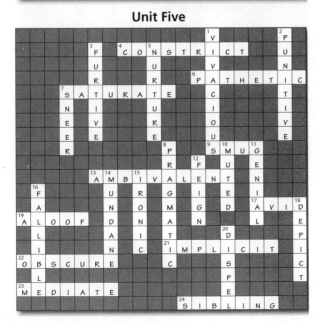

Answers to the Unit Tests: IMPROVING VOCABULARY SKILLS

Unit One	Unit Two	Unit Three	Unit Four	Unit Five

Unit One, Test 1
1. escalates
2. euphemism
3. mercenary
4. inequity
5. obsolete
6. succinct
7. epitome
8. deterrent
9. absolved
10. inclination

11. D	16. D
12. A	17. A
13. C	18. B
14. C	19. B
15. B	20. C

Unit Two, Test 1
1. nocturnal
2. rehabilitate
3. degenerate
4. implausible
5. concurrent
6. immaculate
7. blight
8. dispatch
9. default
10. flagrant

11. C	16. D
12. B	17. A
13. C	18. B
14. C	19. A
15. D	20. C

Unit Three, Test 1
1. intermittent
2. speculate
3. demise
4. curtailed
5. covert
6. Proponents
7. impasse
8. Prone
9. abstain
10. deficit

11. B	16. A
12. C	17. C
13. C	18. A
14. D	19. B
15. B	20. B

Unit Four, Test 1
1. hampered
2. faltered
3. blasé
4. deviated
5. complacent
6. pseudonym
7. elation
8. repertoire
9. diligent
10. libel

11. B	16. D
12. C	17. C
13. D	18. B
14. B	19. C
15. D	20. A

Unit Five, Test 1
1. pretentious
2. explicit
3. depicted
4. implicit
5. esteem
6. formulated
7. exhaustive
8. smug
9. ironic
10. feigned

11. C	16. C
12. D	17. A
13. A	18. D
14. C	19. B
15. D	20. C

Unit One, Test 2
1. K	14. I
2. H	15. C
3. D	16. I
4. M	17. I
5. G	18. C
6. J	19. C
7. A	20. B
8. B	21. C
9. I	22. A
10. F	23. C
11. L	24. A
12. C	25. C
13. E	

Unit Two, Test 2
1. B	14. I
2. G	15. I
3. M	16. I
4. C	17. C
5. I	18. C
6. K	19. I
7. F	20. B
8. A	21. A
9. H	22. B
10. J	23. C
11. L	24. B
12. D	25. C
13. E	

Unit Three, Test 2
1. C	14. C
2. I	15. I
3. D	16. I
4. L	17. C
5. M	18. C
6. J	19. I
7. G	20. C
8. F	21. A
9. H	22. A
10. A	23. B
11. K	24. A
12. B	25. B
13. E	

Unit Four, Test 2
1. J	14. I
2. G	15. C
3. F	16. I
4. K	17. C
5. A	18. C
6. E	19. I
7. L	20. A
8. H	21. B
9. M	22. C
10. C	23. B
11. B	24. A
12. I	25. B
13. D	

Unit Five, Test 2
1. K	14. I
2. D	15. I
3. J	16. C
4. A	17. I
5. C	18. I
6. E	19. C
7. B	20. C
8. I	21. C
9. F	22. A
10. H	23. A
11. M	24. A
12. G	25. C
13. L	

Unit One, Test 3
1. A	11. A
2. D	12. B
3. B	13. A
4. C	14. D
5. A	15. D
6. A	16. A
7. C	17. C
8. C	18. D
9. C	19. D
10. D	20. A

Unit Two, Test 3
1. C	11. A
2. A	12. C
3. B	13. C
4. D	14. D
5. A	15. B
6. B	16. A
7. B	17. A
8. A	18. B
9. B	19. C
10. D	20. D

Unit Three, Test 3
1. D	11. C
2. B	12. D
3. C	13. A
4. A	14. B
5. B	15. B
6. D	16. A
7. C	17. C
8. A	18. D
9. B	19. B
10. B	20. B

Unit Four, Test 3
1. D	11. D
2. B	12. B
3. C	13. C
4. A	14. C
5. D	15. B
6. A	16. D
7. B	17. A
8. D	18. D
9. C	19. C
10. A	20. A

Unit Five, Test 3
1. A	11. A
2. C	12. B
3. D	13. C
4. C	14. D
5. B	15. C
6. C	16. B
7. B	17. B
8. A	18. A
9. D	19. C
10. A	20. D

Unit One, Test 4
(Word Parts)
1. E	11. D
2. I	12. C
3. C	13. H
4. G	14. I
5. J	15. G
6. A	16. A
7. H	17. B
8. B	18. C
9. D	19. B
10. F	20. A

Unit Two, Test 4
(Word Parts)
1. E	11. A
2. J	12. J
3. B	13. F
4. D	14. D
5. I	15. G
6. H	16. B
7. G	17. C
8. A	18. A
9. C	19. B
10. F	20. C

Unit Three, Test 4
(Word Parts)
1. E	11. B
2. A	12. C
3. H	13. D
4. I	14. F
5. C	15. H
6. J	16. C
7. G	17. B
8. D	18. A
9. F	19. C
10. B	20. B

Unit Four, Test 4
(Word Parts)
1. B	11. H
2. F	12. B
3. A	13. A
4. G	14. D
5. H	15. E
6. J	16. C
7. C	17. B
8. I	18. B
9. D	19. C
10. E	20. B

Mastery Test: *Chapter 1 (Joseph Palmer)*

In the space provided, write the word from the box needed to complete each sentence. Then put the **letter** of that word in the column at the left. Use each word once.

A. **absolve**	B. **adamant**	C. **amiable**	D. **amoral**	E. **animosity**
F. **antagonist**	G. **eccentric**	H. **encounter**	I. **epitome**	J. **malign**

_____ 1. Female students who took auto shop classes used to be considered _____. Now, however, it's not considered odd for women to learn to do car repairs.

_____ 2. The husband and wife were such bitter _____s at their divorce hearing that it was hard to believe they had once loved each other.

_____ 3. Frank hates the thought that his teacher believes he cheated. He'll go to any lengths to _____ himself.

_____ 4. Elena intended to ask her father to lend her his car, but when she saw how grouchy he was, she decided to wait until he was in a more _____ mood.

_____ 5. The great baseball player and civil rights leader Jackie Robinson was the _____ of both physical and moral strength.

_____ 6. When Mrs. Haley visited the school she'd attended thirty years before, she unexpectedly had an _____ with one of her former teachers.

_____ 7. Bill is _____ about going to the park for a picnic, even though the weather report is predicting severe thunderstorms.

_____ 8. Although my emotionally disturbed neighbor makes rude comments to my visitors and scatters trash all over my steps, I don't feel any _____ toward her. I just feel sorry for her.

_____ 9. A newborn baby is _____. It's only as a child grows older that he or she develops a sense of "right" and "wrong."

_____ 10. People who say the female crocodile eats her young _____ her. She simply takes them into a protective pouch inside her mouth.

SCORE: (Number correct) _____ × 10 = _____ %

Mastery Test: *Chapter 2 (Telephone Salespeople)*

In the space provided, write the word from the box needed to complete each sentence. Then put the **letter** of that word in the column at the left. Use each word once.

A. **curt**	B. **demoralize**	C. **dilemma**	D. **inclination**	E. **irate**
F. **retort**	G. **sabotage**	H. **subsequent**	I. **wary**	J. **zeal**

_____ 1. Vicky was so _____ when her boyfriend forgot her birthday that she sent him a bunch of dead flowers.

_____ 2. Someone must have wanted to _____ the motorcycle race. Thumbtacks and broken glass are scattered all over the road where the race was going to be held.

_____ 3. At the beginning of her daily shift at the hotel, Helen cleans rooms with great _____. However, after a few hours, she loses most of her enthusiasm.

_____ 4. When I asked my friend if she felt like going shopping, she gave me a _____ answer: "Go away—I'm busy."

_____ 5. Failing his driver's test the first time completely _____(e)d Enrique. He didn't think he'd ever get his license.

_____ 6. Connie was faced with a(n) _____: should she go to work feeling nauseated, or should she call in sick and lose a day's pay?

_____ 7. Ordinarily I would be _____ of strangers asking to use my telephone, but the couple seemed to know my parents, so I let them in.

_____ 8. "Baby, I'm nothing without you," said Jeff. "Jeff, you're not much of anything *with* me," Abby _____(e)d.

_____ 9. Although Wanda's story sounds unlikely, I've never known her to lie, so I have a(n) _____ to believe her.

_____ 10. Ron didn't care for his counselor at their first session, but he learned to like and trust her at _____ meetings.

SCORE: (Number correct) _____ × 10 = _____ %

Mastery Test: *Chapter 3 (A Cruel Sport)*

In the space provided, write the word from the box needed to complete each sentence. Then put the **letter** of that word in the column at the left. Use each word once.

A. **acclaim**	B. **adjacent**	C. **elicit**	D. **engross**	E. **escalate**
F. **exploit**	G. **methodical**	H. **obsolete**	I. **tangible**	J. **terminate**

_____ 1. The mystery story so _____(e)d Donna that she jumped in fright when I entered the room.

_____ 2. Dinah arranges the spices in her kitchen in a(n) _____ way: in alphabetical order.

_____ 3. The landlord would like to _____ the lease of the family in 4-A. Their loud parties and shouting disturb everyone in the building.

_____ 4. My woodworker friend lives _____ to his work. His workshop is next door to his house.

_____ 5. That supervisor knows how to _____ workers. She makes them work overtime without extra pay.

_____ 6. Electronic books are becoming more popular, but I don't think they'll ever make printed books _____.

_____ 7. Peter seems to think he deserves _____ just for showing up for school. His teachers, however, think that's the least he can do.

_____ 8. The protests of some small groups in Eastern Europe _____(e)d into full-scale rebellions against their governments.

_____ 9. Some people enjoy getting praised when they do a good job. I prefer a more _____ reward, like a raise in pay.

_____ 10. Flora is a bad-tempered child. Even the suggestion that she come to the dinner table is enough to _____ a tantrum.

SCORE: (Number correct) _____ × 10 = _____ %

Mastery Test: *Chapter 4 (Bald Is Beautiful)*

In the space provided, write the word from the box needed to complete each sentence. Then put the **letter** of that word in the column at the left. Use each word once.

A. **deterrent**	B. **implication**	C. **inequity**	D. **infirmity**	E. **infringe**
F. **innovation**	G. **revitalize**	H. **sparse**	I. **subjective**	J. **succinct**

_____ 1. When his instructor began telling Todd about the tutoring center, Todd got angry. He didn't like the _____ that he needed extra help.

_____ 2. I may look sick, but I'm just tired. All I need to _____ me is a good night's sleep.

_____ 3. Newspaper reporters must try to keep their opinions out of their news stories, but they are permitted to be more _____ in editorials.

_____ 4. Even though he has arthritis in both legs, my grandfather still walks two miles a day. Obviously he doesn't let his _____ keep him down.

_____ 5. I'd like to learn to ski, but the high cost of renting equipment is a _____ to that ever happening.

_____ 6. Sometimes a very _____ answer sounds rude. So, for example, instead of just saying "no" to a child, parents should say something like "Not now, honey."

_____ 7. When ice-cream parlors began selling frozen yogurt, dieters hurried to try it. They welcomed this dessert _____ that permitted them the taste of ice cream without the calories.

_____ 8. Bev _____s on the Howards' privacy by constantly showing up at their house without an invitation.

_____ 9. Although the crowd at our last home game was _____, the fans made up for their small numbers by waving banners and cheering loudly after each play.

_____ 10. At my mother's workplace, men are paid $12.00 an hour, while women doing the same type of work earn only $10.75. This is an obvious _____.

SCORE: (Number correct) _____ × 10 = _____ %

Mastery Test: *Chapter 5 (No Luck with Women)*

In the space provided, write the word from the box needed to complete each sentence. Then put the **letter** of that word in the column at the left. Use each word once.

A. **allusion**	B. **altruistic**	C. **appease**	D. **arbitrary**	E. **assail**
F. **banal**	G. **euphemism**	H. **mercenary**	I. **syndrome**	J. **taint**

_____ 1. I expected the made-for-TV movie to be another _____ romance, but I was pleasantly surprised. It was both original and funny.

_____ 2. The little boy's slow speech and clumsy movements are all part of a(n) _____ caused by his lack of oxygen at birth.

_____ 3. A heckler in the audience _____(e)d the comedian with rude remarks until the bouncer forced the heckler to leave the club.

_____ 4. I'm afraid my sister is encouraging her children to be _____. Every time they do a chore or an errand, she gives them a dollar. Soon they won't do anything unless they get paid.

_____ 5. Being suspended for drug abuse _____s athletes' reputations.

_____ 6. So many people are afraid of dying that we use _____s to describe it, such as "passing away."

_____ 7. I admire Luis' _____ nature. He is truly more concerned for the welfare of those around him than he is for his own.

_____ 8. Apologizing for tearing Danny's shirt isn't enough. Nothing will _____ him until you buy him a new one.

_____ 9. Hoping to receive a cell phone for her birthday, Jeannie continually makes such _____s to it as "Mom, when I was at the mall today I saw a coat you would have loved! I wish I could have called you to tell you about it."

_____ 10. That judge's sentencing seems completely _____. Yesterday she sent a shoplifter to jail for three months, but today she gave a car thief probation and a suspended sentence.

SCORE: (Number correct) _____ × 10 = _____ %

Mastery Test: *Chapter 7 (Accident and Recovery)*

In the space provided, write the word from the box needed to complete each sentence. Then put the **letter** of that word in the column at the left. Use each word once.

A. **calamity**	B. **comprehensive**	C. **conventional**	D. **flagrant**	E. **fluctuate**
F. **persevere**	G. **ponder**	H. **rehabilitate**	I. **turmoil**	J. **venture**

_____ 1. The movie I saw last weekend really confused me. I have _____(e)d its meaning all week.

_____ 2. When a doctor sees a new patient, the doctor should ask for a _____ health history, beginning with childhood illnesses and ending with the patient's present physical condition.

_____ 3. After breaking his leg in a motorcycle accident, Lenny had to attend physical therapy classes to _____ himself so he could walk normally again.

_____ 4. The birthday party ended in complete _____, as the children ran around the room screaming, breaking balloons, and grabbing presents.

_____ 5. I'm not sure my answer is correct, but I'm feeling brave, so I'll _____ a guess.

_____ 6. While Fran enjoys unusual foods, such as curries and pasta, her husband Nick prefers more _____ dinners, like steak and French fries.

_____ 7. It takes a long time for Julio to know people well enough to trust them. You'll have to _____ if you want to win his friendship.

_____ 8. The recent earthquake was a terrible_____, killing thousands of people and leveling entire towns.

_____ 9. I was shocked by the new student's _____ refusal to observe the dress code at our school.

_____ 10. My feelings about my job _____ according to what kind of day I've had at work. Some days my job is good; some days it's terrible.

SCORE: (Number correct) _____ × 10 = _____ %

Mastery Test: *Chapter 8 (Animal Senses)*

In the space provided, write the word from the box needed to complete each sentence. Then put the **letter** of that word in the column at the left. Use each word once.

A. **attest**	B. **attribute**	C. **discern**	D. **dispatch**	E. **enhance**
F. **enigma**	G. **exemplify**	H. **mobile**	I. **nocturnal**	J. **orient**

_____ 1. Every year our neighbors _____ the appearance of their home. Last year they redecorated the living room; this year, they planted a flowering tree in their front yard.

_____ 2. One interesting _____ of my family is that everyone in it was born in July.

_____ 3. Sailors used to _____ themselves by looking at the positions of the stars. Now they use modern instruments to figure out their location and direction at sea.

_____ 4. For many people, Adolf Hitler and the Nazis _____ the human potential for evil.

_____ 5. We keep our TV in the bedroom, but since it's on wheels, it's _____. We roll it into the living room or kitchen whenever we want to.

_____ 6. The victim's neighbor _____(e)d to the fact that she had never returned from her shopping trip. Her newspapers and mail hadn't been picked up for a week.

_____ 7. My brother's career plans are a(n) _____ to my parents. They can't understand why he wants to move to a small town in Maine and make furniture instead of getting an office job and making money.

_____ 8. I can't _____ any difference between diet soft drinks and the nondiet ones. They taste exactly the same to me.

_____ 9. Cats are _____ animals. They sleep most of the day and are active most of the night.

_____ 10. As soon as the emergency call was received, police and paramedics were _____(e)d to the scene of the accident.

SCORE: (Number correct) _____ × 10 = _____ %

Mastery Test: *Chapter 9 (Money Problems)*

In the space provided, write the word from the box needed to complete each sentence. Then put the **letter** of that word in the column at the left. Use each word once.

A. **concurrent**	B. **confiscate**	C. **constitute**	D. **decipher**	E. **default**
F. **hypothetical**	G. **nominal**	H. **predominant**	I. **prerequisite**	J. **recession**

_____ 1. Myra won her case in small-claims court when the man she was suing _____(e)d by not showing up.

_____ 2. Although the delicious punch is made of a mixture of fruit juices, the _____ flavor is strawberry.

_____ 3. After a water fight broke out in the fourth-grade classroom, the teacher _____(e)d all the squirt guns.

_____ 4. During the _____, when business was bad, more than half the workers in the plastics factory were laid off.

_____ 5. Since Velma couldn't _____ her teacher's handwriting, she had no idea how to go about revising her paper.

_____ 6. I just realized that my school vacation and my sister's wedding are _____. I'll be able to help her get everything ready for the wedding.

_____ 7. Two scoops of vanilla fudge ice cream, hot fudge sauce, marshmallow topping, and walnut pieces _____ my favorite dessert—a walnut-marshmallow-hot-fudge sundae.

_____ 8. Let me ask you a _____ question. If you were teaching this course, what questions would you put on the final exam?

_____ 9. Being at least 16 years old is the usual _____ for obtaining a driver's license.

_____ 10. Although the dog fight looked serious, our German shepherd escaped with only _____ injuries.

SCORE: (Number correct) _____ × 10 = _____ %

Mastery Test: *Chapter 10 (The New French Employee)*

In the space provided, write the word from the box needed to complete each sentence. Then put the **letter** of that word in the column at the left. Use each word once.

A. **degenerate**	B. **implausible**	C. **incoherent**	D. **intercede**	E. **intricate**
F. **sanctuary**	G. **scrutiny**	H. **sinister**	I. **suffice**	J. **vulnerable**

_____ 1. Because the novel's plot was so _____, Alfonso was beginning to get confused. Then he had the bright idea of writing down the names of the many characters and their relationships to one another.

_____ 2. My close friendship with Ellen began to _____ after my school work began taking up most of my time. I then had no spare time in which to see her or have our usual long phone conversations.

_____ 3. Since his divorce, my older brother has felt extremely _____. He's afraid to get involved with anyone and run the risk of getting hurt again.

_____ 4. After the robbery, I gave the apartment a careful inspection to see what had been taken. My _____ extended even to the linen closet, where I counted the towels and sheets.

_____ 5. "I'd love to go shopping with you," Cheryl said, "but my granddad says I have to finish my homework first. If you'd _____, maybe he'll change his mind and let me go."

_____ 6. When Pat learned she had won the lottery, she became _____ with joy. She kept babbling: "You've got to be . . . Oh my . . . If this isn't . . ."

_____ 7. The Women's _____ in town is a shelter for women who are being abused at home.

_____ 8. "Who drew on the wall with crayon?" asked the angry mother. The little boy's _____ answer was, "A man came through the window and did it."

_____ 9. The food in the refrigerator will have to _____ for the rest of the week. There's no grocery money until the next family paycheck.

_____ 10. Everyone was shocked to learn that Mr. Johnson had once spent time in jail for a break-in and robbery. His cheerful, friendly manner gave no hint of his _____ past.

SCORE: (Number correct) _____ × 10 = _____ %

Mastery Test: *Chapter 11 (A Cruel Teacher)*

In the space provided, write the word from the box needed to complete each sentence. Then put the **letter** of that word in the column at the left. Use each word once.

A. **blatant**	B. **blight**	C. **contrive**	D. **garble**	E. **gaunt**
F. **gloat**	G. **immaculate**	H. **plagiarism**	I. **qualm**	J. **retaliate**

_____ 1. When the boss announced that everyone would have to work an hour overtime, the staff _____(e)d by taking a two-hour lunch.

_____ 2. Even though I knew I was doing the right thing, I felt a _____ of conscience as I told Mr. Lane that it was my friend who'd stolen his car.

_____ 3. To the family's amazement, the teenager's room was _____. The bed was made, the records were put away, and there wasn't a single piece of clothing on the floor.

_____ 4. It's hard not to _____ about Sharon being fired when she's been so unpleasant to all her coworkers.

_____ 5. That dogwood tree must be suffering from a _____. It didn't flower this year, and half the branches have no leaves.

_____ 6. Those ten-dollar bills are _____ forgeries. Even a ten-year-old could tell that they're fakes.

_____ 7. My uncle's stroke has _____(e)d his speech. Now it's almost impossible to understand what he's saying.

_____ 8. A writer accused a comedian of _____. He said that the comedian had taken the writer's script and turned it into a movie without paying the writer or giving him credit.

_____ 9. After losing forty pounds, Alice thought her figure was perfect. Actually, though, she looked unpleasantly _____ —as if she'd not quite recovered from a long illness.

_____ 10. Joanne has _____(e)d a clever way of making throw pillows. She sews two fancy washcloths together back to back and then stuffs them with foam rubber.

SCORE: (Number correct) _____ × 10 = _____ %

Mastery Test: *Chapter 13 (Learning to Study)*

In the space provided, write the word from the box needed to complete each sentence. Then put the **letter** of that word in the column at the left. Use each word once.

A. **curtail**	B. **devastate**	C. **digress**	D. **incentive**	E. **incorporate**
F. **indispensable**	G. **intermittent**	H. **rigor**	I. **squander**	J. **succumb**

_____ 1. My fantasy apartment _____s several very desirable features: a huge living room for parties, an all-electronic kitchen, a whirlpool, and a balcony overlooking the ocean.

_____ 2. The _____s of camping are too much for Elaine. She likes to sleep on a sturdy mattress in a safe, warm room, not in a flimsy tent with biting insects.

_____ 3. My grandmother refused to _____ even one bit of food. Today's leftovers always became tomorrow's soup or hash.

_____ 4. Are you going to stick to your diet, or are you going to _____ to temptation and have a piece of chocolate fudge cake?

_____ 5. I don't understand how people got along without VCR's. I find my VCR _____; without it, I'd never get to see my favorite shows at the few times I have to watch them.

_____ 6. A bad case of flu forced Gerald to _____ his vacation. He came home after only three days and spent the rest of the week lying in bed.

_____ 7. When employers offer their workers _____s, such as vacations or a share in the profits, the employees usually work harder.

_____ 8. Rico was _____(e)d to learn that he hadn't gotten the promotion. He had already planned how he would spend the extra money.

_____ 9. My e-mails to my friend Steve are _____. Sometimes I write once a month, other times once a year.

_____ 10. The candidate for the state senate must not know much about taxes. Every time she's asked about this topic, she _____(e)s and talks about other matters, like the homeless or public transportation.

SCORE: (Number correct) _____ × 10 = _____ %

Mastery Test: *Chapter 14 (The Mad Monk)*

In the space provided, write the word from the box needed to complete each sentence. Then put the **letter** of that word in the column at the left. Use each word once.

A. **alleviate**	B. **benefactor**	C. **covert**	D. **cynic**	E. **demise**
F. **infamous**	G. **intrinsic**	H. **revulsion**	I. **speculate**	J. **virile**

_____ 1. Everyone was shocked to learn of the sudden _____ of Michael Jackson, famous worldwide as the "King of Pop." He died at the age of only 50 while rehearsing for a series of concerts.

_____ 2. My family photo album has little _____ value, but to me, it is worth more than any amount of money.

_____ 3. Nicotine gum can _____ the withdrawal symptoms of quitting smoking.

_____ 4. Someone once helped my uncle pay for college. Now that he can afford it, he's become a _____ to struggling students.

_____ 5. Brenda took a(n) _____ look at her watch, hoping her hosts didn't notice her glance and think she was anxious to leave.

_____ 6. Benjamin Franklin must have been a _____. He showed a lack of faith in human nature when he wrote, "Three may keep a secret if two of them are dead."

_____ 7. In her lecture, the history teacher _____(e)d about why countries go to war. She came up with three reasons: to get territory, to gain natural resources such as oil, and to have power over others.

_____ 8. In the past, men who cried or showed their emotions weren't considered _____. Today, though, it's acceptable for "real men" to be sensitive.

_____ 9. My husband was filled with such _____ during the horror movie that he had to leave the theater. He couldn't bear to watch the scientist turn into a giant fly.

_____ 10. Nearly every American has heard of John Wilkes Booth. He is _____ for murdering President Abraham Lincoln.

SCORE: (Number correct) _____ × 10 = _____ %

Mastery Test: *Chapter 15 (Conflict Over Holidays)*

In the space provided, write the word from the box needed to complete each sentence. Then put the **letter** of that word in the column at the left. Use each word once.

A. **abstain**	B. **affiliate**	C. **agnostic**	D. **aspire**	E. **benevolent**
F. **deficit**	G. **dissent**	H. **diversion**	I. **lucrative**	J. **mandatory**

_____ 1. The famous American lawyer, Clarence Darrow, said it was impossible to know if God exists. "I do not consider it an insult, but a compliment, to be called an _____. I do not pretend to know where many ignorant men are sure."

_____ 2. Laura loves salty foods, but she has to _____ from them. Her blood pressure is high, and salt makes it higher.

_____ 3. Organizations such as the Boy Scouts and Girl Scouts reward their members for performing _____ actions like volunteering at a hospital or a shelter for the homeless.

_____ 4. The Taylors were considering a divorce around Christmas time, so there was a noticeable _____ of good cheer in their house.

_____ 5. To get a construction job, workers usually have to _____ with the union. Few bosses are willing to risk hiring non-union employees.

_____ 6. The Johnsons were sorry to lose their favorite babysitter, but they understood that she needed a more _____ job in order to earn money for college.

_____ 7. That teacher won't put up with any _____ in her classroom. The only opinions she likes to listen to are her own.

_____ 8. Many Little League players _____ to become major league ballplayers. That's why they take the game so seriously.

_____ 9. At this school, a course in writing is _____. Even art students must take it.

_____ 10. JoJo the Clown visits Children's Hospital every Saturday to provide a(n) _____ for children who are bedridden or about to undergo operations.

SCORE: (Number correct) _____ × 10 = _____ %

Mastery Test: *Chapter 16 (Dr. Martin Luther King, Jr.)*

In the space provided, write the word from the box needed to complete each sentence. Then put the **letter** of that word in the column at the left. Use each word once.

A. **charisma**	B. **contemporary**	C. **contend**	D. **conversely**	E. **extrovert**
F. **poignant**	G. **prevalent**	H. **proponent**	I. **quest**	J. **traumatic**

_____ 1. My little sister doesn't enjoy old classic movies like *The Wizard of Oz* or *Gone with the Wind*. She'd rather see something more _____, with actors who are still alive.

_____ 2. My friend Bob is so outgoing that he can joke and make friends easily. I wish I were as much of a(n) _____ as he is.

_____ 3. Holly's most _____ childhood experience was getting lost in a department store. She's never forgotten how frightened and upset she was before her parents found her.

_____ 4. Many people in our community object to the plan to build a shopping mall in the center of town. They _____ that it will create too much traffic and noise, and they also insist it will be bad for the environment.

_____ 5. Squirrels are _____ in our neighborhood. We see them everywhere.

_____ 6. Gold was discovered in California in January, 1848. The following year, 80,000 people traveled there in a(n) _____ for the precious metal.

_____ 7. My mother raised my brother and me after getting her college degree. _____, my aunt raised a family before getting her degree.

_____ 8. Some sports stars have so much _____ that their fans will wait outside the stadium for hours just to get a look at them.

_____ 9. Donna and Greg's wedding ceremony was full of touching details. An especially _____ moment came when the bride and groom gave a rose to each other's parents.

_____ 10. Our doctor is a(n) _____ of home care. She sends patients home from the hospital as soon as possible, believing they'll recover more quickly in familiar surroundings.

SCORE: (Number correct) _____ × 10 = _____ %

Mastery Test: *Chapter 17 (Relating to Parents)*

In the space provided, write the word from the box needed to complete each sentence. Then put the **letter** of that word in the column at the left. Use each word once.

A. **congenial**	B. **flippant**	C. **impasse**	D. **perception**	E. **prompt**
F. **prone**	G. **rapport**	H. **rationale**	I. **relentless**	J. **reprisal**

_____ 1. We were at a frustrating _____. Our old car needed major repairs in order to keep running, but it wasn't really worth saving. However, a new car would simply cost too much.

_____ 2. The rain has been _____. It has poured down every day for the past week.

_____ 3. Reba's _____ of big cities is that they're exciting, interesting places. Her husband, however, sees them only as noisy, dirty places to avoid.

_____ 4. Why am I more _____ to upset stomachs on the days I have tests? I wish I didn't get so tense then.

_____ 5. In the days when parents arranged their children's marriages, it could take a long time for the newlyweds to develop a _____.

_____ 6. When the fourth-grade teacher asked her class, "Who discovered America?" my little brother gave the _____ answer, "Not me, Teacher!"

_____ 7. The boss's _____ for not letting us leave the building during our lunch hour is "It gives you the chance to get to know each other better." We don't think that's a good enough reason for keeping us cooped up.

_____ 8. The sing-along at Sally's party was so much fun that it _____(e)d my father to get out his dusty old guitar when we got home.

_____ 9. Henry is such a _____ fellow that all the other waiters at the restaurant like him, even though he does get more tips than any of them.

_____ 10. The Thompsons, our next-door neighbors, didn't invite us to their Fourth of July barbecue. In _____, we didn't invite them to our Labor Day picnic.

SCORE: (Number correct) _____ × 10 = _____ %

Mastery Test: *Chapter 19 (Interview with a Rude Star)*

In the space provided, write the word from the box needed to complete each sentence. Then put the **letter** of that word in the column at the left. Use each word once.

A. **benign**	B. **blasé**	C. **comprise**	D. **condescend**	E. **facade**
F. **glib**	G. **haughty**	H. **libel**	I. **pseudonym**	J. **redundant**

_____ 1. "Mark Twain" is the _____ of writer Samuel Longhorne Clemens.

_____ 2. The tough look on the principal's face frightens students at first, but his encouraging manner soon reveals his _____ nature.

_____ 3. Our property _____s the house, a barn, and an old butcher house where neighbors used to bring their cows for slaughter.

_____ 4. The used car salesman wasn't at all _____. When I asked about a car, he hesitated and gave my question some thought before answering.

_____ 5. Gary tried to act _____ about his first airplane trip, but I could tell he was excited by the way he kept looking out the window.

_____ 6. When a newspaper printed damaging lies about her, the actress sued the paper for _____.

_____ 7. Despite her great success as an actress, Lida wasn't _____. When she returned home to visit old friends, she was just as modest and friendly as ever.

_____ 8. The executives in that company eat in their own lunchroom. They wouldn't _____ to eat with "ordinary" workers.

_____ 9. The restaurant's _____ is modest, but inside, the dining area is large and elegant.

_____ 10. Ken's essay on self-reliance is _____. For example, he mentions three times that his grandparents raised all their own food.

SCORE: (Number correct) _____ × 10 = _____ %

Mastery Test: *Chapter 20 (The Nightmare of Gym)*

In the space provided, write the word from the box needed to complete each sentence. Then put the **letter** of that word in the column at the left. Use each word once.

A. **averse**	B. **detract**	C. **disdain**	D. **divulge**	E. **elation**
F. **endow**	G. **expulsion**	H. **mortified**	I. **nullified**	J. **ominous**

_____ 1. My parents couldn't give me much materially, but they did _____ me with a healthy self-confidence.

_____ 2. Patti's _____ at being elected class president was lessened by the knowledge that her best friend had lost the election for class secretary.

_____ 3. Some superstitious people are _____ to anything with the number thirteen on it.

_____ 4. The still air and strangely green sky were signs of a(n) _____ change in the weather.

_____ 5. Elise felt _____ when she jumped on the trampoline and her shorts fell off, but everyone else laughed.

_____ 6. A year in college has made Gina feel superior. She now looks with _____ upon old friends who haven't gone beyond high school.

_____ 7. Officials _____(e)d the results of the race when they learned that the winning horse had been given an illegal drug.

_____ 8. Rudy's noisy and insulting behavior resulted in his _____ from the restaurant.

_____ 9. The continual crying of a baby in the auditorium _____(e)d from our enjoyment of the movie.

_____ 10. Because the Academy Awards program is so long, I fall asleep long before the names of the top winners are _____(e)d.

SCORE: (Number correct) _____ × 10 = _____ %

Mastery Test: *Chapter 21 (Skipping Church)*

In the space provided, write the word from the box needed to complete each sentence. Then put the **letter** of that word in the column at the left. Use each word once.

A. **credible**	B. **cursory**	C. **designate**	D. **deviate**	E. **improvise**
F. **interim**	G. **latent**	H. **secular**	I. **shun**	J. **simulate**

_____ 1. My little sister did such a _____ job of packing for the pajama party that she didn't even take her pajamas.

_____ 2. The school year ends two weeks before the YMCA summer day camp begins, so the Adamses have to find a babysitter to take care of their children during the _____.

_____ 3. I always keep some pasta, spaghetti sauce, and frozen vegetables on hand so that I can quickly _____ a meal for unexpected guests.

_____ 4. We often get ads in the mail for jewelry with lab-produced gems that _____ real diamonds.

_____ 5. Instead of performing a religious play, the church theater group decided to perform a _____ one this year.

_____ 6. The prom committee _____(e)d Jed to be in charge of the decorations because of his artistic ability.

_____ 7. The energy in a log is _____ until the log is burned and the wood's matter changes to heat.

_____ 8. Jan never just tells a story from beginning to end. She always _____s from her story into completely new topics as they occur to her.

_____ 9. Nell's story about being kidnapped seemed _____ at first, but the way she keeps changing the facts makes it harder to believe.

_____ 10. The chances of coming in contact with ticks are reduced if you _____ areas where they are usually found, such as patches of tall grass.

SCORE: (Number correct) _____ × 10 = _____ %

Mastery Test: *Chapter 22 (A Model Teacher)*

In the space provided, write the word from the box needed to complete each sentence. Then put the **letter** of that word in the column at the left. Use each word once.

A. **commemorate**	B. **complacent**	C. **consensus**	D. **deplete**	E. **diligent**
F. **empathy**	G. **menial**	H. **niche**	I. **transcend**	J. **waive**

_____ 1. Although we have only one house guest, his huge appetite quickly _____s our supplies of certain foods. I've had to make three trips to the supermarket this week.

_____ 2. To be a good therapist, one must have _____ for others.

_____ 3. Tony never became _____ about his store's success. He continued to work as hard as he did the first day it was opened.

_____ 4. To _____ my aunt and uncle's wedding anniversary, I made a donation to one of their favorite charities.

_____ 5. Amy isn't skilled at dealing with people, but she has found a(n) _____ as a computer repair specialist, working mainly with machines, not humans.

_____ 6. There was rarely a(n) _____ in our large family on where to eat. Three of us always wanted Mexican food, and the others usually preferred Italian or Chinese.

_____ 7. With special training, Philip was able to _____ his learning disability and become a successful accountant.

_____ 8. Ben cheerfully accepted a job as a dishwasher at a summer resort. He didn't mind the _____ work as long as he could enjoy the beautiful resort in his free time.

_____ 9. Once the librarian gets to know you, she _____s the requirement that you show your student identification every time you wish to take out a book.

_____ 10. Herb is not at the top of the honor roll month after month because he's so brilliant, but because he's very _____ about his school work.

SCORE: (Number correct) _____ × 10 = _____ %

Mastery Test: *Chapter 23 (My Talented Roommate)*

In the space provided, write the word from the box needed to complete each sentence. Then put the **letter** of that word in the column at the left. Use each word once.

A. **bizarre**	B. **conducive**	C. **falter**	D. **flaunt**	E. **frenzy**
F. **gist**	G. **hamper**	H. **paradox**	I. **repertoire**	J. **viable**

_____ 1. Visitors to the park always want to see the "Strangled Tree," a _____-looking oak with two arm-like branches that seem to be choking itself.

_____ 2. Brushing and flossing teeth regularly is _____ to good dental health.

_____ 3. Gino's lack of discipline _____s his development as an athlete. He only practices when he feels like it, so his skills don't improve very much.

_____ 4. An irritating _____ to many job seekers is that they can't be hired without experience, but they can't gain experience without being hired.

_____ 5. To be _____, any agreement between the company and the union must give each some benefits.

_____ 6. Uncle Jim's memory seems to be getting worse. When we bumped into each other this morning, he _____(e)d as he tried to come up with my name.

_____ 7. The _____ of the story of Pinocchio is that a wooden puppet earns the right to become a real boy.

_____ 8. Evie's friends wouldn't resent her marrying a rich man if she acted modestly about it. Instead she _____s her huge diamond ring and talks about money all the time.

_____ 9. When the basketball game went into second overtime, the already excited fans went into such a _____ that the players were nearly deafened by their screams and clapping.

_____ 10. Actress Meryl Streep is known for her large _____ of accents. Voices she has mastered for her movies include those of a Polish refugee and an upper-class Englishwoman.

SCORE: (Number correct) _____ × 10 = _____ %

Mastery Test: *Chapter 25 (Cal and His Sisters)*

In the space provided, write the word from the box needed to complete each sentence. Then put the **letter** of that word in the column at the left. Use each word once.

A. **devoid**	B. **implore**	C. **infuriate**	D. **intimidate**	E. **introvert**
F. **jeopardize**	G. **sibling**	H. **smug**	I. **sneer**	J. **vivacious**

_____ 1. I was feeling quite _____ about having gotten a perfect score on the quiz until I noticed that almost everyone else in class had gotten the same score.

_____ 2. When it comes to herself, Ellen has no sense of humor. Being laughed at _____s her.

_____ 3. We don't use the old pump in the backyard because the well out there has been _____ of water for years.

_____ 4. When I was younger, I would _____ my parents for days before my birthday to tell me what present they'd bought me.

_____ 5. Sonia may be a senior citizen, but she's the most _____ person I know. She's enthusiastic about all sorts of interests—from concerts to politics to sports—and she never runs out of energy.

_____ 6. Although Greg is really a gentle soul, his loud voice and his piercing eyes often _____ people.

_____ 7. Anna is losing friends because of her rude behavior. For instance, she _____(e)d at one girl's clothes, saying, "I'd be embarrassed to wear my sister's hand-me-downs."

_____ 8. While dealing with many people at work may exhaust a(n) _____, it will energize an outgoing person.

_____ 9. Her bank's refusal to lend her money has _____(e)d Sue's plans to open a clothing store.

_____ 10. When Ken's parents told him he was adopted, they also said he'd been one of five brothers and sisters. He then decided to do all he could to find his four _____s.

SCORE: (Number correct) _____ × 10 = _____ %

Mastery Test: *Chapter 26 (Shoplifter)*

In the space provided, write the word from the box needed to complete each sentence. Then put the **letter** of that word in the column at the left. Use each word once.

A. **condone**	B. **contemplate**	C. **feasible**	D. **feign**	E. **fiscal**
F. **furtive**	G. **gape**	H. **pathetic**	I. **precedent**	J. **punitive**

_____ 1. Although Dr. Simpson often seems rude, we _____ his bad manners because of the many kind things he's done for our family over the years.

_____ 2. The _____ rules at some banks allowed them to lend huge amounts of money. When the economy turned bad and the loans weren't repaid, those banks failed.

_____ 3. Many young people _____ joining the Army because of the free career training it could provide them.

_____ 4. Should prisons only be _____? Or should they also teach prisoners useful skills?

_____ 5. We _____(e)d in astonishment at the huge hole in the ground left by the earthquake.

_____ 6. Alex's attempts to repair his car were so _____ that he made the situation even worse.

_____ 7. Lawyers rely heavily on legal _____. When a question arises, they look for past cases in which similar questions were dealt with.

_____ 8. Little Emily tried to act as if she wasn't thinking about her Christmas presents, but she kept taking _____ glances at the beautifully wrapped packages under the tree.

_____ 9. I wonder if it will someday be _____ for an average person to take a vacation somewhere in space.

_____ 10. When I open one of Grandma's birthday presents, I usually have to _____ delighted surprise. She often gives me something that's either ugly or useless.

SCORE: (Number correct) _____ × 10 = _____ %

Mastery Test: *Chapter 27 (A Nutty Newspaper Office)*

In the space provided, write the word from the box needed to complete each sentence. Then put the **letter** of that word in the column at the left. Use each word once.

A. **cryptic**	B. **deficient**	C. **depict**	D. **detrimental**	E. **implicit**
F. **inhibition**	G. **ironic**	H. **rupture**	I. **saturate**	J. **vindictive**

_____ 1. The _____ note my girlfriend left on my door said only, "A bridge over troubled waters."

_____ 2. Throughout the hilarious movie, my visiting cousin didn't laugh once or even crack a smile. He seemed completely _____ in a sense of humor.

_____ 3. Most plants need as much sunshine as possible. But for shade-loving plants, direct sunlight is actually _____ to their well-being.

_____ 4. The expensive two-week, eight-hour-a-day language course _____s students' minds with the new language.

_____ 5. "Wouldn't you be more comfortable on the couch?" was a(n) _____ request for the 300-pound guest not to sit on Jane's fragile antique chair.

_____ 6. Celia felt as if she'd kept all her anger at her roommate trapped in a box inside her. Suddenly, the box _____(e)d, and angry words came spilling out of her mouth.

_____ 7. Although Denzel Washington was in the same elevator with me, my _____ against bothering celebrities kept me from asking for his autograph.

_____ 8. "It's a(n) _____ fact of life," said Aunt Lucy, "that we are often attracted to our mates by the very qualities that later drive us crazy."

_____ 9. Bertha had _____(e)d her father as such a monster that when I finally met him, I was surprised to find him soft-spoken and pleasant.

_____ 10. Mona was angry because her brother had refused to lend her a favorite CD. Feeling _____, Mona went through her brother's room and removed everything she had ever given him.

SCORE: (Number correct) _____ × 10 = _____ %

Mastery Test: *Chapter 28 (Roughing It)*

In the space provided, write the word from the box needed to complete each sentence. Then put the **letter** of that word in the column at the left. Use each word once.

A. **constrict**	B. **exhaustive**	C. **fallible**	D. **formulate**	E. **genial**
F. **habitat**	G. **pragmatic**	H. **pretentious**	I. **reconcile**	J. **vile**

_____ 1. The octopus is very good at squeezing into small spaces. It can _____ its flexible legs and body enough to slip into what seems an impossibly small area.

_____ 2. My fifth-grade teacher's _____ manner disguised a truly unpleasant personality.

_____ 3. Instead of denying it when she makes a mistake, our English teacher simply says, "Like everyone else, I'm _____."

_____ 4. Jan doesn't often mention the fact that she has two doctoral degrees because she doesn't want to seem _____.

_____ 5. I don't really like my biology lab partner, but he asked me out so suddenly that I didn't have time to _____ an excuse. Instead I just stammered, "Uh, well, I guess so."

_____ 6. Although several specialists ran a(n) _____ series of tiring tests and exams, they could discover no cause for Eric's terrible headaches.

_____ 7. My twelve-year-old sister enjoyed creating a natural _____ inside a large aquarium for her hermit crab.

_____ 8. It's more _____ to buy clothing that can be mixed and matched into various outfits than to buy clothes that can be worn in only one outfit.

_____ 9. When Sara decided to stay home with the baby, she and Andy _____(e)d themselves to living on considerably less money for a while.

_____ 10. Why do millions of people enjoy seeing movies about such _____ subjects as chain-saw murders?

SCORE: (Number correct) _____ × 10 = _____ %

Mastery Test: *Chapter 29 (Getting Scared)*

In the space provided, write the word from the box needed to complete each sentence. Then put the **letter** of that word in the column at the left. Use each word once.

A. **avid**	B. **dwindle**	C. **esteem**	D. **evoke**	E. **legacy**
F. **mediate**	G. **muted**	H. **nurture**	I. **pacify**	J. **transient**

_____ 1. If we aren't careful, our _____ to our children and grandchildren may be an environment damaged beyond saving.

_____ 2. The children were annoyed to return from lunch and find that their formerly huge snowman had _____(e)d under the midday sun to only a stump.

_____ 3. "I don't know what to say!" gasped the woman when she met her favorite actor. "I'm your most _____ fan. I've seen each of your movies at least three times."

_____ 4. The smell of lilac cologne always _____s memories in me of my grandmother.

_____ 5. Kay looks more attractive now that she's traded in her harsh, bright make-up for more _____ colors.

_____ 6. It was hard for Toni to see the restaurant she had _____(e)d from a tiny take-out stand to a thriving pizzeria disappear in a blaze of fire.

_____ 7. Al was about to offer to _____ the dispute between his two angry neighbors, but when he noticed one of them had a knife, he decided instead to call the police.

_____ 8. My _____ for my rich uncle grew when I learned how much work he did for charities and how much money he gave them.

_____ 9. When my brother is really angry, nothing I say can _____ him. I just listen until he's had his say, and then he quickly calms down again.

_____ 10. My joy at seeing an A at the top of the returned math paper was _____, disappearing quickly when I realized the teacher had mistakenly given me someone else's paper.

SCORE: (Number correct) _____ × 10 = _____ %

Mastery Test: *Chapter 30 (My Sister's Date)*

In the space provided, write the word from the box needed to complete each sentence. Then put the **letter** of that word in the column at the left. Use each word once.

A. **aloof**	B. **ambivalent**	C. **augment**	D. **dispel**	E. **explicit**
F. **longevity**	G. **magnitude**	H. **mundane**	I. **obscure**	J. **render**

_____ 1. I've tried to _____ superstitions from my mind, but I still find myself walking around ladders, not under them.

_____ 2. I don't know how Tom could have made such a mess of painting the garage. He was given _____ instructions as to how it was to be done.

_____ 3. Perry decided to _____ his muscles by lifting weights every other day.

_____ 4. Cats are usually thought of as more _____ than dogs, keeping their distance from everyone but a chosen few.

_____ 5. Doug is _____ about the job offer he's received. The job itself sounds great, but accepting it would mean moving far from his family and friends.

_____ 6. Many scientists believe our sun will die someday, but since that event wouldn't happen for millions of years, it seems of little _____ today.

_____ 7. People often marry expecting never-ending romance and excitement. However, marriages are full of _____ details like bill-paying and finding baby sitters.

_____ 8. After staying awake all night, Duane wrote what he thought was a brilliant letter to his girlfriend. But this morning he found it so _____ that even he couldn't understand it all.

_____ 9. A new coat of off-white paint _____(e)d the old kitchen much brighter and more attractive.

_____ 10. Just when you are determined to stop all unhealthy habits, you read about some lively 100-year-old who says his or her _____ stems from daily doses of whiskey and cigars.

SCORE: (Number correct) _____ × 10 = _____ %

Answers to the Mastery Tests: IMPROVING VOCABULARY SKILLS

Chapter 1 (Joseph Palmer)

1. G		6. H	
2. F		7. B	
3. A		8. E	
4. C		9. D	
5. I		10. J	

Chapter 2 (Telephone Salespeople)

1. E		6. C	
2. G		7. I	
3. J		8. F	
4. A		9. D	
5. B		10. H	

Chapter 3 (A Cruel Sport)

1. D		6. H	
2. G		7. A	
3. J		8. E	
4. B		9. I	
5. F		10. C	

Chapter 4 (Bald Is Beautiful)

1. B		6. J	
2. G		7. F	
3. I		8. E	
4. D		9. H	
5. A		10. C	

Chapter 5 (No Luck with Women)

1. F		6. G	
2. I		7. B	
3. E		8. C	
4. H		9. A	
5. J		10. D	

Chapter 7 (Accident and Recovery)

1. G		6. C	
2. B		7. F	
3. H		8. A	
4. I		9. D	
5. J		10. E	

Chapter 8 (Animal Senses)

1. E		6. A	
2. B		7. F	
3. J		8. C	
4. G		9. I	
5. H		10. D	

Chapter 9 (Money Problems)

1. E		6. A	
2. H		7. C	
3. B		8. F	
4. J		9. I	
5. D		10. G	

Chapter 10 (The New French Employee)

1. E		6. C	
2. A		7. F	
3. J		8. B	
4. G		9. I	
5. D		10. H	

Chapter 11 (A Cruel Teacher)

1. J		6. A	
2. I		7. D	
3. G		8. H	
4. F		9. E	
5. B		10. C	

Chapter 13 (Learning to Study)

1. E		6. A	
2. H		7. D	
3. I		8. B	
4. J		9. G	
5. F		10. C	

Chapter 14 (The Mad Monk)

1. E		6. D	
2. G		7. I	
3. A		8. J	
4. B		9. H	
5. C		10. F	

Chapter 15 (Conflict Over Holidays)

1. C		6. I	
2. A		7. G	
3. E		8. D	
4. F		9. J	
5. B		10. H	

Chapter 16 (Dr. Martin Luther King, Jr.)

1.	B	6.	I
2.	E	7.	D
3.	J	8.	A
4.	C	9.	F
5.	G	10.	H

Chapter 17 (Relating to Parents)

1.	C	6.	B
2.	I	7.	H
3.	D	8.	E
4.	F	9.	A
5.	G	10.	J

Chapter 19 (Interview with a Rude Star)

1.	I	6.	H
2.	A	7.	G
3.	C	8.	D
4.	F	9.	E
5.	B	10.	J

Chapter 20 (The Nightmare of Gym)

1.	F	6.	C
2.	E	7.	I
3.	A	8.	G
4.	J	9.	B
5.	H	10.	D

Chapter 21 (Skipping Church)

1.	B	6.	C
2.	F	7.	G
3.	E	8.	D
4.	J	9.	A
5.	H	10.	I

Chapter 22 (A Model Teacher)

1.	D	6.	C
2.	F	7.	I
3.	B	8.	G
4.	A	9.	J
5.	H	10.	E

Chapter 23 (My Talented Roommate)

1.	A	6.	C
2.	B	7.	F
3.	G	8.	D
4.	H	9.	E
5.	J	10.	I

Chapter 25 (Cal and His Sisters)

1.	H	6.	D
2.	C	7.	I
3.	A	8.	E
4.	B	9.	F
5.	J	10.	G

Chapter 26 (Shoplifter)

1.	A	6.	H
2.	E	7.	I
3.	B	8.	F
4.	J	9.	C
5.	G	10.	D

Chapter 27 (A Nutty Newspaper Office)

1.	A	6.	H
2.	B	7.	F
3.	D	8.	G
4.	I	9.	C
5.	E	10.	J

Chapter 28 (Roughing It)

1.	A	6.	B
2.	E	7.	F
3.	C	8.	G
4.	H	9.	I
5.	D	10.	J

Chapter 29 (Getting Scared)

1.	E	6.	H
2.	B	7.	F
3.	A	8.	C
4.	D	9.	I
5.	G	10.	J

Chapter 30 (My Sister's Date)

1.	D	6.	G
2.	E	7.	H
3.	C	8.	I
4.	A	9.	J
5.	B	10.	F

Mastery Test: *Unit One*

PART A
Complete each sentence in a way that clearly shows you understand the meaning of the **boldfaced** word. Take a minute to plan your answer before you write.

Example: _____*Four feet of snow on the ground*_____would be a **deterrent** to getting to school.

1. Typewriters are now almost **obsolete** because _____

   _____.

2. I might be **demoralized** if _____

   _____.

3. One **tangible** symbol of affection is _____

   _____.

4. One behavior that makes me **irate** is _____

   _____.

5. I think that _____

   _____ **infringes** on other people's rights.

6. The **eccentric** teacher has a habit of _____

   _____.

7. This year I face a **dilemma**: _____

   _____.

8. The most **altruistic** thing I ever saw anyone do was to _____

   _____.

9. The actor received this **acclaim** for his performance: " _____

   _____."

10. My uncle is **wary** of driving at night, so he _____

    _____.

(Continues on next page)

PART B

Use each of the following ten words in sentences of your own. Make it clear that you know the meaning of the word you use. Feel free to use the past tense or plural form of a word.

A. **absolve**	B. **adjacent**	C. **animosity**	D. **appease**	E. **curt**
F. **engross**	G. **epitome**	H. **innovation**	I. **methodical**	J. **zeal**

11. _____

_____

12. _____

_____

13. _____

_____

14. _____

_____

15. _____

_____

16. _____

_____

17. _____

_____

18. _____

_____

19. _____

_____

20. _____

_____

SCORE: (Number correct) _____ × 5 = _____ %

Mastery Test: *Unit Two*

PART A
Complete each sentence in a way that clearly shows you understand the meaning of the **boldfaced** word. Take a minute to plan your answer before you write.

Example: Being **nocturnal** animals, raccoons _____ raid our garbage cans only at night _____.

1. The news reported a **calamity** in which _____

   _____.

2. Ray **dispatched** his younger brother to _____

   _____.

3. When I'm alone, I often **ponder** _____

   _____.

4. When Carolyn saw her essay grade, she **gloated**, saying, " _____

   _____."

5. My apartment is so **immaculate** that _____

   _____.

6. Three personal **attributes** that I possess are _____

   _____.

7. The novel's main character is a **sinister** doctor who _____

   _____.

8. When our neighbor cut lilacs off our bush for her home, we **retaliated** by _____

   _____.

9. One advantage of a **mobile** library might be _____

   _____.

10. I plan to **persevere** in _____

    _____.

(Continues on next page)

PART B

Use each of the following ten words in sentences of your own. Make it clear that you know the meaning of the word you use. Feel free to use the past tense or plural form of a word.

A. **blight**	B. **decipher**	C. **fluctuate**	D. **implausible**	E. **predominant**
F. **qualm**	G. **rehabilitate**	H. **sanctuary**	I. **turmoil**	J. **vulnerable**

11. _____

_____

12. _____

_____

13. _____

_____

14. _____

_____

15. _____

_____

16. _____

_____

17. _____

_____

18. _____

_____

19. _____

_____

20. _____

_____

SCORE: (Number correct) _____ × 5 = _____ %

Mastery Test: *Unit Three*

PART A

Complete each sentence in a way that clearly shows you understand the meaning of the **boldfaced** word. Take a minute to plan your answer before you write.

Example: As an **incentive** to work better, the company _____ *gives bonuses to workers who show special effort* _____.

1. One sight that makes me feel **revulsion** is _____

_____.

2. A good way to **squander** your money is to _____

_____.

3. Jon, who is a **proponent** of daily exercise, advised me, " _____

_____."

4. At our school, it is **mandatory** to _____

_____.

5. I **aspire** to _____

_____.

6. During the math class, the teacher **digressed** by _____

_____.

7. Our father told us how **traumatic** it was for him to _____

_____.

8. My **rationale** for going to college is _____

_____.

9. The reason the plan was **covert** was that _____

_____.

10. When asked by the restaurant owner to pay his bill, the young man's **flippant** reply was " _____

_____."

(Continues on next page)

PART B

Use each of the following ten words in sentences of your own. Make it clear that you know the meaning of the word you use. Feel free to use the past tense or plural form of a word.

| A. affiliate | B. contend | C. curtail | D. cynic | E. diversion |
| F. perception | G. rapport | H. relentless | I. speculate | J. virile |

11. _____

_____

12. _____

_____

13. _____

_____

14. _____

_____

15. _____

_____

16. _____

_____

17. _____

_____

18. _____

_____

19. _____

_____

20. _____

_____

SCORE: (Number correct) _____ × 5 = _____ %

150

Mastery Test: *Unit Four*

PART A
Complete each sentence in a way that clearly shows you understand the meaning of the **boldfaced** word. Take a minute to plan your answer before you write.

Example: Sam **flaunted** his new convertible by _____*driving it back and forth past the school with its top down*_____ .

1. My favorite **secular** holiday is _____

_____ .

2. An author might use a **pseudonym** because _____

_____ .

3. A stiff arm **hampers** _____

_____ .

4. My father showed his **elation** at the news by _____

_____ .

5. The children are so **blasé** about fireworks that _____

_____ .

6. A secretary's job can include such **menial** tasks as _____

_____ .

7. I find it **detracts** from a restaurant meal when _____

_____ .

8. Lamont is **averse** to city life because _____

_____ .

9. One of the most **bizarre** sights I've ever seen in a restaurant is _____

_____ .

10. I was **mortified** when _____

_____ .

(Continues on next page)

PART B

Use each of the following ten words in sentences of your own. Make it clear that you know the meaning of the word you use. Feel free to use the past tense or plural form of a word.

A. **condescend**	B. **consensus**	C. **deplete**	D. **deviate**	E. **diligent**
F. **empathy**	G. **gist**	H. **interim**	I. **niche**	J. **waive**

11. _____

_____

12. _____

_____

13. _____

_____

14. _____

_____

15. _____

_____

16. _____

_____

17. _____

_____

18. _____

_____

19. _____

_____

20. _____

_____

SCORE: (Number correct) _____ × 5 = _____ %

Mastery Test: *Unit Five*

PART A

Complete each sentence in a way that clearly shows you understand the meaning of the **boldfaced** word. Take a minute to plan your answer before you write.

Example: To increase your **longevity**, _____ *exercise frequently and avoid alcohol, tobacco, and high-fat foods* _____.

1. One thing the nursery-school teacher did to **nurture** each child each day was _____

    _____.

2. **Pragmatic** Ramona spends her money on such things as _____

    _____.

3. The critic summed up how **pathetic** the actor's performance was with this comment: "_____

    _____."

4. Lionel **implored** his parents to _____

    _____.

5. The **magnitude** of Carol's musical talent became clear to us when _____

    _____.

6. A student **deficient** in study skills might _____

    _____.

7. We learned how **fallible** the house builder was when _____

    _____.

8. To **mediate** the argument between my sister and me, _____

    _____.

9. Enrique was **rendered** helpless when _____

    _____.

10. When Mary Lou asked the fortuneteller, "What will my career be?" the **cryptic** reply was "_____

    _____."

(Continues on next page)

PART B

Use each of the following ten words in sentences of your own. Make it clear that you know the meaning of the word you use. Feel free to use the past tense or plural form of a word.

A. **condone**	B. **esteem**	C. **feign**	D. **habitat**	E. **inhibition**
F. **ironic**	G. **pacify**	H. **sibling**	I. **smug**	J. **vindictive**

11. _____

_____

12. _____

_____

13. _____

_____

14. _____

_____

15. _____

_____

16. _____

_____

17. _____

_____

18. _____

_____

19. _____

_____

20. _____

_____

SCORE: (Number correct) _____ × 5 = _____ %

ADVANCING VOCABULARY SKILLS

NAME: _____

SECTION: _____ DATE: _____

SCORE: _____

Pretest

> This test contains 100 items. In the space provided, write the letter of the choice that is closest in meaning to the **boldfaced** word.
>
> *Important:* Keep in mind that this test is for diagnostic purposes only. **If you do not know a word, leave the space blank rather than guess at it.**

____ 1. **scrupulous**   a) sociable   b) careless   c) clean   d) conscientious

____ 2. **vicarious**   a) experienced indirectly   b) lively   c) inactive   d) occasional

____ 3. **facetious**   a) ill-mannered   b) joking   c) careless   d) depressed

____ 4. **discretion**   a) independence   b) gladness   c) slyness   d) tact

____ 5. **gregarious**   a) wordy   b) depressed   c) sociable   d) religious

____ 6. **despondent**   a) depressed   b) tired   c) encouraged   d) well-behaved

____ 7. **rudimentary**   a) rude   b) planned   c) partial   d) elementary

____ 8. **retrospect**   a) expecting   b) repetition   c) removal   d) looking back

____ 9. **instigate**   a) stir to action   b) investigate   c) prepare   d) suppress

____ 10. **venerate**   a) protect   b) create   c) make unfriendly   d) respect

____ 11. **subsidize**   a) support financially   b) lift up   c) fall over   d) calculate

____ 12. **dissident**   a) political supporter   b) visitor   c) candidate   d) one who disagrees

____ 13. **juxtapose**   a) replace   b) place side by side   c) remove   d) imagine

____ 14. **embellish**   a) remove   b) keep   c) decorate   d) hide

____ 15. **inadvertent**   a) unintentional   b) not for sale   c) distant   d) near

____ 16. **relinquish**   a) enjoy   b) gather   c) criticize   d) give up

____ 17. **impetuous**   a) lazy   b) calm   c) teasing   d) impulsive

____ 18. **euphoric**   a) undecided   b) depressed   c) lonely   d) overjoyed

____ 19. **infallible**   a) incapable of error   b) accident-prone   c) human   d) wild

____ 20. **regress**   a) make progress   b) restrict   c) return to previous behavior   d) adjust

____ 21. **fortuitous**   a) lucky   b) sad   c) having never happened before   d) brave

____ 22. **sham**   a) type   b) imitation   c) disturbance   d) belief

____ 23. **predisposed**   a) against   b) reluctant to speak   c) undecided   d) tending beforehand

____ 24. **propensity**   a) relation   b) job   c) tendency   d) hobby

____ 25. **reprehensible**   a) blameworthy   b) well-filled   c) affordable   d) admirable

(Continues on next page)

_____ 26. **attrition**   **a)** becoming fewer   **b)** connection   **c)** multiplying   **d)** imitation

_____ 27. **reticent**   **a)** forgiving   **b)** sad   **c)** reluctant to speak   **d)** contrary to reason

_____ 28. **circumvent**   **a)** avoid   **b)** fail to notice   **c)** distribute   **d)** socialize

_____ 29. **inundate**   **a)** delay   **b)** flood   **c)** swallow   **d)** approve

_____ 30. **oblivious**   **a)** courageous   **b)** unaware   **c)** quiet   **d)** reliable

_____ 31. **inquisitive**   **a)** cheerful   **b)** nervous   **c)** curious   **d)** in pain

_____ 32. **relegate**   **a)** bring back into use   **b)** assign to a lesser place   **c)** blend   **d)** raise

_____ 33. **bolster**   **a)** support   **b)** protect   **c)** protest   **d)** hide

_____ 34. **terse**   **a)** nervous   **b)** sad   **c)** brief   **d)** cool

_____ 35. **sedentary**   **a)** sitting   **b)** excessive   **c)** harmless   **d)** repeated

_____ 36. **superfluous**   **a)** extra   **b)** unclear   **c)** useful   **d)** ahead

_____ 37. **exonerate**   **a)** encourage   **b)** condemn   **c)** hide   **d)** free from blame

_____ 38. **contingency**   **a)** contest   **b)** disapproval   **c)** theory   **d)** possibility

_____ 39. **clandestine**   **a)** well-lit   **b)** secret   **c)** noble   **d)** harmless

_____ 40. **liability**   **a)** drawback   **b)** hatred   **c)** favor   **d)** indirect remark

_____ 41. **austere**   **a)** wealthy   **b)** plain   **c)** complex   **d)** far

_____ 42. **perfunctory**   **a)** unenthusiastic   **b)** troubled   **c)** on time   **d)** well-prepared

_____ 43. **provocative**   **a)** careful   **b)** able to improve   **c)** inconsistent   **d)** arousing interest

_____ 44. **esoteric**   **a)** public   **b)** uniform   **c)** well-written   **d)** understood by few

_____ 45. **metamorphosis**   **a)** journey   **b)** change   **c)** secret plot   **d)** fantasy

_____ 46. **verbose**   **a)** wordy   **b)** active   **c)** noisy   **d)** forceful

_____ 47. **connoisseur**   **a)** one who likes to suffer   **b)** egotist   **c)** expert   **d)** painter

_____ 48. **contrite**   **a)** indecent   **b)** sorry   **c)** lacking confidence   **d)** careful

_____ 49. **plight**   **a)** difficult situation   **b)** minor weakness   **c)** environment   **d)** travel

_____ 50. **distraught**   **a)** educated   **b)** too noticeable   **c)** troubled   **d)** rehearsed

(Continues on next page)

_____ 51. **encompass**   **a)** include   **b)** draw   **c)** separate   **d)** purchase

_____ 52. **stringent**   **a)** dry   **b)** strict   **c)** loose   **d)** long

_____ 53. **eradicate**   **a)** wipe out   **b)** scold   **c)** restore   **d)** hold onto

_____ 54. **sordid**   **a)** slow   **b)** unprepared   **c)** morally low   **d)** injured

_____ 55. **presumptuous**   **a)** indecent   **b)** lacking standards of selection   **c)** nervous   **d)** too bold

_____ 56. **meticulous**   **a)** broken-down   **b)** curious   **c)** careful and exact   **d)** irregular

_____ 57. **magnanimous**   **a)** nameless   **b)** proud   **c)** generous in forgiving   **d)** lacking standards

_____ 58. **exhort**   **a)** strongly urge   **b)** travel   **c)** escape   **d)** hint

_____ 59. **innocuous**   **a)** delightful   **b)** harmless   **c)** dangerous   **d)** disappointing

_____ 60. **masochist**   **a)** one who likes to suffer   **b)** egotist   **c)** fan
d) one who expects the worst

_____ 61. **deplore**   **a)** command   **b)** disapprove of   **c)** encourage   **d)** prevent

_____ 62. **atrophy**   **a)** weaken   **b)** reward   **c)** expand   **d)** strengthen

_____ 63. **unprecedented**   **a)** overly noticeable   **b)** without authority   **c)** unexpected
d) having never happened before

_____ 64. **mitigate**   **a)** make worse   **b)** make less severe   **c)** remove   **d)** hide

_____ 65. **exacerbate**   **a)** make worse   **b)** remove   **c)** bring closer   **d)** strengthen

_____ 66. **exorbitant**   **a)** absorbent   **b)** excessive   **c)** quarrelsome   **d)** well-timed

_____ 67. **facilitate**   **a)** approve   **b)** serve   **c)** make easier   **d)** clear from blame

_____ 68. **synchronize**   **a)** spread throughout   **b)** separate   **c)** reduce   **d)** cause to occur together

_____ 69. **extricate**   **a)** run away   **b)** confuse   **c)** free from difficulty   **d)** complicate

_____ 70. **exhilaration**   **a)** freedom   **b)** thirst   **c)** wisdom   **d)** gladness

_____ 71. **proficient**   **a)** proud   **b)** wise   **c)** skilled   **d)** well-known

_____ 72. **annihilate**   **a)** guide   **b)** misunderstand   **c)** carry out   **d)** destroy

_____ 73. **criterion**   **a)** philosophy   **b)** standard for judgment   **c)** political theory
d) state of mind

_____ 74. **vindicate**   **a)** clear from blame   **b)** ridicule   **c)** escape   **d)** formally question

_____ 75. **subversive**   **a)** being a servant   **b)** acting to overthrow   **c)** willing
d) planning to build

(Continues on next page)

_____ 76. **forestall**   **a)** prevent   **b)** predict   **c)** rent   **d)** hurry

_____ 77. **retribution**   **a)** donation   **b)** looking back   **c)** evil   **d)** punishment

_____ 78. **insinuate**   **a)** demand   **b)** state   **c)** deny   **d)** hint

_____ 79. **disparity**   **a)** sadness   **b)** inequality   **c)** blemish   **d)** similarity

_____ 80. **opportune**   **a)** generous   **b)** more important   **c)** well-timed   **d)** belittling

_____ 81. **fastidious**   **a)** not planned   **b)** attentive to details   **c)** quick   **d)** inferior

_____ 82. **heinous**   **a)** evil   **b)** mischievous   **c)** stubborn   **d)** depressed

_____ 83. **implement**   **a)** encourage   **b)** carry out   **c)** insult   **d)** prevent

_____ 84. **complement**   **a)** praise   **b)** sin   **c)** make fun of   **d)** add what is needed

_____ 85. **impromptu**   **a)** forceful   **b)** unplanned   **c)** delayed   **d)** on time

_____ 86. **transgress**   **a)** follow   **b)** round out   **c)** travel   **d)** break a law

_____ 87. **extenuating**   **a)** excusing   **b)** inferior   **c)** forceful   **d)** overly noticeable

_____ 88. **vehement**   **a)** forceful   **b)** wicked   **c)** rude   **d)** calm

_____ 89. **auspicious**   **a)** threatening   **b)** lazy   **c)** favorable   **d)** not trusting

_____ 90. **rebuke**   **a)** compromise   **b)** fix   **c)** scold   **d)** admire

_____ 91. **macabre**   **a)** frightful   **b)** depressed   **c)** cheerful   **d)** common

_____ 92. **fabricate**   **a)** misinterpret   **b)** put away   **c)** clothe   **d)** invent

_____ 93. **turbulent**   **a)** ambitious   **b)** wildly disturbed   **c)** mixed   **d)** fast

_____ 94. **impending**   **a)** about to happen   **b)** illegal   **c)** historical   **d)** usual

_____ 95. **paramount**   **a)** dramatic   **b)** disturbed   **c)** unknown   **d)** chief

_____ 96. **emulate**   **a)** be tardy   **b)** misunderstand   **c)** imitate   **d)** prepare

_____ 97. **antithesis**   **a)** disorder   **b)** theory   **c)** effect   **d)** opposite

_____ 98. **incapacitate**   **a)** disable   **b)** allow   **c)** increase   **d)** fight

_____ 99. **abrasive**   **a)** rough   **b)** friendly   **c)** mild   **d)** foolish

_____ 100. **prognosis**   **a)** hope   **b)** memory   **c)** opposite   **d)** prediction

---

STOP. This is the end of the test. If there is time remaining, you may go back and recheck your answers. When the time is up, hand in both your answer sheet and this test booklet to your instructor.

ADVANCING VOCABULARY SKILLS

Posttest

This test contains 100 items. In the space provided, write the letter of the choice that is closest in meaning to the **boldfaced** word.

_____ 1. **juxtapose**   a) place side by side   b) replace   c) remove   d) imagine

_____ 2. **embellish**   a) remove   b) decorate   c) keep   d) hide

_____ 3. **facetious**   a) joking   b) ill-mannered   c) careless   d) depressed

_____ 4. **infallible**   a) wild   b) accident-prone   c) incapable of error   d) human

_____ 5. **discretion**   a) independence   b) tact   c) slyness   d) gladness

_____ 6. **inadvertent**   a) near   b) not for sale   c) distant   d) unintentional

_____ 7. **gregarious**   a) religious   b) sociable   c) depressed   d) wordy

_____ 8. **rudimentary**   a) rude   b) planned   c) partial   d) elementary

_____ 9. **retrospect**   a) repetition   b) looking back   c) removal   d) expecting

_____ 10. **regress**   a) restrict   b) make progress   c) adjust   d) return to previous behavior

_____ 11. **instigate**   a) stir to action   b) suppress   c) prepare   d) investigate

_____ 12. **venerate**   a) protect   b) respect   c) make unfriendly   d) create

_____ 13. **propensity**   a) hobby   b) relation   c) job   d) tendency

_____ 14. **subsidize**   a) fall over   b) lift up   c) support financially   d) calculate

_____ 15. **dissident**   a) political supporter   b) candidate   c) visitor   d) one who disagrees

_____ 16. **despondent**   a) tired   b) depressed   c) encouraged   d) well-behaved

_____ 17. **relinquish**   a) give up   b) criticize   c) gather   d) enjoy

_____ 18. **scrupulous**   a) clean   b) careless   c) sociable   d) conscientious

_____ 19. **sham**   a) type   b) imitation   c) disturbance   d) belief

_____ 20. **impetuous**   a) impulsive   b) lazy   c) teasing   d) calm

_____ 21. **fortuitous**   a) having never happened before   b) brave   c) lucky   d) sad

_____ 22. **predisposed**   a) against   b) reluctant to speak   c) tending beforehand   d) undecided

_____ 23. **reprehensible**   a) affordable   b) well-filled   c) blameworthy   d) admirable

_____ 24. **vicarious**   a) occasional   b) experienced indirectly   c) lively   d) inactive

_____ 25. **euphoric**   a) undecided   b) depressed   c) lonely   d) overjoyed

(Continues on next page)

____ 26. **contrite**   **a)** careful   **b)** lacking confidence   **c)** sorry   **d)** indecent

____ 27. **attrition**   **a)** becoming fewer   **b)** imitation   **c)** multiplying   **d)** connection

____ 28. **terse**   **a)** nervous   **b)** sad   **c)** brief   **d)** cool

____ 29. **esoteric**   **a)** public   **b)** uniform   **c)** well-written   **d)** understood by few

____ 30. **clandestine**   **a)** secret   **b)** well-lit   **c)** noble   **d)** harmless

____ 31. **inquisitive**   **a)** cheerful   **b)** curious   **c)** nervous   **d)** in pain

____ 32. **contingency**   **a)** contest   **b)** disapproval   **c)** theory   **d)** possibility

____ 33. **relegate**   **a)** blend   **b)** assign to a lesser place   **c)** bring back into use   **d)** raise

____ 34. **verbose**   **a)** noisy   **b)** active   **c)** wordy   **d)** forceful

____ 35. **exonerate**   **a)** encourage   **b)** hide   **c)** condemn   **d)** free from blame

____ 36. **connoisseur**   **a)** one who likes to suffer   **b)** egotist   **c)** expert   **d)** painter

____ 37. **liability**   **a)** hatred   **b)** drawback   **c)** indirect remark   **d)** favor

____ 38. **circumvent**   **a)** distribute   **b)** socialize   **c)** avoid   **d)** fail to notice

____ 39. **bolster**   **a)** hide   **b)** protest   **c)** protect   **d)** support

____ 40. **austere**   **a)** far   **b)** wealthy   **c)** plain   **d)** complex

____ 41. **reticent**   **a)** forgiving   **b)** reluctant to speak   **c)** sad   **d)** contrary to reason

____ 42. **distraught**   **a)** troubled   **b)** too noticeable   **c)** educated   **d)** rehearsed

____ 43. **superfluous**   **a)** useful   **b)** unclear   **c)** extra   **d)** ahead

____ 44. **provocative**   **a)** careful   **b)** arousing interest   **c)** inconsistent   **d)** able to improve

____ 45. **metamorphosis**   **a)** secret plot   **b)** fantasy   **c)** journey   **d)** change

____ 46. **sedentary**   **a)** excessive   **b)** sitting   **c)** repeated   **d)** harmless

____ 47. **oblivious**   **a)** courageous   **b)** unaware   **c)** quiet   **d)** reliable

____ 48. **plight**   **a)** minor weakness   **b)** difficult situation   **c)** travel   **d)** environment

____ 49. **inundate**   **a)** flood   **b)** delay   **c)** approve   **d)** swallow

____ 50. **perfunctory**   **a)** unenthusiastic   **b)** on time   **c)** troubled   **d)** well-prepared

(Continues on next page)

_____ 51. **encompass**   **a)** separate   **b)** draw   **c)** include   **d)** purchase

_____ 52. **vindicate**   **a)** ridicule   **b)** escape   **c)** clear from blame   **d)** formally question

_____ 53. **meticulous**   **a)** irregular   **b)** broken-down   **c)** curious   **d)** careful and exact

_____ 54. **annihilate**   **a)** destroy   **b)** misunderstand   **c)** carry out   **d)** guide

_____ 55. **exacerbate**   **a)** bring closer   **b)** strengthen   **c)** make worse   **d)** remove

_____ 56. **magnanimous**   **a)** nameless   **b)** generous in forgiving   **c)** proud   **d)** lacking standards

_____ 57. **exhort**   **a)** hint   **b)** strongly urge   **c)** travel   **d)** escape

_____ 58. **stringent**   **a)** long   **b)** loose   **c)** strict   **d)** dry

_____ 59. **innocuous**   **a)** delightful   **b)** harmless   **c)** dangerous   **d)** disappointing

_____ 60. **facilitate**   **a)** make easier   **b)** serve   **c)** approve   **d)** clear from blame

_____ 61. **presumptuous**   **a)** indecent   **b)** lacking standards of selection   **c)** nervous   **d)** too bold

_____ 62. **unprecedented**   **a)** overly noticeable   **b)** without authority   **c)** unexpected
    d) having never happened before

_____ 63. **mitigate**   **a)** make less severe   **b)** make worse   **c)** hide   **d)** remove

_____ 64. **subversive**   **a)** being a servant   **b)** willing   **c)** planning to build   **d)** acting to overthrow

_____ 65. **atrophy**   **a)** strengthen   **b)** reward   **c)** expand   **d)** weaken

_____ 66. **sordid**   **a)** slow   **b)** morally low   **c)** unprepared   **d)** injured

_____ 67. **extricate**   **a)** run away   **b)** free from difficulty   **c)** confuse   **d)** complicate

_____ 68. **exhilaration**   **a)** gladness   **b)** freedom   **c)** thirst   **d)** wisdom

_____ 69. **masochist**   **a)** one who expects the worst   **b)** egotist   **c)** fan
    d) one who likes to suffer

_____ 70. **eradicate**   **a)** wipe out   **b)** scold   **c)** restore   **d)** hold onto

_____ 71. **proficient**   **a)** wise   **b)** proud   **c)** well-known   **d)** skilled

_____ 72. **exorbitant**   **a)** excessive   **b)** absorbent   **c)** quarrelsome   **d)** well-timed

_____ 73. **synchronize**   **a)** cause to occur together   **b)** separate   **c)** reduce   **d)** spread throughout

_____ 74. **deplore**   **a)** command   **b)** encourage   **c)** disapprove of   **d)** prevent

_____ 75. **criterion**   **a)** philosophy   **b)** political theory   **c)** standard for judgment
    d) state of mind

(Continues on next page)

_____	76. **forestall**	**a)** rent	**b)** predict	**c)** prevent	**d)** hurry
_____	77. **complement**	**a)** sin	**b)** praise	**c)** add what is needed	**d)** make fun of
_____	78. **prognosis**	**a)** memory	**b)** hope	**c)** prediction	**d)** opposite
_____	79. **vehement**	**a)** wicked	**b)** forceful	**c)** calm	**d)** rude
_____	80. **auspicious**	**a)** threatening	**b)** lazy	**c)** not trusting	**d)** favorable
_____	81. **disparity**	**a)** sadness	**b)** similarity	**c)** inequality	**d)** blemish
_____	82. **heinous**	**a)** depressed	**b)** evil	**c)** mischievous	**d)** stubborn
_____	83. **impromptu**	**a)** forceful	**b)** on time	**c)** delayed	**d)** unplanned
_____	84. **antithesis**	**a)** disorder	**b)** theory	**c)** opposite	**d)** effect
_____	85. **incapacitate**	**a)** allow	**b)** disable	**c)** increase	**d)** fight
_____	86. **implement**	**a)** carry out	**b)** encourage	**c)** insult	**d)** prevent
_____	87. **insinuate**	**a)** demand	**b)** state	**c)** deny	**d)** hint
_____	88. **rebuke**	**a)** compromise	**b)** scold	**c)** fix	**d)** admire
_____	89. **impending**	**a)** illegal	**b)** about to happen	**c)** historical	**d)** usual
_____	90. **abrasive**	**a)** foolish	**b)** rough	**c)** friendly	**d)** mild
_____	91. **fastidious**	**a)** not planned	**b)** attentive to details	**c)** quick	**d)** inferior
_____	92. **macabre**	**a)** depressed	**b)** frightful	**c)** common	**d)** cheerful
_____	93. **opportune**	**a)** well-timed	**b)** more important	**c)** generous	**d)** belittling
_____	94. **turbulent**	**a)** wildly disturbed	**b)** ambitious	**c)** mixed	**d)** fast
_____	95. **transgress**	**a)** round out	**b)** follow	**c)** break a law	**d)** travel
_____	96. **extenuating**	**a)** overly noticeable	**b)** excusing	**c)** inferior	**d)** forceful
_____	97. **paramount**	**a)** disturbed	**b)** dramatic	**c)** chief	**d)** unknown
_____	98. **fabricate**	**a)** put away	**b)** misinterpret	**c)** invent	**d)** clothe
_____	99. **retribution**	**a)** looking back	**b)** donation	**c)** punishment	**d)** evil
_____	100. **emulate**	**a)** be tardy	**b)** imitate	**c)** misunderstand	**d)** prepare

STOP. This is the end of the test. If there is time remaining, you may go back and recheck your answers. When the time is up, hand in both your answer sheet and this test booklet to your instructor.

Name: _____

Unit One: *Pretest*

In the space provided, write the letter of the choice that is closest in meaning to the **boldfaced** word.

_____ 1. **optimum**   **a)** highest   **b)** most favorable   **c)** brightest   **d)** heaviest

_____ 2. **dexterous**   **a)** young   **b)** accidental   **c)** skillful   **d)** skinny

_____ 3. **scrupulous**   **a)** sociable   **b)** careless   **c)** clean   **d)** conscientious

_____ 4. **vicarious**   **a)** experienced indirectly   **b)** lively   **c)** inactive   **d)** occasional

_____ 5. **sensory**   **a)** in the mind   **b)** sensible   **c)** of the senses   **d)** on the surface

_____ 6. **facetious**   **a)** ill-mannered   **b)** joking   **c)** careless   **d)** depressed

_____ 7. **discretion**   **a)** independence   **b)** gladness   **c)** slyness   **d)** tact

_____ 8. **ostentatious**   **a)** showy   **b)** lazy   **c)** courageous   **d)** playfully witty

_____ 9. **gregarious**   **a)** wordy   **b)** depressed   **c)** sociable   **d)** religious

_____ 10. **detriment**   **a)** outward behavior   **b)** something damaging   **c)** failure   **d)** silence

_____ 11. **despondent**   **a)** depressed   **b)** tired   **c)** encouraged   **d)** well-behaved

_____ 12. **rudimentary**   **a)** rude   **b)** planned   **c)** partial   **d)** elementary

_____ 13. **zealot**   **a)** dictator   **b)** person devoted to a cause   **c)** casual person   **d)** leader

_____ 14. **collaborate**   **a)** respect   **b)** work hard   **c)** search   **d)** work together

_____ 15. **resilient**   **a)** able to recover quickly   **b)** strong   **c)** heavy   **d)** light

_____ 16. **squelch**   **a)** make fun of   **b)** stretch   **c)** suppress   **d)** approve

_____ 17. **retrospect**   **a)** expecting   **b)** repetition   **c)** removal   **d)** looking back

_____ 18. **instigate**   **a)** stir to action   **b)** investigate   **c)** prepare   **d)** suppress

_____ 19. **scoff**   **a)** impress   **b)** inquire   **c)** make fun of   **d)** show off

_____ 20. **venerate**   **a)** protect   **b)** create   **c)** make unfriendly   **d)** respect

_____ 21. **ambiguous**   **a)** under   **b)** not clear   **c)** widespread   **d)** too large

_____ 22. **sporadic**   **a)** tiny   **b)** particular   **c)** occasional   **d)** wasteful

_____ 23. **subsidize**   **a)** support financially   **b)** lift up   **c)** fall over   **d)** calculate

_____ 24. **inane**   **a)** brilliant   **b)** measurable   **c)** causing pain   **d)** silly

_____ 25. **lethargy**   **a)** strength   **b)** highest point   **c)** hunger   **d)** lack of energy

(Continues on next page)

_____ 26. **dissident**   a) political supporter   b) visitor   c) candidate   d) one who disagrees

_____ 27. **juxtapose**   a) replace   b) place side by side   c) remove   d) imagine

_____ 28. **fritter**   a) waste   b) prove   c) wander   d) collect

_____ 29. **embellish**   a) remove   b) keep   c) decorate   d) hide

_____ 30. **inadvertent**   a) unintentional   b) not for sale   c) distant   d) near

_____ 31. **relinquish**   a) enjoy   b) gather   c) criticize   d) give up

_____ 32. **estrange**   a) state again   b) depart   c) keep away   d) enter

_____ 33. **maudlin**   a) kind   b) sentimental   c) useful   d) clever

_____ 34. **impetuous**   a) lazy   b) calm   c) teasing   d) impulsive

_____ 35. **ubiquitous**   a) existing everywhere   b) all-knowing   c) all-powerful   d) perfect

_____ 36. **euphoric**   a) undecided   b) depressed   c) lonely   d) overjoyed

_____ 37. **zenith**   a) cure-all   b) peak   c) drawback   d) authority

_____ 38. **infallible**   a) incapable of error   b) accident-prone   c) human   d) wild

_____ 39. **regress**   a) make progress   b) restrict   c) return to previous behavior   d) adjust

_____ 40. **berate**   a) urge   b) criticize   c) branch off   d) lie

_____ 41. **charlatan**   a) impostor   b) actor   c) business investor   d) one who wastes

_____ 42. **proliferation**   a) support   b) research   c) removal   d) rapid spread

_____ 43. **corroborate**   a) imitate   b) support with proof   c) plot   d) study carefully

_____ 44. **diverge**   a) branch off   b) uncover   c) escape   d) hide

_____ 45. **irrevocable**   a) not likely   b) unable to be cancelled   c) sacred
   d) existing everywhere

_____ 46. **precipitate**   a) hold   b) become different   c) plan   d) bring on

_____ 47. **dormant**   a) inactive   b) lively   c) inside   d) troubled

_____ 48. **disseminate**   a) act as   b) scatter widely   c) reveal   d) produce

_____ 49. **hoist**   a) hold onto   b) bury   c) let go of   d) lift

_____ 50. **illicit**   a) illegal   b) secret   c) unspoken   d) public

SCORE: (Number correct) _____ × 2 = _____ %

Unit One: *Posttest*

In the space provided, write the letter of the choice that is closest in meaning to the **boldfaced** word.

_____ 1. **dormant**   **a)** inside   **b)** lively   **c)** inactive   **d)** troubled

_____ 2. **dexterous**   **a)** skinny   **b)** young   **c)** accidental   **d)** skillful

_____ 3. **relinquish**   **a)** give up   **b)** gather   **c)** criticize   **d)** enjoy

_____ 4. **subsidize**   **a)** lift up   **b)** support financially   **c)** fall over   **d)** calculate

_____ 5. **gregarious**   **a)** sociable   **b)** depressed   **c)** wordy   **d)** religious

_____ 6. **corroborate**   **a)** plot   **b)** support with proof   **c)** imitate   **d)** study carefully

_____ 7. **despondent**   **a)** encouraged   **b)** tired   **c)** depressed   **d)** well-behaved

_____ 8. **zealot**   **a)** dictator   **b)** person devoted to a cause   **c)** casual person   **d)** leader

_____ 9. **optimum**   **a)** heaviest   **b)** brightest   **c)** highest   **d)** most favorable

_____ 10. **collaborate**   **a)** respect   **b)** work together   **c)** search   **d)** work hard

_____ 11. **berate**   **a)** lie   **b)** urge   **c)** criticize   **d)** branch off

_____ 12. **ostentatious**   **a)** showy   **b)** courageous   **c)** lazy   **d)** playfully witty

_____ 13. **instigate**   **a)** prepare   **b)** investigate   **c)** stir to action   **d)** suppress

_____ 14. **zenith**   **a)** cure-all   **b)** authority   **c)** drawback   **d)** peak

_____ 15. **ambiguous**   **a)** widespread   **b)** not clear   **c)** under   **d)** too large

_____ 16. **scrupulous**   **a)** sociable   **b)** careless   **c)** clean   **d)** conscientious

_____ 17. **detriment**   **a)** silence   **b)** something damaging   **c)** failure   **d)** outward behavior

_____ 18. **euphoric**   **a)** overjoyed   **b)** depressed   **c)** lonely   **d)** undecided

_____ 19. **dissident**   **a)** political supporter   **b)** candidate   **c)** visitor   **d)** one who disagrees

_____ 20. **rudimentary**   **a)** planned   **b)** partial   **c)** elementary   **d)** rude

_____ 21. **disseminate**   **a)** reveal   **b)** scatter widely   **c)** act as   **d)** produce

_____ 22. **fritter**   **a)** waste   **b)** prove   **c)** wander   **d)** collect

_____ 23. **vicarious**   **a)** inactive   **b)** occasional   **c)** experienced indirectly   **d)** lively

_____ 24. **venerate**   **a)** create   **b)** respect   **c)** make unfriendly   **d)** protect

_____ 25. **estrange**   **a)** state again   **b)** enter   **c)** keep away   **d)** depart

(Continues on next page)

_____ 26. **irrevocable**   a) sacred   b) unable to be cancelled   c) not likely   d) existing everywhere

_____ 27. **inane**   a) silly   b) brilliant   c) causing pain   d) measurable

_____ 28. **sensory**   a) on the surface   b) of the senses   c) sensible   d) in the mind

_____ 29. **resilient**   a) able to recover quickly   b) heavy   c) strong   d) light

_____ 30. **infallible**   a) accident-prone   b) wild   c) human   d) incapable of error

_____ 31. **juxtapose**   a) remove   b) place side by side   c) replace   d) imagine

_____ 32. **regress**   a) make progress   b) restrict   c) return to previous behavior   d) adjust

_____ 33. **charlatan**   a) one who wastes   b) actor   c) business investor   d) imposter

_____ 34. **squelch**   a) make fun of   b) stretch   c) suppress   d) approve

_____ 35. **lethargy**   a) highest point   b) strength   c) hunger   d) lack of energy

_____ 36. **ubiquitous**   a) existing everywhere   b) all-knowing   c) all-powerful   d) perfect

_____ 37. **proliferation**   a) removal   b) research   c) support   d) rapid spread

_____ 38. **discretion**   a) independence   b) gladness   c) slyness   d) tact

_____ 39. **inadvertent**   a) near   b) not for sale   c) unintentional   d) distant

_____ 40. **diverge**   a) hide   b) branch off   c) uncover   d) escape

_____ 41. **scoff**   a) impress   b) inquire   c) make fun of   d) show off

_____ 42. **precipitate**   a) bring on   b) become different   c) plan   d) hold

_____ 43. **retrospect**   a) expecting   b) looking back   c) removal   d) repetition

_____ 44. **sporadic**   a) tiny   b) particular   c) occasional   d) wasteful

_____ 45. **maudlin**   a) clever   b) sentimental   c) useful   d) kind

_____ 46. **embellish**   a) decorate   b) hide   c) remove   d) keep

_____ 47. **illicit**   a) secret   b) illegal   c) unspoken   d) public

_____ 48. **impetuous**   a) calm   b) lazy   c) impulsive   d) teasing

_____ 49. **hoist**   a) lift   b) let go of   c) bury   d) hold onto

_____ 50. **facetious**   a) ill-mannered   b) careless   c) joking   d) depressed

---

SCORE: (Number correct) _____ × 2 = _____ %

Name: _____

Unit Two: *Pretest*

In the space provided, write the letter of the choice that is closest in meaning to the **boldfaced** word.

_____ 1. **solace**   **a)** relaxation   **b)** comfort   **c)** sleep   **d)** comedy

_____ 2. **fortuitous**   **a)** lucky   **b)** sad   **c)** having never happened before   **d)** brave

_____ 3. **impeccable**   **a)** built-in   **b)** unnecessary   **c)** mischievous   **d)** faultless

_____ 4. **sham**   **a)** type   **b)** imitation   **c)** disturbance   **d)** belief

_____ 5. **liaison**   **a)** reference   **b)** plan   **c)** go-between   **d)** accusation

_____ 6. **equivocate**   **a)** be vague on purpose   **b)** dedicate   **c)** approve   **d)** agree

_____ 7. **predisposed**   **a)** against   **b)** reluctant to speak   **c)** undecided   **d)** tending beforehand

_____ 8. **solicitous**   **a)** trying to impress   **b)** sitting   **c)** showing concern   **d)** negative

_____ 9. **propensity**   **a)** relation   **b)** job   **c)** tendency   **d)** hobby

_____ 10. **reprehensible** **a)** blameworthy   **b)** well-filled   **c)** affordable   **d)** admirable

_____ 11. **vociferous**   **a)** vicious   **b)** talented   **c)** noisy   **d)** busy

_____ 12. **grievous**   **a)** funny   **b)** boring   **c)** impressive   **d)** causing pain

_____ 13. **attrition**   **a)** becoming fewer   **b)** connection   **c)** multiplying   **d)** imitation

_____ 14. **reticent**   **a)** forgiving   **b)** sad   **c)** reluctant to speak   **d)** contrary to reason

_____ 15. **robust**   **a)** extremely careful   **b)** vigorous   **c)** tall   **d)** loyal

_____ 16. **circumvent**   **a)** avoid   **b)** fail to notice   **c)** distribute   **d)** socialize

_____ 17. **cohesive**   **a)** slippery   **b)** risky   **c)** separating   **d)** sticking together

_____ 18. **sanction**   **a)** present   **b)** prepare   **c)** authorize   **d)** free from a difficulty

_____ 19. **inundate**   **a)** delay   **b)** flood   **c)** swallow   **d)** approve

_____ 20. **oblivious**   **a)** courageous   **b)** unaware   **c)** quiet   **d)** reliable

_____ 21. **inquisitive**   **a)** cheerful   **b)** nervous   **c)** curious   **d)** in pain

_____ 22. **tenet**   **a)** principle   **b)** apartment dweller   **c)** disadvantage   **d)** peculiarity

_____ 23. **depreciate**   **a)** set free   **b)** come forth   **c)** support   **d)** fall in value

_____ 24. **relegate**   **a)** bring back into use   **b)** assign to a lesser place   **c)** blend   **d)** raise

_____ 25. **bolster**   **a)** support   **b)** protect   **c)** protest   **d)** hide

(Continues on next page)

_____ 26. **terse**   **a)** nervous   **b)** sad   **c)** brief   **d)** cool

_____ 27. **replete**   **a)** unclear   **b)** well-filled   **c)** finished   **d)** empty

_____ 28. **sedentary**   **a)** sitting   **b)** excessive   **c)** harmless   **d)** repeated

_____ 29. **indiscriminate**   **a)** self-centered   **b)** especially generous   **c)** painful
     d) not choosing carefully

_____ 30. **nebulous**   **a)** contrary to reason   **b)** unclear   **c)** complete   **d)** calm

_____ 31. **raucous**   **a)** unfriendly   **b)** spacious   **c)** disorderly   **d)** stubborn

_____ 32. **autonomy**   **a)** independence   **b)** personal risk   **c)** transportation   **d)** group

_____ 33. **tenacious**   **a)** undecided   **b)** social   **c)** holding firmly   **d)** nervous

_____ 34. **utopia**   **a)** remedy   **b)** strong desire   **c)** master plan   **d)** perfect place

_____ 35. **recourse**   **a)** changed direction   **b)** source of help   **c)** possible event   **d)** class

_____ 36. **reiterate**   **a)** repeat   **b)** begin again   **c)** motivate   **d)** decide

_____ 37. **mandate**   **a)** mood   **b)** government   **c)** voters' wishes   **d)** record

_____ 38. **bureaucratic**   **a)** excited   **b)** mixed   **c)** unthinking   **d)** insisting on the rules

_____ 39. **ostracize**   **a)** exclude   **b)** prepare   **c)** scold   **d)** decide on

_____ 40. **tantamount to**   **a)** highest   **b)** the same as   **c)** beside   **d)** near

_____ 41. **prolific**   **a)** wise   **b)** overly cautious   **c)** fertile   **d)** holding firmly

_____ 42. **superfluous**   **a)** extra   **b)** unclear   **c)** useful   **d)** ahead

_____ 43. **exonerate**   **a)** encourage   **b)** condemn   **c)** hide   **d)** free from blame

_____ 44. **indigenous**   **a)** underground   **b)** native   **c)** following established rules   **d)** distant

_____ 45. **contingency**   **a)** contest   **b)** disapproval   **c)** theory   **d)** possibility

_____ 46. **reinstate**   **a)** make more severe   **b)** suggest   **c)** restore   **d)** visit

_____ 47. **incongruous**   **a)** not noticeable   **b)** inborn   **c)** inconsistent   **d)** gathered together

_____ 48. **egocentric**   **a)** unbalanced   **b)** circular   **c)** square   **d)** self-centered

_____ 49. **clandestine**   **a)** well-lit   **b)** secret   **c)** noble   **d)** harmless

_____ 50. **liability**   **a)** drawback   **b)** hatred   **c)** favor   **d)** indirect remark

---

**SCORE:** (Number correct) _____ × 2 = _____ %

Unit Two: *Posttest*

In the space provided, write the letter of the choice that is closest in meaning to the **boldfaced** word.

_____ 1. **propensity**   a) relation   b) job   c) tendency   d) hobby

_____ 2. **raucous**   a) stubborn   b) disorderly   c) spacious   d) unfriendly

_____ 3. **contingency**   a) possibility   b) disapproval   c) theory   d) contest

_____ 4. **vociferous**   a) busy   b) talented   c) noisy   d) vicious

_____ 5. **recourse**   a) changed direction   b) source of help   c) possible event   d) class

_____ 6. **fortuitous**   a) brave   b) sad   c) having never happened before   d) lucky

_____ 7. **depreciate**   a) set free   b) fall in value   c) support   d) come forth

_____ 8. **egocentric**   a) unbalanced   b) self-centered   c) square   d) circular

_____ 9. **robust**   a) extremely careful   b) loyal   c) tall   d) vigorous

_____ 10. **liaison**   a) accusation   b) plan   c) go-between   d) reference

_____ 11. **reprehensible**   a) admirable   b) well-filled   c) blameworthy   d) affordable

_____ 12. **bolster**   a) support   b) protest   c) protect   d) hide

_____ 13. **inquisitive**   a) in pain   b) cheerful   c) nervous   d) curious

_____ 14. **solicitous**   a) trying to impress   b) negative   c) showing concern   d) sitting

_____ 15. **grievous**   a) funny   b) boring   c) impressive   d) causing pain

_____ 16. **reiterate**   a) repeat   b) motivate   c) begin again   d) decide

_____ 17. **autonomy**   a) transportation   b) personal risk   c) independence   d) group

_____ 18. **sanction**   a) authorize   b) prepare   c) present   d) free from a difficulty

_____ 19. **reticent**   a) forgiving   b) sad   c) reluctant to speak   d) contrary to reason

_____ 20. **ostracize**   a) scold   b) prepare   c) decide on   d) exclude

_____ 21. **terse**   a) brief   b) sad   c) nervous   d) cool

_____ 22. **prolific**   a) overly cautious   b) wise   c) fertile   d) holding firmly

_____ 23. **superfluous**   a) ahead   b) unclear   c) extra   d) useful

_____ 24. **solace**   a) sleep   b) comfort   c) relaxation   d) comedy

_____ 25. **attrition**   a) becoming fewer   b) multiplying   c) connection   d) imitation

(Continues on next page)

_____ 26. **inundate**   **a)** delay   **b)** flood   **c)** swallow   **d)** approve

_____ 27. **utopia**   **a)** master plan   **b)** strong desire   **c)** remedy   **d)** perfect place

_____ 28. **relegate**   **a)** bring back into use   **b)** assign to a lesser place   **c)** blend   **d)** raise

_____ 29. **impeccable**   **a)** unnecessary   **b)** built-in   **c)** mischievous   **d)** faultless

_____ 30. **replete**   **a)** empty   **b)** unclear   **c)** well-filled   **d)** finished

_____ 31. **nebulous**   **a)** contrary to reason   **b)** unclear   **c)** complete   **d)** calm

_____ 32. **equivocate**   **a)** agree   **b)** dedicate   **c)** approve   **d)** be vague on purpose

_____ 33. **bureaucratic**   **a)** unthinking   **b)** excited   **c)** mixed   **d)** insisting on the rules

_____ 34. **sedentary**   **a)** sitting   **b)** excessive   **c)** harmless   **d)** repeated

_____ 35. **tantamount to** **a)** beside   **b)** near   **c)** highest   **d)** the same as

_____ 36. **liability**   **a)** drawback   **b)** favor   **c)** hatred   **d)** indirect remark

_____ 37. **circumvent**   **a)** socialize   **b)** avoid   **c)** distribute   **d)** fail to notice

_____ 38. **exonerate**   **a)** encourage   **b)** condemn   **c)** hide   **d)** free from blame

_____ 39. **indigenous**   **a)** native   **b)** underground   **c)** following established rules   **d)** distant

_____ 40. **predisposed**   **a)** undecided   **b)** reluctant to speak   **c)** against   **d)** tending beforehand

_____ 41. **tenet**   **a)** peculiarity   **b)** principle   **c)** disadvantage   **d)** apartment dweller

_____ 42. **mandate**   **a)** record   **b)** voters' wishes   **c)** government   **d)** mood

_____ 43. **tenacious**   **a)** undecided   **b)** social   **c)** holding firmly   **d)** nervous

_____ 44. **reinstate**   **a)** make more severe   **b)** restore   **c)** suggest   **d)** visit

_____ 45. **incongruous**   **a)** not noticeable   **b)** gathered together   **c)** inconsistent   **d)** inborn

_____ 46. **oblivious**   **a)** courageous   **b)** unaware   **c)** quiet   **d)** reliable

_____ 47. **clandestine**   **a)** well-lit   **b)** harmless   **c)** noble   **d)** secret

_____ 48. **sham**   **a)** belief   **b)** type   **c)** imitation   **d)** disturbance

_____ 49. **cohesive**   **a)** sticking together   **b)** risky   **c)** separating   **d)** slippery

_____ 50. **indiscriminate** **a)** not choosing carefully   **b)** especially generous   **c)** painful
             d) self-centered

SCORE: (Number correct) _____ × 2 = _____ %

170

Name: _____

Unit Three: *Pretest*

In the space provided, write the letter of the choice that is closest in meaning to the **boldfaced** word.

_____ 1. **inclusive** a) surrounding b) adding c) including much d) reducing

_____ 2. **preposterous** a) unprepared b) ridiculous c) proud d) about to happen

_____ 3. **advocate** a) surround b) fascinate c) subtract d) support

_____ 4. **idiosyncrasy** a) secret plot b) crazy idea c) personal peculiarity d) mockery

_____ 5. **jurisdiction** a) range of authority b) exact copy c) law d) secret plot

_____ 6. **antipathy** a) disease b) difficult situation c) high regard d) strong dislike

_____ 7. **imminent** a) recent b) about to happen c) current d) late

_____ 8. **emancipate** a) redirect b) ridicule c) display d) set free

_____ 9. **precarious** a) risky b) crowded c) careless d) distant

_____ 10. **impede** a) wipe out b) stretch c) get in the way of d) urge

_____ 11. **austere** a) wealthy b) plain c) complex d) far

_____ 12. **travesty** a) mockery b) copy c) campaign d) ill will

_____ 13. **notorious** a) too bold b) written c) known widely but unfavorably
d) lacking skill

_____ 14. **facsimile** a) authority b) copy c) comparison d) accusation

_____ 15. **grotesque** a) harmless b) unclear c) dirty d) distorted

_____ 16. **perfunctory** a) unenthusiastic b) troubled c) on time d) well-prepared

_____ 17. **mesmerize** a) wipe out b) control c) hypnotize d) slow down

_____ 18. **provocative** a) careful b) able to improve c) inconsistent d) arousing interest

_____ 19. **esoteric** a) public b) uniform c) well-written d) understood by few

_____ 20. **metamorphosis** a) journey b) change c) secret plot d) fantasy

_____ 21. **verbose** a) wordy b) active c) noisy d) forceful

_____ 22. **connoisseur** a) one who likes to suffer b) egotist c) expert d) painter

_____ 23. **contrite** a) indecent b) sorry c) lacking confidence d) careful

_____ 24. **lucid** a) clear b) generous in forgiving c) careful d) bold

_____ 25. **conspiracy** a) robbery b) revenge c) project d) secret plot

(Continues on next page)

_____ 26. **germane**   **a)** evil   **b)** chief   **c)** relevant   **d)** growing

_____ 27. **superficially**   **a)** strictly   **b)** carefully   **c)** totally   **d)** hastily

_____ 28. **plight**   **a)** difficult situation   **b)** minor weakness   **c)** environment   **d)** travel

_____ 29. **distraught**   **a)** educated   **b)** too noticeable   **c)** troubled   **d)** rehearsed

_____ 30. **symmetrical**   **a)** extra   **b)** balanced   **c)** frightening   **d)** colorful

_____ 31. **standardize**   **a)** allow   **b)** simplify   **c)** limit   **d)** make uniform

_____ 32. **encompass**   **a)** include   **b)** draw   **c)** separate   **d)** purchase

_____ 33. **homogeneous**   **a)** pure   **b)** smooth   **c)** uniform   **d)** separate

_____ 34. **stringent**   **a)** dry   **b)** strict   **c)** loose   **d)** long

_____ 35. **adept**   **a)** forceful   **b)** exact   **c)** balanced   **d)** skilled

_____ 36. **eradicate**   **a)** wipe out   **b)** scold   **c)** restore   **d)** hold onto

_____ 37. **sordid**   **a)** slow   **b)** unprepared   **c)** morally low   **d)** injured

_____ 38. **entrepreneur**   **a)** lawyer   **b)** business investor   **c)** college educator   **d)** police officer

_____ 39. **stint**   **a)** period of work   **b)** sequence of events   **c)** exercise   **d)** stunt

_____ 40. **presumptuous**   **a)** indecent   **b)** lacking standards of selection   **c)** nervous   **d)** too bold

_____ 41. **meticulous**   **a)** broken-down   **b)** curious   **c)** careful and exact   **d)** irregular

_____ 42. **repugnant**   **a)** scornful   **b)** offensive   **c)** harmful   **d)** impressive

_____ 43. **foible**   **a)** character flaw   **b)** ambition   **c)** noble quality   **d)** accident

_____ 44. **recrimination**   **a)** environment   **b)** ambition   **c)** robbery   **d)** countercharge

_____ 45. **magnanimous**   **a)** nameless   **b)** proud   **c)** generous in forgiving   **d)** lacking standards

_____ 46. **exhort**   **a)** strongly urge   **b)** travel   **c)** escape   **d)** hint

_____ 47. **rancor**   **a)** pride   **b)** fear   **c)** strong desire   **d)** ill will

_____ 48. **innocuous**   **a)** delightful   **b)** harmless   **c)** dangerous   **d)** disappointing

_____ 49. **flamboyant**   **a)** talkative   **b)** courageous   **c)** showy   **d)** exact

_____ 50. **masochist**   **a)** one who likes to suffer   **b)** egotist   **c)** fan   **d)** one who expects the worst

_____

SCORE: (Number correct) _____ × 2 = _____ %

Unit Three: *Posttest*

In the space provided, write the letter of the choice that is closest in meaning to the **boldfaced** word.

_____ 1. **contrite**   **a)** lacking confidence   **b)** indecent   **c)** sorry   **d)** careful

_____ 2. **emancipate**   **a)** redirect   **b)** ridicule   **c)** display   **d)** set free

_____ 3. **esoteric**   **a)** understood by few   **b)** uniform   **c)** well-written   **d)** public

_____ 4. **entrepreneur**   **a)** police officer   **b)** lawyer   **c)** business investor   **d)** college educator

_____ 5. **magnanimous**   **a)** generous in forgiving   **b)** nameless   **c)** proud   **d)** lacking standards

_____ 6. **precarious**   **a)** careless   **b)** crowded   **c)** risky   **d)** distant

_____ 7. **masochist**   **a)** one who likes to suffer   **b)** egotist   **c)** fan
      d) one who expects the worst

_____ 8. **impede**   **a)** urge   **b)** stretch   **c)** get in the way of   **d)** wipe out

_____ 9. **lucid**   **a)** careful   **b)** bold   **c)** generous in forgiving   **d)** clear

_____ 10. **sordid**   **a)** injured   **b)** unprepared   **c)** morally low   **d)** slow

_____ 11. **preposterous**   **a)** unprepared   **b)** ridiculous   **c)** proud   **d)** about to happen

_____ 12. **mesmerize**   **a)** wipe out   **b)** hypnotize   **c)** control   **d)** slow down

_____ 13. **exhort**   **a)** strongly urge   **b)** escape   **c)** hint   **d)** travel

_____ 14. **advocate**   **a)** fascinate   **b)** support   **c)** subtract   **d)** surround

_____ 15. **inclusive**   **a)** including much   **b)** adding   **c)** surrounding   **d)** reducing

_____ 16. **connoisseur**   **a)** one who likes to suffer   **b)** egotist   **c)** expert   **d)** painter

_____ 17. **stringent**   **a)** long   **b)** dry   **c)** strict   **d)** loose

_____ 18. **perfunctory**   **a)** troubled   **b)** unenthusiastic   **c)** on time   **d)** well-prepared

_____ 19. **provocative**   **a)** inconsistent   **b)** able to improve   **c)** careful   **d)** arousing interest

_____ 20. **rancor**   **a)** ill will   **b)** fear   **c)** strong desire   **d)** pride

_____ 21. **conspiracy**   **a)** project   **b)** robbery   **c)** revenge   **d)** secret plot

_____ 22. **idiosyncrasy**   **a)** fault   **b)** crazy idea   **c)** personal peculiarity   **d)** mockery

_____ 23. **adept**   **a)** exact   **b)** forceful   **c)** balanced   **d)** skilled

_____ 24. **innocuous**   **a)** dangerous   **b)** harmless   **c)** delightful   **d)** disappointing

_____ 25. **austere**   **a)** complex   **b)** far   **c)** wealthy   **d)** plain

(Continues on next page)

_____ 26. **symmetrical**   a) frightening   b) balanced   c) extra   d) colorful

_____ 27. **standardize**   a) make uniform   b) allow   c) simplify   d) limit

_____ 28. **verbose**   a) noisy   b) active   c) wordy   d) forceful

_____ 29. **recrimination**   a) environment   b) robbery   c) countercharge   d) ambition

_____ 30. **encompass**   a) purchase   b) draw   c) separate   d) include

_____ 31. **grotesque**   a) harmless   b) unclear   c) dirty   d) distorted

_____ 32. **jurisdiction**   a) range of authority   b) exact copy   c) secret plot   d) law

_____ 33. **travesty**   a) campaign   b) ill will   c) mockery   d) copy

_____ 34. **stint**   a) period of work   b) sequence of events   c) exercise   d) stunt

_____ 35. **presumptuous**   a) nervous   b) lacking standards of selection   c) indecent   d) too bold

_____ 36. **meticulous**   a) broken-down   b) careful and exact   c) curious   d) irregular

_____ 37. **distraught**   a) troubled   b) rehearsed   c) educated   d) too noticeable

_____ 38. **repugnant**   a) harmful   b) offensive   c) scornful   d) impressive

_____ 39. **metamorphosis**   a) secret plot   b) journey   c) change   d) fantasy

_____ 40. **foible**   a) character flaw   b) ambition   c) noble quality   d) accident

_____ 41. **antipathy**   a) difficult situation   b) high regard   c) disease   d) strong dislike

_____ 42. **eradicate**   a) wipe out   b) restore   c) scold   d) hold onto

_____ 43. **plight**   a) travel   b) difficult situation   c) minor weakness   d) environment

_____ 44. **facsimile**   a) accusation   b) authority   c) copy   d) comparison

_____ 45. **superficially**   a) strictly   b) carefully   c) totally   d) hastily

_____ 46. **imminent**   a) about to happen   b) recent   c) current   d) late

_____ 47. **flamboyant**   a) showy   b) exact   c) talkative   d) courageous

_____ 48. **germane**   a) evil   b) chief   c) relevant   d) growing

_____ 49. **homogeneous**   a) separate   b) uniform   c) smooth   d) pure

_____ 50. **notorious**   a) written   b) lacking skill   c) known widely but unfavorably   d) too bold

SCORE: (Number correct) _____ × 2 = _____ %

Unit Four: *Pretest*

In the space provided, write the letter of the choice that is closest in meaning to the **boldfaced** word.

_____ 1. **integral**   **a)** simple   **b)** beyond what is reasonable   **c)** necessary to the whole
d) one-sided

_____ 2. **commensurate**   **a)** overly valued   **b)** remembered   **c)** secondary   **d)** in proportion

_____ 3. **chide**   **a)** approve   **b)** scold   **c)** joke   **d)** remind

_____ 4. **yen**   **a)** strong desire   **b)** acceptance   **c)** gladness   **d)** dislike

_____ 5. **diabolic**   **a)** excessive   **b)** mischievous   **c)** odd   **d)** wicked

_____ 6. **scenario**   **a)** fiction   **b)** comparison   **c)** imagined sequence   **d)** scenic view

_____ 7. **coalition**   **a)** union   **b)** cure-all   **c)** injury   **d)** conduct

_____ 8. **noxious**   **a)** unnecessary   **b)** excessive   **c)** disorganized   **d)** harmful to health

_____ 9. **connotation**   **a)** disapproval   **b)** law   **c)** suggested meaning   **d)** standard for judgment

_____ 10. **dilapidated**   **a)** ill-fed   **b)** broken-down   **c)** stubborn   **d)** improved

_____ 11. **panacea**   **a)** cure-all   **b)** state of uncertainty   **c)** reward   **d)** false medicine

_____ 12. **utilitarian**   **a)** useless   **b)** built-in   **c)** practical   **d)** beautiful

_____ 13. **deplore**   **a)** command   **b)** disapprove of   **c)** encourage   **d)** prevent

_____ 14. **atrophy**   **a)** weaken   **b)** reward   **c)** expand   **d)** strengthen

_____ 15. **unprecedented**   **a)** overly noticeable   **b)** without authority   **c)** unexpected
d) having never happened before

_____ 16. **mitigate**   **a)** make worse   **b)** make less severe   **c)** remove   **d)** hide

_____ 17. **deprivation**   **a)** lack of a basic necessity   **b)** depth   **c)** disapproval   **d)** privacy

_____ 18. **imperative**   **a)** thoughtful   **b)** more harmful than at first evident   **c)** likely   **d)** necessary

_____ 19. **objective**   **a)** useful   **b)** poorly supported   **c)** based on facts   **d)** emotional

_____ 20. **exacerbate**   **a)** make worse   **b)** remove   **c)** bring closer   **d)** strengthen

_____ 21. **rejuvenate**   **a)** set free   **b)** grow   **c)** refresh   **d)** make easier

_____ 22. **exorbitant**   **a)** absorbent   **b)** excessive   **c)** quarrelsome   **d)** well-timed

_____ 23. **decorum**   **a)** correctness in manners   **b)** talent   **c)** repayment   **d)** indirect remark

_____ 24. **facilitate**   **a)** approve   **b)** serve   **c)** make easier   **d)** clear from blame

_____ 25. **synchronize**   **a)** spread throughout   **b)** separate   **c)** reduce   **d)** cause to occur together

(Continues on next page)

_____ 26. **espouse**   a) prolong   b) support   c) delay   d) marry

_____ 27. **extricate**   a) run away   b) confuse   c) free from difficulty   d) complicate

_____ 28. **tenuous**   a) weak   b) boring   c) showy   d) well-supported

_____ 29. **exhilaration**   a) freedom   b) thirst   c) wisdom   d) gladness

_____ 30. **orthodox**   a) firm   b) favorable   c) traditional   d) new

_____ 31. **assimilate**   a) exercise   b) adjust to a culture   c) examine   d) ease the progress of

_____ 32. **inherent**   a) built-in   b) plain   c) common   d) local

_____ 33. **unilateral**   a) late   b) demanding   c) having authority   d) one-sided

_____ 34. **demeanor**   a) choice   b) disguise   c) conduct   d) method

_____ 35. **dissipate**   a) strengthen   b) scatter   c) blame   d) collect

_____ 36. **nonchalant**   a) casual   b) uncertain   c) careful   d) frozen

_____ 37. **denunciation**   a) concern   b) approval   c) manner of speaking   d) act of condemning

_____ 38. **unassuming**   a) slow   b) modest   c) cautious   d) thorough

_____ 39. **indolent**   a) poor   b) about to happen   c) lazy   d) hot

_____ 40. **belligerent**   a) quarrelsome   b) musical   c) most important   d) humble

_____ 41. **proficient**   a) proud   b) wise   c) skilled   d) well-known

_____ 42. **annihilate**   a) guide   b) misunderstand   c) carry out   d) destroy

_____ 43. **criterion**   a) philosophy   b) standard for judgment   c) political theory
d) state of mind

_____ 44. **vindicate**   a) clear from blame   b) ridicule   c) escape   d) formally question

_____ 45. **emanate**   a) go above   b) run through   c) go down   d) come forth

_____ 46. **holistic**   a) democratic   b) secretive   c) emphasizing the whole   d) little-known

_____ 47. **subversive**   a) being a servant   b) acting to overthrow   c) willing
d) planning to build

_____ 48. **staunch**   a) loyal   b) in doubt   c) proud   d) easy to handle

_____ 49. **analogy**   a) original   b) sample   c) summary   d) comparison

_____ 50. **placebo**   a) standard   b) harmless substance used as medicine   c) wish
d) the whole

> *SCORE:* (Number correct) _____ × 2 = _____ %

Unit Four: *Posttest*

In the space provided, write the letter of the choice that is closest in meaning to the **boldfaced** word.

_____ 1. **scenario**   a) scenic view   b) fiction   c) comparison   d) imagined sequence

_____ 2. **dilapidated**   a) improved   b) broken-down   c) ill-fed   d) stubborn

_____ 3. **analogy**   a) summary   b) sample   c) original   d) comparison

_____ 4. **denunciation**   a) act of condemning   b) approval   c) manner of speaking   d) concern

_____ 5. **diabolic**   a) odd   b) mischievous   c) excessive   d) wicked

_____ 6. **staunch**   a) easy to handle   b) loyal   c) proud   d) in doubt

_____ 7. **unprecedented**   a) overly noticeable   b) without authority   c) having never happened before
      d) unexpected

_____ 8. **unassuming**   a) thorough   b) slow   c) modest   d) cautious

_____ 9. **deprivation**   a) lack of a basic necessity   b) disapproval   c) depth   d) privacy

_____ 10. **coalition**   a) injury   b) cure-all   c) union   d) conduct

_____ 11. **mitigate**   a) remove   b) hide   c) make worse   d) make less severe

_____ 12. **integral**   a) one-sided   b) beyond what is reasonable   c) necessary to the whole
      d) simple

_____ 13. **placebo**   a) wish   b) harmless substance used as medicine   c) the whole
      d) standard

_____ 14. **rejuvenate**   a) set free   b) grow   c) refresh   d) make easier

_____ 15. **dissipate**   a) blame   b) scatter   c) strengthen   d) collect

_____ 16. **proficient**   a) skilled   b) proud   c) wise   d) well-known

_____ 17. **decorum**   a) repayment   b) indirect remark   c) correctness in manners   d) talent

_____ 18. **panacea**   a) reward   b) state of uncertainty   c) cure-all   d) false medicine

_____ 19. **demeanor**   a) conduct   b) choice   c) disguise   d) method

_____ 20. **facilitate**   a) make easier   b) serve   c) approve   d) clear from blame

_____ 21. **imperative**   a) likely   b) more harmful than at first evident   c) thoughtful
      d) necessary

_____ 22. **synchronize**   a) spread throughout   b) reduce   c) cause to occur together   d) separate

_____ 23. **commensurate**   a) in proportion   b) secondary   c) remembered   d) overly valued

_____ 24. **utilitarian**   a) built-in   b) practical   c) useless   d) beautiful

_____ 25. **unilateral**   a) having authority   b) one-sided   c) late   d) demanding

(Continues on next page)

_____ 26. **extricate**   a) run away   b) free from difficulty   c) confuse   d) complicate

_____ 27. **objective**   a) emotional   b) poorly supported   c) based on facts   d) useful

_____ 28. **tenuous**   a) showy   b) boring   c) weak   d) well-supported

_____ 29. **nonchalant**   a) casual   b) uncertain   c) careful   d) frozen

_____ 30. **exhilaration**   a) wisdom   b) thirst   c) freedom   d) gladness

_____ 31. **subversive**   a) being a servant   b) acting to overthrow   c) willing
d) planning to build

_____ 32. **deplore**   a) encourage   b) prevent   c) command   d) disapprove of

_____ 33. **exacerbate**   a) remove   b) make worse   c) strengthen   d) bring closer

_____ 34. **annihilate**   a) carry out   b) misunderstand   c) guide   d) destroy

_____ 35. **orthodox**   a) new   b) favorable   c) traditional   d) firm

_____ 36. **assimilate**   a) examine   b) adjust to a culture   c) exercise   d) ease the progress of

_____ 37. **inherent**   a) built-in   b) common   c) local   d) plain

_____ 38. **chide**   a) remind   b) approve   c) scold   d) joke

_____ 39. **holistic**   a) emphasizing the whole   b) secretive   c) democratic   d) little-known

_____ 40. **atrophy**   a) expand   b) reward   c) weaken   d) strengthen

_____ 41. **yen**   a) strong desire   b) acceptance   c) dislike   d) gladness

_____ 42. **emanate**   a) go down   b) come forth   c) go above   d) run through

_____ 43. **indolent**   a) lazy   b) about to happen   c) poor   d) hot

_____ 44. **espouse**   a) delay   b) prolong   c) support   d) marry

_____ 45. **belligerent**   a) most important   b) musical   c) quarrelsome   d) humble

_____ 46. **criterion**   a) standard for judgment   b) philosophy   c) state of mind
d) political theory

_____ 47. **connotation**   a) disapproval   b) law   c) standard for judgment   d) suggested meaning

_____ 48. **exorbitant**   a) quarrelsome   b) excessive   c) absorbent   d) well-timed

_____ 49. **vindicate**   a) formally question   b) escape   c) ridicule   d) clear from blame

_____ 50. **noxious**   a) harmful to health   b) disorganized   c) unnecessary   d) excessive

**SCORE:** (Number correct) _____ × 2 = _____ %

178

Unit Five: *Pretest*

In the space provided, write the letter of the choice that is closest in meaning to the **boldfaced** word.

_____ 1. **forestall**   a) prevent   b) predict   c) rent   d) hurry

_____ 2. **retribution**   a) donation   b) looking back   c) evil   d) punishment

_____ 3. **interrogate**   a) put into practice   b) invent   c) formally question   d) blame sharply

_____ 4. **permeate**   a) imitate   b) spread throughout   c) pollute   d) deny the authority of

_____ 5. **insidious**   a) more harmful than at first evident   b) sly
c) more noticeable than desired   d) slow

_____ 6. **insinuate**   a) demand   b) state   c) deny   d) hint

_____ 7. **disparity**   a) sadness   b) inequality   c) blemish   d) similarity

_____ 8. **omnipotent**   a) all-powerful   b) forgiving   c) altogether   d) cure-all

_____ 9. **opportune**   a) generous   b) more important   c) well-timed   d) belittling

_____ 10. **fastidious**   a) not planned   b) attentive to details   c) quick   d) inferior

_____ 11. **heinous**   a) evil   b) mischievous   c) stubborn   d) depressed

_____ 12. **obtrusive**   a) about to happen   b) too near   c) undesirably noticeable   d) shocking

_____ 13. **implement**   a) encourage   b) carry out   c) insult   d) prevent

_____ 14. **discreet**   a) tactful   b) intense   c) knowledgeable   d) open

_____ 15. **inference**   a) rumor   b) meeting   c) assumption   d) speech

_____ 16. **flout**   a) beat   b) surprise   c) suggest   d) disobey

_____ 17. **impromptu**   a) forceful   b) unplanned   c) delayed   d) on time

_____ 18. **transgress**   a) follow   b) round out   c) travel   d) break a law

_____ 19. **expedite**   a) speed up   b) explore   c) sadden   d) elect

_____ 20. **innuendo**   a) threat   b) challenge   c) impression   d) indirect remark

_____ 21. **redeem**   a) show to be true   b) restore to favor   c) select   d) ignore

_____ 22. **vehement**   a) forceful   b) wicked   c) rude   d) calm

_____ 23. **auspicious**   a) threatening   b) lazy   c) favorable   d) not trusting

_____ 24. **subordinate**   a) irritating   b) inferior   c) quiet   d) chief

_____ 25. **rebuke**   a) compromise   b) fix   c) scold   d) admire

(Continues on next page)

_____ 26. **validate**   a) dislike   b) prove   c) discover   d) notice

_____ 27. **macabre**   a) frightful   b) depressed   c) cheerful   d) common

_____ 28. **deride**   a) repair   b) take   c) ridicule   d) ease

_____ 29. **fabricate**   a) misinterpret   b) put away   c) clothe   d) invent

_____ 30. **misconstrue**   a) misunderstand   b) dislike   c) reject   d) admire

_____ 31. **derogatory**   a) healthful   b) unable to be repaired   c) belittling   d) proud

_____ 32. **turbulent**   a) ambitious   b) wildly disturbed   c) mixed   d) fast

_____ 33. **impending**   a) about to happen   b) illegal   c) historical   d) usual

_____ 34. **paramount**   a) dramatic   b) disturbed   c) unknown   d) chief

_____ 35. **platitude**   a) prediction   b) commonplace remark   c) highest point   d) noisy disorder

_____ 36. **spontaneous**   a) cheerful   b) full of wild disorder   c) done on impulse   d) fiery

_____ 37. **adroit**   a) skillful   b) funny   c) conscientious   d) easy to discipline

_____ 38. **contention**   a) guard   b) meeting   c) rise   d) claim

_____ 39. **stigma**   a) prediction   b) disgrace   c) claim   d) peak

_____ 40. **repudiate**   a) deny the truth of   b) compliment   c) hinder   d) state again

_____ 41. **irreparable**   a) untrue   b) unable to create   c) able to recover quickly   d) unable to be repaired

_____ 42. **pinnacle**   a) choice   b) peak   c) blemish   d) opposite

_____ 43. **emulate**   a) be tardy   b) misunderstand   c) imitate   d) prepare

_____ 44. **abrasive**   a) rough   b) friendly   c) mild   d) foolish

_____ 45. **docile**   a) violent   b) early   c) easy to discipline   d) irritating

_____ 46. **antithesis**   a) disorder   b) theory   c) effect   d) opposite

_____ 47. **incapacitate**   a) disable   b) allow   c) increase   d) fight

_____ 48. **admonish**   a) imitate   b) scold   c) publicize   d) frighten

_____ 49. **prognosis**   a) hope   b) memory   c) opposite   d) prediction

_____ 50. **culmination**   a) country   b) highest point   c) edge   d) bottom

SCORE: (Number correct) _____ × 2 = _____ %

Unit Five: *Posttest*

In the space provided, write the letter of the choice that is closest in meaning to the **boldfaced** word.

____ 1. **misconstrue**   a) dislike   b) misunderstand   c) reject   d) admire

____ 2. **irreparable**   a) able to recover quickly   b) unable to create   c) untrue
d) unable to be repaired

____ 3. **rebuke**   a) compromise   b) fix   c) scold   d) admire

____ 4. **retribution**   a) punishment   b) donation   c) looking back   d) evil

____ 5. **fastidious**   a) not planned   b) quick   c) attentive to details   d) inferior

____ 6. **forestall**   a) prevent   b) predict   c) rent   d) hurry

____ 7. **obtrusive**   a) shocking   b) too near   c) undesirably noticeable   d) about to happen

____ 8. **disparity**   a) blemish   b) similarity   c) sadness   d) inequality

____ 9. **prognosis**   a) prediction   b) memory   c) opposite   d) hope

____ 10. **contention**   a) guard   b) meeting   c) claim   d) rise

____ 11. **inference**   a) rumor   b) assumption   c) meeting   d) speech

____ 12. **derogatory**   a) belittling   b) healthful   c) unable to be repaired   d) proud

____ 13. **expedite**   a) elect   b) speed up   c) explore   d) sadden

____ 14. **interrogate**   a) put into practice   b) invent   c) formally question   d) blame sharply

____ 15. **antithesis**   a) disorder   b) opposite   c) effect   d) theory

____ 16. **impending**   a) illegal   b) historical   c) usual   d) about to happen

____ 17. **impromptu**   a) forceful   b) unplanned   c) delayed   d) on time

____ 18. **redeem**   a) restore to favor   b) show to be true   c) select   d) ignore

____ 19. **heinous**   a) stubborn   b) mischievous   c) evil   d) depressed

____ 20. **permeate**   a) imitate   b) spread throughout   c) deny the authority of   d) pollute

____ 21. **abrasive**   a) foolish   b) friendly   c) mild   d) rough

____ 22. **auspicious**   a) threatening   b) lazy   c) favorable   d) not trusting

____ 23. **opportune**   a) generous   b) more important   c) belittling   d) well-timed

____ 24. **emulate**   a) imitate   b) be tardy   c) misunderstand   d) prepare

____ 25. **flout**   a) beat   b) surprise   c) disobey   d) suggest

(Continues on next page)

_____ 26. **culmination**   **a)** country   **b)** highest point   **c)** edge   **d)** bottom

_____ 27. **deride**   **a)** repair   **b)** take   **c)** ease   **d)** ridicule

_____ 28. **insidious**   **a)** sly   **b)** more harmful than at first evident   **c)** more noticeable than desired
d) slow

_____ 29. **implement**   **a)** encourage   **b)** insult   **c)** carry out   **d)** prevent

_____ 30. **admonish**   **a)** scold   **b)** imitate   **c)** publicize   **d)** frighten

_____ 31. **fabricate**   **a)** misinterpret   **b)** put away   **c)** clothe   **d)** invent

_____ 32. **turbulent**   **a)** wildly disturbed   **b)** ambitious   **c)** mixed   **d)** fast

_____ 33. **validate**   **a)** notice   **b)** prove   **c)** discover   **d)** dislike

_____ 34. **docile**   **a)** violent   **b)** early   **c)** easy to discipline   **d)** irritating

_____ 35. **paramount**   **a)** dramatic   **b)** chief   **c)** disturbed   **d)** unknown

_____ 36. **discreet**   **a)** tactful   **b)** intense   **c)** open   **d)** knowledgeable

_____ 37. **macabre**   **a)** depressed   **b)** frightful   **c)** cheerful   **d)** common

_____ 38. **platitude**   **a)** prediction   **b)** commonplace remark   **c)** highest point
d) noisy disorder

_____ 39. **omnipotent**   **a)** forgiving   **b)** altogether   **c)** cure-all   **d)** all-powerful

_____ 40. **repudiate**   **a)** deny the truth of   **b)** compliment   **c)** hinder   **d)** state again

_____ 41. **innuendo**   **a)** impression   **b)** challenge   **c)** threat   **d)** indirect remark

_____ 42. **subordinate**   **a)** irritating   **b)** chief   **c)** quiet   **d)** inferior

_____ 43. **stigma**   **a)** prediction   **b)** disgrace   **c)** claim   **d)** peak

_____ 44. **transgress**   **a)** round out   **b)** follow   **c)** travel   **d)** break a law

_____ 45. **spontaneous**   **a)** cheerful   **b)** full of wild disorder   **c)** done on impulse   **d)** fiery

_____ 46. **incapacitate**   **a)** increase   **b)** allow   **c)** disable   **d)** fight

_____ 47. **vehement**   **a)** forceful   **b)** wicked   **c)** calm   **d)** rude

_____ 48. **adroit**   **a)** easy to discipline   **b)** funny   **c)** skillful   **d)** conscientious

_____ 49. **pinnacle**   **a)** choice   **b)** peak   **c)** blemish   **d)** opposite

_____ 50. **insinuate**   **a)** deny   **b)** demand   **c)** state   **d)** hint

_____
| *SCORE:* (Number correct) _____ × 2 = _____ % |
_____

ADVANCING VOCABULARY SKILLS

Pretest / Posttest

ANSWER SHEET

1. ____	26. ____	51. ____	76. ____
2. ____	27. ____	52. ____	77. ____
3. ____	28. ____	53. ____	78. ____
4. ____	29. ____	54. ____	79. ____
5. ____	30. ____	55. ____	80. ____
6. ____	31. ____	56. ____	81. ____
7. ____	32. ____	57. ____	82. ____
8. ____	33. ____	58. ____	83. ____
9. ____	34. ____	59. ____	84. ____
10. ____	35. ____	60. ____	85. ____
11. ____	36. ____	61. ____	86. ____
12. ____	37. ____	62. ____	87. ____
13. ____	38. ____	63. ____	88. ____
14. ____	39. ____	64. ____	89. ____
15. ____	40. ____	65. ____	90. ____
16. ____	41. ____	66. ____	91. ____
17. ____	42. ____	67. ____	92. ____
18. ____	43. ____	68. ____	93. ____
19. ____	44. ____	69. ____	94. ____
20. ____	45. ____	70. ____	95. ____
21. ____	46. ____	71. ____	96. ____
22. ____	47. ____	72. ____	97. ____
23. ____	48. ____	73. ____	98. ____
24. ____	49. ____	74. ____	99. ____
25. ____	50. ____	75. ____	100. ____

ANSWER KEY

1. d	26. a	51. a	76. a
2. a	27. c	52. b	77. d
3. b	28. a	53. a	78. d
4. d	29. b	54. c	79. b
5. c	30. b	55. d	80. c
6. a	31. c	56. c	81. b
7. d	32. b	57. c	82. a
8. d	33. a	58. a	83. b
9. a	34. c	59. b	84. d
10. d	35. a	60. a	85. b
11. a	36. a	61. b	86. d
12. d	37. d	62. a	87. a
13. b	38. d	63. d	88. a
14. c	39. b	64. b	89. c
15. a	40. a	65. a	90. c
16. d	41. b	66. b	91. a
17. d	42. a	67. c	92. d
18. d	43. d	68. d	93. b
19. a	44. d	69. c	94. a
20. c	45. b	70. d	95. d
21. a	46. a	71. c	96. c
22. b	47. c	72. d	97. d
23. d	48. b	73. b	98. a
24. c	49. a	74. a	99. a
25. a	50. c	75. b	100. d

Posttest

ANSWER KEY

1.	a	26.	c	51.	c	76.	c
2.	b	27.	a	52.	c	77.	c
3.	a	28.	c	53.	d	78.	c
4.	c	29.	d	54.	a	79.	b
5.	b	30.	a	55.	c	80.	d
6.	d	31.	b	56.	b	81.	c
7.	b	32.	d	57.	b	82.	b
8.	d	33.	b	58.	c	83.	d
9.	b	34.	c	59.	b	84.	c
10.	d	35.	d	60.	a	85.	b
11.	a	36.	c	61.	d	86.	a
12.	b	37.	b	62.	d	87.	d
13.	d	38.	c	63.	a	88.	b
14.	c	39.	d	64.	d	89.	b
15.	d	40.	c	65.	d	90.	b
16.	b	41.	b	66.	b	91.	b
17.	a	42.	a	67.	b	92.	b
18.	d	43.	c	68.	a	93.	a
19.	b	44.	b	69.	d	94.	a
20.	a	45.	d	70.	a	95.	c
21.	c	46.	b	71.	d	96.	b
22.	c	47.	b	72.	a	97.	c
23.	c	48.	b	73.	a	98.	c
24.	b	49.	a	74.	c	99.	c
25.	d	50.	a	75.	c	100.	b

Answers to the Pretests and Posttests: ADVANCING VOCABULARY SKILLS

Unit One		Unit Two		Unit Three		Unit Four		Unit Five	
Pretest	*Posttest*	*Pretest*	*Posttest*	*Pretest*	*Posttest*	*Pretest*	*Posttest*	*Pretest*	*Posttest*
1. b	1. c	1. b	1. c	1. c	1. c	1. c	1. d	1. a	1. b
2. c	2. d	2. a	2. b	2. b	2. d	2. d	2. b	2. d	2. d
3. d	3. a	3. d	3. a	3. d	3. a	3. b	3. d	3. c	3. c
4. a	4. b	4. b	4. c	4. c	4. c	4. a	4. a	4. b	4. a
5. c	5. a	5. c	5. b	5. a	5. a	5. d	5. d	5. a	5. c
6. b	6. b	6. a	6. d	6. d	6. c	6. c	6. b	6. d	6. a
7. d	7. c	7. d	7. b	7. b	7. a	7. a	7. c	7. b	7. c
8. a	8. b	8. c	8. b	8. d	8. c	8. d	8. c	8. a	8. d
9. c	9. d	9. c	9. d	9. a	9. d	9. c	9. a	9. c	9. a
10. b	10. b	10. a	10. c	10. c	10. c	10. b	10. c	10. b	10. c
11. a	11. c	11. c	11. c	11. b	11. b	11. a	11. d	11. a	11. b
12. d	12. a	12. d	12. a	12. a	12. b	12. c	12. c	12. c	12. a
13. b	13. c	13. a	13. d	13. c	13. a	13. b	13. b	13. b	13. b
14. d	14. d	14. c	14. c	14. b	14. b	14. a	14. c	14. a	14. c
15. a	15. b	15. b	15. d	15. d	15. a	15. d	15. b	15. c	15. b
16. c	16. d	16. a	16. a	16. a	16. c	16. b	16. a	16. d	16. d
17. d	17. b	17. d	17. c	17. c	17. c	17. a	17. c	17. b	17. b
18. a	18. a	18. c	18. a	18. d	18. b	18. d	18. c	18. d	18. a
19. c	19. d	19. b	19. c	19. d	19. d	19. c	19. a	19. a	19. c
20. d	20. c	20. b	20. d	20. b	20. a	20. a	20. a	20. d	20. b
21. b	21. b	21. c	21. a	21. a	21. d	21. c	21. d	21. b	21. d
22. c	22. a	22. a	22. c	22. c	22. c	22. b	22. c	22. a	22. c
23. a	23. c	23. d	23. c	23. b	23. d	23. a	23. a	23. c	23. d
24. d	24. b	24. b	24. b	24. a	24. b	24. c	24. b	24. b	24. a
25. d	25. c	25. a	25. a	25. d	25. d	25. d	25. b	25. c	25. c
26. d	26. b	26. c	26. b	26. c	26. b	26. b	26. b	26. b	26. b
27. b	27. a	27. b	27. d	27. d	27. a	27. c	27. c	27. a	27. d
28. a	28. b	28. a	28. b	28. a	28. c	28. a	28. c	28. c	28. b
29. c	29. a	29. d	29. d	29. c	29. c	29. d	29. a	29. d	29. c
30. a	30. d	30. b	30. c	30. b	30. d	30. c	30. d	30. a	30. a
31. d	31. b	31. c	31. b	31. d	31. d	31. b	31. b	31. c	31. d
32. c	32. c	32. a	32. d	32. c	32. a	32. a	32. d	32. b	32. a
33. b	33. d	33. c	33. d	33. c	33. c	33. d	33. b	33. a	33. b
34. d	34. c	34. d	34. a	34. b	34. a	34. c	34. d	34. d	34. c
35. a	35. d	35. b	35. d	35. d	35. d	35. b	35. c	35. b	35. b
36. d	36. a	36. a	36. a	36. a	36. b	36. a	36. b	36. c	36. a
37. b	37. d	37. c	37. b	37. c	37. a	37. d	37. a	37. a	37. b
38. a	38. d	38. d	38. d	38. b	38. b	38. b	38. c	38. d	38. b
39. c	39. c	39. a	39. a	39. a	39. c	39. c	39. a	39. b	39. d
40. b	40. b	40. b	40. d	40. d	40. a	40. a	40. c	40. a	40. a
41. a	41. c	41. c	41. b	41. c	41. d	41. c	41. a	41. d	41. d
42. d	42. a	42. a	42. b	42. b	42. a	42. d	42. b	42. b	42. d
43. b	43. b	43. d	43. c	43. a	43. b	43. b	43. a	43. c	43. b
44. a	44. c	44. b	44. b	44. d	44. c	44. a	44. c	44. a	44. d
45. b	45. b	45. d	45. c	45. c	45. d	45. d	45. c	45. c	45. c
46. d	46. a	46. c	46. b	46. a	46. a	46. c	46. a	46. d	46. c
47. a	47. b	47. c	47. d	47. d	47. a	47. b	47. d	47. a	47. a
48. b	48. c	48. d	48. c	48. b	48. c	48. a	48. b	48. b	48. c
49. d	49. a	49. b	49. a	49. c	49. b	49. d	49. d	49. d	49. b
50. a	50. c	50. a	50. a	50. a	50. c	50. b	50. a	50. b	50. d

Answers to the Chapter Activities: ADVANCING VOCABULARY SKILLS

Chapter 1 (Apartment Problems)

Ten Words in Context	Matching Words/Defs	Sentence Check 1	Sentence Check 2	Final Check
1. C 6. A	1. 4 6. 2	1. C 6. G	1–2. C, H	1. E 6. I
2. A 7. B	2. 7 7. 8	2. A 7. J	3–4. D, B	2. C 7. J
3. B 8. A	3. 6 8. 5	3. B 8. F	5–6. F, A	3. A 8. D
4. C 9. A	4. 1 9. 3	4. E 9. I	7–8. E, G	4. B 9. H
5. B 10. B	5. 10 10. 9	5. H 10. D	9–10. I, J	5. G 10. F

Chapter 2 (Hardly a Loser)

Ten Words in Context	Matching Words/Defs	Sentence Check 1	Sentence Check 2	Final Check
1. C 6. A	1. 3 6. 8	1. F 6. G	1–2. F, A	1. C 6. D
2. B 7. A	2. 6 7. 9	2. B 7. A	3–4. G, D	2. F 7. A
3. C 8. B	3. 4 8. 2	3. C 8. H	5–6. I, B	3. G 8. J
4. C 9. B	4. 1 9. 5	4. J 9. E	7–8. C, E	4. H 9. I
5. A 10. A	5. 10 10. 7	5. I 10. D	9–10. H, J	5. B 10. E

Chapter 3 (Grandfather at the Art Museum)

Ten Words in Context	Matching Words/Defs	Sentence Check 1	Sentence Check 2	Final Check
1. A 6. A	1. 7 6. 3	1. H 6. C	1–2. H, I	1. E 6. H
2. A 7. B	2. 8 7. 10	2. I 7. G	3–4. G, B	2. B 7. J
3. B 8. A	3. 1 8. 4	3. J 8. B	5–6. J, C	3. G 8. D
4. C 9. B	4. 6 9. 5	4. E 9. A	7–8. D, F	4. C 9. F
5. C 10. A	5. 2 10. 9	5. D 10. F	9–10. A, E	5. A 10. I

Chapter 4 (My Brother's Mental Illness)

Ten Words in Context	Matching Words/Defs	Sentence Check 1	Sentence Check 2	Final Check
1. C 6. C	1. 8 6. 10	1. G 6. E	1–2. E, H	1. C 6. F
2. B 7. A	2. 4 7. 2	2. J 7. A	3–4. D, A	2. J 7. I
3. A 8. B	3. 6 8. 5	3. C 8. I	5–6. I, F	3. E 8. B
4. A 9. C	4. 1 9. 3	4. H 9. F	7–8. B, G	4. D 9. A
5. A 10. C	5. 9 10. 7	5. B 10. D	9–10. J, C	5. H 10. G

Chapter 5 (A Get-Rich-Quick Scam)

Ten Words in Context	Matching Words/Defs	Sentence Check 1	Sentence Check 2	Final Check
1. C 6. C	1. 5 6. 9	1. D 6. G	1–2. B	1. A 6. B
2. B 7. B	2. 3 7. 6	2. A 7. F	3–4. E, G	2. J 7. F
3. A 8. A	3. 8 8. 1	3. H 8. C	5–6. F, H	3. C 8. G
4. A 9. A	4. 10 9. 4	4. E 9. B	7–8. C, I	4. E 9. D
5. A 10. C	5. 2 10. 7	5. I 10. J	9–10. J, A	5. I 10. H

Chapter 6 (Holiday Blues)

Ten Word Pts in Context	Matching Words/Defs	Sentence Check 1	Sentence Check 2	Final Check
1. C 6. C	1. 9 6. 1	1. A 6. F	1–2. J, I	1. D 6. E
2. A 7. A	2. 6 7. 10	2. I 7. H	3–4. C, B	2. B 7. G
3. B 8. B	3. 2 8. 5	3. G 8. C	5–6. E, D	3. F 8. I
4. C 9. A	4. 8 9. 7	4. D 9. J	7–8. H, A	4. J 9. C
5. C 10. B	5. 4 10. 3	5. E 10. B	9–10. F, G	5. A 10. H

Chapter 7 (A Phony Friend)

Ten Words in Context	Matching Words/Defs	Sentence Check 1	Sentence Check 2	Final Check
1. B 6. B	1. 6 6. 1	1. I 6. H	1–2. F, A	1. D 6. J
2. A 7. A	2. 7 7. 3	2. C 7. F	3–4. I, D	2. F 7. C
3. A 8. A	3. 2 8. 10	3. E 8. B	5–6. E, J	3. E 8. B
4. C 9. C	4. 9 9. 5	4. J 9. D	7–8. B, G	4. I 9. H
5. B 10. B	5. 4 10. 8	5. G 10. A	9–10. C, H	5. A 10. G

Chapter 8 (Coco the Gorilla)

Ten Words in Context	Matching Words/Defs	Sentence Check 1	Sentence Check 2	Final Check
1. B 6. B	1. 9 6. 3	1. F 6. C	1–2. E, F	1. A 6. J
2. A 7. B	2. 5 7. 10	2. J 7. D	3–4. I, A	2. C 7. H
3. A 8. C	3. 2 8. 1	3. I 8. E	5–6. D, G	3. F 8. B
4. C 9. A	4. 7 9. 4	4. H 9. A	7–8. H, B	4. I 9. E
5. A 10. C	5. 8 10. 6	5. B 10. G	9–10. J, C	5. G 10. D

Chapter 9 (Our Annual Garage Sale)

Ten Words in Context	Matching Words/Defs	Sentence Check 1	Sentence Check 2	Final Check
1. C 6. A	1. 2 6. 1	1. J 6. G	1–2. B, E	1. F 6. G
2. B 7. B	2. 3 7. 5	2. C 7. F	3–4. F, H	2. A 7. J
3. C 8. C	3. 8 8. 7	3. A 8. E	5–6. D, A	3. H 8. C
4. C 9. A	4. 9 9. 5	4. B 9. H	7–8. G, I	4. I 9. D
5. A 10. C	5. 10 10. 6	5. I 10. D	9–10. J, C	5. E 10. B

Chapter 10 (A Debate on School Uniforms)

Ten Words in Context	Matching Words/Defs	Sentence Check 1	Sentence Check 2	Final Check
1. B 6. A	1. 10 6. 1	1. A 6. I	1–2. J, A	1. C 6. J
2. A 7. A	2. 5 7. 3	2. D 7. J	3–4. B, G	2. A 7. F
3. C 8. B	3. 6 8. 4	3. G 8. B	5–6. C, F	3. B 8. E
4. A 9. A	4. 2 9. 8	4. H 9. C	7–8. I, H	4. H 9. I
5. B 10. C	5. 7 10. 9	5. E 10. F	9–10. D, E	5. D 10. G

Chapter 11 (My Large Family)

Ten Words in Context	Matching Words/Defs	Sentence Check 1	Sentence Check 2	Final Check
1. C 6. B	1. 7 6. 10	1. E 6. D	1–2. E, F	1. F 6. C
2. A 7. B	2. 1 7. 8	2. I 7. H	3–4. D, I	2. H 7. G
3. A 8. A	3. 5 8. 4	3. G 8. A	5–6. H, J	3. J 8. A
4. C 9. C	4. 2 9. 3	4. F 9. J	7–8. C, G	4. I 9. E
5. A 10. A	5. 6 10. 9	5. B 10. C	9–10. A, B	5. D 10. B

Chapter 12 (Alex's Search)

Ten Word Pts in Context	Matching Words/Defs	Sentence Check 1	Sentence Check 2	Final Check
1. B 6. C	1. 4 6. 10	1. C 6. B	1–2. G, F	1. D 6. F
2. A 7. A	2. 3 7. 9	2. J 7. I	3–4. D, B	2. B 7. A
3. B 8. C	3. 8 8. 5	3. F 8. D	5–6. I, H	3. I 8. C
4. A 9. B	4. 1 9. 6	4. G 9. A	7–8. A, J	4. E 9. H
5. B 10. C	5. 7 10. 2	5. H 10. E	9–10. E, C	5. G 10. J

Chapter 13 (Ann's Love of Animals)

Ten Words in Context	Matching Words/Defs	Sentence Check 1	Sentence Check 2	Final Check
1. B 6. B	1. 6 6. 3	1. I 6. C	1–2. A, G	1. G 6. C
2. A 7. A	2. 7 7. 10	2. A 7. H	3–4. D, F	2. F 7. J
3. C 8. C	3. 1 8. 4	3. G 8. B	5–6. I, E	3. D 8. I
4. A 9. A	4. 8 9. 9	4. E 9. J	7–8. C, H	4. B 9. E
5. C 10. C	5. 2 10. 5	5. F 10. D	9–10. B, J	5. H 10. A

Chapter 14 (A Costume Party)

Ten Words in Context	Matching Words/Defs	Sentence Check 1	Sentence Check 2	Final Check
1. B 6. A	1. 5 6. 9	1. J 6. B	1–2. D, J	1. H 6. E
2. A 7. A	2. 6 7. 3	2. G 7. E	3–4. G, E	2. A 7. B
3. C 8. A	3. 10 8. 2	3. I 8. H	5–6. I, E	3. I 8. F
4. A 9. C	4. 8 9. 1	4. D 9. A	7–8. H, F	4. C 9. J
5. B 10. A	5. 7 10. 4	5. C 10. F	9–10. C, B	5. G 10. D

Chapter 15 (The Missing Painting)

Ten Words in Context	Matching Words/Defs	Sentence Check 1	Sentence Check 2	Final Check
1. B 6. A	1. 4 6. 3	1. C 6. B	1–2. D, B	1. D 6. I
2. A 7. C	2. 10 7. 9	2. G 7. E	3–4. A, H	2. A 7. H
3. C 8. B	3. 8 8. 1	3. I 8. D	5–6. C, G	3. F 8. B
4. A 9. C	4. 5 9. 7	4. A 9. F	7–8. E, I	4. G 9. E
5. B 10. B	5. 6 10. 2	5. J 10. H	9–10. J, F	5. J 10. C

Chapter 16 (An Ohio Girl in New York)

Ten Words in Context	Matching Words/Defs	Sentence Check 1	Sentence Check 2	Final Check
1. A 6. A	1. 3 6. 10	1. F 6. E	1–2. C, A	1. I 6. C
2. C 7. B	2. 1 7. 8	2. A 7. B	3–4. I, J	2. G 7. F
3. A 8. B	3. 9 8. 2	3. G 8. J	5–6. D, G	3. E 8. H
4. C 9. A	4. 6 9. 5	4. I 9. C	7–8. F, B	4. J 9. B
5. B 10. C	5. 4 10. 7	5. D 10. H	9–10. H, E	5. A 10. D

Chapter 17 (How Neat Is Neat Enough)

Ten Words in Context	Matching Words/Defs	Sentence Check 1	Sentence Check 2	Final Check
1. C 6. B	1. 8 6. 3	1. J 6. D	1–2. A, G	1. G 6. A
2. A 7. A	2. 4 7. 9	2. E 7. H	3–4. H, E	2. E 7. J
3. B 8. B	3. 10 8. 1	3. F 8. I	5–6. F, J	3. C 8. F
4. A 9. C	4. 6 9. 5	4. C 9. G	7–8. C, D	4. B 9. I
5. A 10. A	5. 2 10. 7	5. A 10. B	9–10. I, B	5. D 10. H

Chapter 18 (A Cult Community)

Ten Word Pts in Context	Matching Words/Defs	Sentence Check 1	Sentence Check 2	Final Check
1. C 6. A	1. 8 6. 2	1. B 6. F	1–2. E, F	1. B 6. I
2. A 7. A	2. 9 7. 1	2. C 7. G	3–4. C, B	2. C 7. G
3. C 8. C	3. 10 8. 3	3. I 8. H	5–6. J, I	3. J 8. A
4. B 9. B	4. 7 9. 6	4. E 9. A	7–8. H, D	4. H 9. D
5. A 10. B	5. 5 10. 4	5. J 10. D	9–10. G, A	5. E 10. F

Chapter 19 (Halloween Troubles)

Ten Words in Context	Matching Words/Defs	Sentence Check 1	Sentence Check 2	Final Check
1. B 6. C	1. 8 6. 7	1. A 6. C	1–2. A, B	1. G 6. B
2. C 7. A	2. 9 7. 2	2. E 7. D	3–4. H, C	2. D 7. C
3. C 8. B	3. 5 8. 3	3. G 8. F	5–6. F, E	3. I 8. H
4. A 9. A	4. 1 9. 4	4. B 9. H	7–8. I, G	4. E 9. J
5. C 10. A	5. 10 10. 6	5. J 10. I	9–10. J, D	5. F 10. A

Chapter 20 (Thomas Dooley)

Ten Words in Context	Matching Words/Defs	Sentence Check 1	Sentence Check 2	Final Check
1. B 6. A	1. 4 6. 3	1. C 6. J	1–2. F, C	1. A 6. G
2. A 7. B	2. 6 7. 5	2. F 7. G	3–4. B, I	2. D 7. H
3. A 8. C	3. 9 8. 7	3. D 8. H	5–6. D, A	3. B 8. F
4. C 9. A	4. 8 9. 10	4. I 9. E	7–8. G, E	4. C 9. J
5. C 10. B	5. 1 10. 2	5. B 10. A	9–10. J, H	5. E 10. I

Chapter 21 (Twelve Grown Men in a Bug)

Ten Words in Context	Matching Words/Defs	Sentence Check 1	Sentence Check 2	Final Check
1. C 6. C	1. 3 6. 2	1. A 6. F	1–2. C, I	1. G 6. A
2. A 7. B	2. 5 7. 9	2. J 7. E	3–4. G, J	2. B 7. F
3. B 8. C	3. 10 8. 6	3. H 8. B	5–6. D, H	3. H 8. I
4. C 9. A	4. 1 9. 7	4. D 9. I	7–8. A, E	4. D 9. E
5. A 10. A	5. 8 10. 4	5. C 10. G	9–10. B, F	5. J 10. C

Chapter 22 (Adjusting to a Group Home)

Ten Words in Context	Matching Words/Defs	Sentence Check 1	Sentence Check 2	Final Check
1. A 6. C	1. 3 6. 1	1. G 6. F	1–2. C, B	1. C 6. J
2. B 7. C	2. 6 7. 10	2. E 7. C	3–4. J, E	2. B 7. I
3. A 8. A	3. 9 8. 7	3. B 8. I	5–6. G, H	3. D 8. A
4. C 9. C	4. 5 9. 2	4. D 9. A	7–8. D, F	4. H 9. E
5. B 10. B	5. 8 10. 4	5. H 10. J	9–10. I, A	5. F 10. G

Chapter 23 (A Different Kind of Doctor)

Ten Words in Context	Matching Words/Defs	Sentence Check 1	Sentence Check 2	Final Check
1. B 6. A	1. 10 6. 3	1. I 6. E	1–2. D, B	1. E 6. B
2. C 7. A	2. 6 7. 9	2. B 7. D	3–4. C, G	2. A 7. J
3. A 8. C	3. 4 8. 8	3. H 8. A	5–6. J, I	3. D 8. G
4. B 9. B	4. 1 9. 5	4. C 9. J	7–8. E, A	4. I 9. H
5. B 10. A	5. 2 10. 7	5. G 10. F	9–10. H, F	5. F 10. C

Chapter 24 (Grandpa and Music)

Ten Word Pts in Context	Matching Words/Defs	Sentence Check 1	Sentence Check 2	Final Check
1. B 6. A	1. 2 6. 4	1. J 6. E	1–2. A, J	1. B 6. I
2. C 7. A	2. 7 7. 6	2. D 7. C	3–4. E, I	2. D 7. E
3. A 8. C	3. 9 8. 10	3. A 8. H	5–6. H, G	3. C 8. J
4. C 9. A	4. 3 9. 1	4. B 9. I	7–8. F, B	4. A 9. H
5. B 10. A	5. 8 10. 5	5. F 10. G	9–10. C, D	5. F 10. G

Chapter 25 (My Devilish Older Sister)

Ten Words in Context	Matching Words/Defs	Sentence Check 1	Sentence Check 2	Final Check
1. B 6. B	1. 6 6. 9	1. I 6. A	1–2. A, D	1. A 6. D
2. A 7. C	2. 4 7. 8	2. B 7. C	3–4. C, I	2. G 7. I
3. B 8. A	3. 10 8. 2	3. H 8. G	5–6. J, H	3. F 8. E
4. A 9. B	4. 1 9. 7	4. E 9. D	7–8. G, B	4. B 9. C
5. A 10. C	5. 3 10. 5	5. J 10. F	9–10. E, F	5. H 10. J

Chapter 26 (Harriet Tubman)

Ten Words in Context	Matching Words/Defs	Sentence Check 1	Sentence Check 2	Final Check
1. A 6. B	1. 4 6. 7	1. I 6. F	1–2. I, C	1. E 6. F
2. B 7. A	2. 9 7. 5	2. D 7. C	3–4. A, G	2. J 7. G
3. C 8. B	3. 6 8. 8	3. E 8. A	5–6. B, H	3. A 8. B
4. A 9. C	4. 10 9. 1	4. G 9. H	7–8. F, E	4. I 9. H
5. A 10. A	5. 2 10. 3	5. B 10. J	9–10. D, J	5. C 10. D

Chapter 27 (Tony's Rehabilitation)

Ten Words in Context	Matching Words/Defs	Sentence Check 1	Sentence Check 2	Final Check
1. C 6. A	1. 5 6. 1	1. H 6. A	1–2. I, G	1. I 6. F
2. A 7. B	2. 2 7. 3	2. I 7. J	3–4. F, D	2. C 7. B
3. A 8. A	3. 6 8. 9	3. D 8. F	5–6. A, C	3. D 8. J
4. B 9. C	4. 10 9. 8	4. B 9. E	7–8. J, H	4. A 9. E
5. C 10. A	5. 4 10. 7	5. G 10. C	9–10. E, B	5. H 10. G

Chapter 28 (Rumors)

Ten Words in Context	Matching Words/Defs	Sentence Check 1	Sentence Check 2	Final Check
1. B 6. A	1. 9 6. 6	1. E 6. C	1–2. I, G	1. C 6. E
2. A 7. A	2. 5 7. 1	2. G 7. J	3–4. H, E	2. F 7. H
3. C 8. A	3. 8 8. 3	3. D 8. H	5–6. J, C	3. B 8. I
4. A 9. A	4. 2 9. 4	4. F 9. I	7–8. D, B	4. A 9. G
5. C 10. B	5. 10 10. 7	5. B 10. A	9–10. F, A	5. D 10. J

Chapter 29 (The End of a Political Career)

Ten Words in Context	Matching Words/Defs	Sentence Check 1	Sentence Check 2	Final Check
1. B 6. B	1. 4 6. 7	1. G 6. E	1–2. J, D	1. A 6. E
2. A 7. B	2. 1 7. 5	2. H 7. I	3–4. C, F	2. B 7. C
3. C 8. C	3. 10 8. 2	3. J 8. C	5–6. A, E	3. I 8. H
4. B 9. A	4. 8 9. 6	4. D 9. B	7–8. B, I	4. F 9. J
5. A 10. A	5. 9 10. 3	5. A 10. F	9–10. H, G	5. G 10. D

Chapter 30 (Firing Our Boss)

Ten Words in Context	Matching Words/Defs	Sentence Check 1	Sentence Check 2	Final Check
1. B 6. B	1. 10 6. 2	1. J 6. B	1–2. C, E	1. B 6. E
2. B 7. A	2. 8 7. 3	2. A 7. I	3–4. I, H	2. A 7. D
3. A 8. C	3. 5 8. 4	3. H 8. E	5–6. G, D	3. C 8. G
4. C 9. A	4. 1 9. 6	4. C 9. D	7–8. F, A	4. F 9. J
5. A 10. B	5. 9 10. 7	5. G 10. F	9–10. J, B	5. H 10. I

Answers to the Unit Reviews: ADVANCING VOCABULARY SKILLS

Unit One

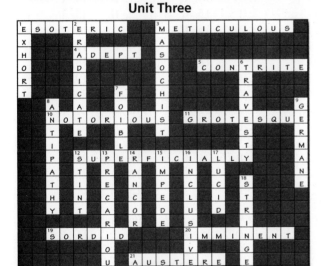

Across: EMBELLISH, CHARLATAN, SCRUPULOUS, OPTIMUM, ILLICIT, INANE, DESPONDENT, DIVERGE, REGRESS, FACETIOUS, SQUELCH, DEXTEROUS

Unit Two

Across: VOCIFEROUS, ATTRITION, SOLICITOUS, LIABILITY, REPLETE, BOLSTER, INQUISITIVE, REINSTATE, SOLACE, UTOPIA, EGOCENTRIC, EXONERATE, RETICENT

Unit Three

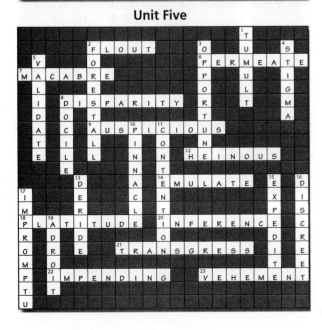

Across: ESOTERIC, METICULOUS, ADEPT, CONTRITE, NOTORIOUS, GROTESQUE, SUPERFICIALLY, SORDID, IMMINENT, AUSTERE, VERBOSE

Unit Four

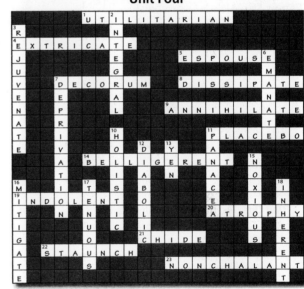

Across: UTILITARIAN, EXTRICATE, ESPOUSE, DECORUM, DISSIPATE, ANNIHILATE, PLACEBO, BELLIGERENT, INDOLENT, ATROPHY, CHIDE, STAUNCH, NONCHALANT

Unit Five

Across: FLOUT, PERMEATE, MACABRE, DISPARITY, AUSPICIOUS, HEINOUS, EMULATE, PLATITUDE, INFERENCE, TRANSGRESS, IMPENDING, VEHEMENT

189

Answers to the Unit Tests: ADVANCING VOCABULARY SKILLS

Unit One	Unit Two	Unit Three	Unit Four	Unit Five

Unit One, Test 1
1. corroborate
2. venerate
3. instigates
4. diverges
5. proliferation
6. sensory
7. facetious
8. squelch
9. scrupulous
10. dormant
11. A 16. A
12. A 17. D
13. C 18. D
14. B 19. A
15. B 20. C

Unit Two, Test 1
1. propensity
2. cohesive
3. liability
4. robust
5. equivocated
6. tenacious
7. reiterated
8. clandestine
9. sanction
10. replete
11. D 16. D
12. C 17. D
13. A 18. B
14. A 19. C
15. D 20. A

Unit Three, Test 1
1. sordid
2. standardized
3. precarious
4. jurisdiction
5. connoisseur
6. notorious
7. travesty
8. stint
9. grotesque
10. idiosyncrasy
11. B 16. A
12. A 17. C
13. D 18. C
14. D 19. B
15. D 20. A

Unit Four, Test 1
1. diabolic
2. exhilaration
3. emanates
4. synchronize
5. decorum
6. dilapidated
7. subversive
8. denunciation
9. annihilate
10. noxious
11. B 16. C
12. D 17. B
13. A 18. B
14. A 19. C
15. B 20. D

Unit Five, Test 1
1. incapacitates
2. promiscuous
3. subordinate
4. rebuked
5. permeated
6. constituents
7. expedite
8. omnipotent
9. prognosis
10. complement
11. A 16. B
12. D 17. C
13. A 18. C
14. A 19. B
15. C 20. A

Unit One, Test 2
1. M 14. I
2. F 15. C
3. G 16. I
4. I 17. C
5. K 18. C
6. J 19. I
7. C 20. A
8. D 21. C
9. E 22. C
10. B 23. B
11. A 24. C
12. H 25. B
13. L

Unit Two, Test 2
1. L 14. I
2. E 15. I
3. C 16. I
4. A 17. C
5. K 18. C
6. B 19. C
7. G 20. C
8. F 21. C
9. J 22. B
10. D 23. B
11. M 24. C
12. I 25. A
13. H

Unit Three, Test 2
1. M 14. I
2. J 15. C
3. H 16. I
4. B 17. I
5. G 18. C
6. C 19. I
7. E 20. C
8. F 21. A
9. I 22. C
10. A 23. B
11. K 24. A
12. D 25. A
13. L

Unit Four, Test 2
1. H 14. I
2. I 15. C
3. D 16. C
4. F 17. I
5. G 18. I
6. K 19. C
7. E 20. C
8. A 21. A
9. L 22. A
10. M 23. C
11. B 24. B
12. C 25. B
13. J

Unit Five, Test 2
1. B 14. I
2. H 15. I
3. A 16. C
4. L 17. I
5. C 18. C
6. I 19. C
7. E 20. B
8. D 21. C
9. J 22. A
10. K 23. B
11. F 24. C
12. G 25. A
13. M

Unit One, Test 3
1. D 11. B
2. A 12. A
3. B 13. D
4. A 14. C
5. C 15. A
6. D 16. D
7. B 17. C
8. B 18. C
9. A 19. A
10. D 20. D

Unit Two, Test 3
1. C 11. C
2. B 12. A
3. A 13. D
4. B 14. A
5. D 15. B
6. C 16. C
7. D 17. D
8. B 18. A
9. C 19. C
10. D 20. B

Unit Three, Test 3
1. D 11. C
2. C 12. D
3. D 13. C
4. B 14. D
5. B 15. B
6. D 16. C
7. B 17. A
8. A 18. B
9. C 19. D
10. B 20. C

Unit Four, Test 3
1. D 11. A
2. C 12. A
3. B 13. C
4. A 14. A
5. D 15. B
6. C 16. C
7. C 17. B
8. B 18. C
9. D 19. D
10. C 20. B

Unit Five, Test 3
1. C 11. B
2. B 12. D
3. A 13. C
4. C 14. C
5. D 15. B
6. A 16. A
7. C 17. D
8. B 18. C
9. C 19. D
10. A 20. B

Unit One, Test 4
(Word Parts)
1. H 11. E
2. A 12. B
3. E 13. I
4. C 14. G
5. I 15. D
6. J 16. B
7. G 17. A
8. F 18. C
9. D 19. C
10. B 20. A

Unit Two, Test 4
(Word Parts)
1. C 11. B
2. H 12. D
3. G 13. A
4. F 14. F
5. D 15. I
6. B 16. B
7. A 17. A
8. E 18. A
9. J 19. C
10. I 20. C

Unit Three, Test 4
(Word Parts)
1. I 11. B
2. G 12. C
3. F 13. I
4. E 14. E
5. C 15. A
6. B 16. B
7. J 17. C
8. D 18. C
9. H 19. A
10. A 20. B

Unit Four, Test 4
(Word Parts)
1. D 11. E
2. I 12. B
3. E 13. C
4. G 14. A
5. H 15. G
6. B 16. A
7. C 17. B
8. A 18. A
9. F 19. C
10. G 20. B

Mastery Test: *Chapter 1 (Apartment Problems)*

In the space provided, write the word from the box needed to complete each sentence. Then put the **letter** of that word in the column at the left. Use each word once.

A. **detriment**	B. **dexterous**	C. **discretion**	D. **facetious**	E. **gregarious**
F. **optimum**	G. **ostentatious**	H. **scrupulous**	I. **sensory**	J. **vicarious**

_____   1. Babies benefit from a great deal of _____ stimulation: different textures to feel, shapes and colors to look at, and various sounds to hear.

_____   2. The boys' club has made Hank more comfortable with others. In the past, he usually stayed by himself, but now he's much more _____.

_____   3. Anita is _____ about not wasting her employer's time. Although she uses a computer all day, she never sends personal e-mail or plays computer games until she gets home.

_____   4. When Brian said he spent all the money I had lent him on a new sports car, I wasn't sure if he was being serious or _____.

_____   5. It will be many years before I can afford to travel much, but in the meantime, I get _____ pleasure from hearing about my friends' exciting vacations.

_____   6. Not being able to read well is a(n) _____ to most careers.

_____   7. To be great performers, piano players must be _____ with their hands.

_____   8. Experts say that the _____ age for receiving the measles vaccine is 15 months. Children younger than that aren't well protected by the injection.

_____   9. It's_____ of the Millers to build a huge fancy vacation home that they'll use only once or twice a year. Why must they make such a show of having money?

_____   10. It's difficult to make a child understand the need for _____. What parent hasn't had the experience of hearing his child yell out some true, but embarrassing fact, such as "Look! That man doesn't have any hair on his head!"

SCORE: (Number correct) _____ × 10 = _____ %

Mastery Test: *Chapter 2 (Hardly a Loser)*

In the space provided, write the word from the box needed to complete each sentence. Then put the **letter** of that word in the column at the left. Use each word once.

A. **collaborate**	B. **despondent**	C. **instigate**	D. **resilient**	E. **retrospect**
F. **rudimentary**	G. **scoff**	H. **squelch**	I. **venerate**	J. **zealot**

_____ 1. In _____, Tim believes his marriage to Lily could have been saved. But at the time, he was convinced that they should split up.

_____ 2. The world _____s Isaac Newton for discovering the laws of gravity.

_____ 3. After breaking her hip, Mrs. Murphy was _____, but she became more hopeful and cheerful when she was discharged from the hospital.

_____ 4. Our neighbor is a _____ about keeping his yard neat. When a single leaf falls off a tree, he rushes out of his house to rake it up.

_____ 5. Winnie was a happy, fun-loving girl when she got married. But five years of living with her sour, serious husband has _____(e)d her bubbly personality.

_____ 6. Joan didn't take part in the snowball fight, but she _____(e)d it by giving the boys huge piles of snowballs.

_____ 7. John Lennon and Paul McCartney _____(e)d in writing many of the Beatles' hit songs, including "Yesterday" and "Yellow Submarine."

_____ 8. People with AIDS are much less _____ than others. A flu attack that most of us can easily shake off is life-threatening to them.

_____ 9. Anyone with even a(n) _____ understanding of electricity knows it's not a good idea to use a metal fork to take a piece of toast from the toaster.

_____ 10. My little sister's friends _____(e)d at her when she claimed she could do magic tricks. Their laughter stopped, however, when she made a pair of pigeons appear from nowhere.

> ***SCORE:*** (Number correct) _____ × 10 = _____ %

Name: _____

Mastery Test: *Chapter 3 (Grandfather at the Art Museum)*

In the space provided, write the word from the box needed to complete each sentence. Then put the **letter** of that word in the column at the left. Use each word once.

A. **ambiguous**	B. **dissident**	C. **embellish**	D. **fritter**	E. **inadvertent**
F. **inane**	G. **juxtapose**	H. **lethargy**	I. **sporadic**	J. **subsidize**

_____ 1. Nita allows her son to _____ away his weekly allowance on junk. She says he'll soon learn that it's better to save his money for something he really wants.

_____ 2. We watched in wonder as the baker _____(e)d the wedding cake with colorful flowers, hearts, and birds.

_____ 3. Dr. Green was disturbed to see such _____ in young Lisa. Usually, children her age have a great amount of energy.

_____ 4. Here's one of the _____ excuses people have given on insurance forms for accidents: "Coming home, I drove into the wrong driveway and hit a tree I don't have."

_____ 5. Every member of the school board but one voted to hire the new teacher. The _____ kept saying, "There's something about him that I just don't like."

_____ 6. The laundry soap ad _____(e)d an ugly, stained shirt with a beautiful, bright shirt that had supposedly been washed in the soap.

_____ 7. The town business association has established a scholarship to _____ a needy business student each year at the local college.

_____ 8. Instead of having a steady job, Lila stays home with her children and makes a little extra money now and then by doing _____ sewing jobs for friends.

_____ 9. Cora's failure to send Rachel a wedding invitation was entirely_____. As soon as Cora realized her mistake, she telephoned Rachel to invite her.

_____ 10. One famous psychological test involves showing people inkblots in shapes purposely made _____ enough so that a variety of different things can be "seen" in each design.

SCORE: (Number correct) _____ × 10 = _____ %

Mastery Test: *Chapter 4 (My Brother's Mental Illness)*

In the space provided, write the word from the box needed to complete each sentence. Then put the **letter** of that word in the column at the left. Use each word once.

A. **berate**	B. **estrange**	C. **euphoric**	D. **impetuous**	E. **infallible**
F. **maudlin**	G. **regress**	H. **relinquish**	I. **ubiquitous**	J. **zenith**

_____ 1. McDonald's is certainly a(n) _____ restaurant chain. It's almost impossible to find a city that doesn't contain a set of the "golden arches."

_____ 2. "Don't _____ the child so," Mrs. Lopez told her husband. "He'll learn more if you just explain what he's done wrong instead of scolding him so harshly."

_____ 3. My older brother seems to believe he's really _____. Whenever someone disagrees with him, he won't even consider the possibility that he's mistaken.

_____ 4. Since so many people who diet eventually _____ to their old weights, wouldn't it make more sense simply to eat sensibly than to diet constantly?

_____ 5. The young woman _____(e)d custody of her baby to adoptive parents because she wanted the child to have a good home, and she knew she wasn't able to provide one.

_____ 6. Timmy was _____ when his parents, at last, agreed to let him have the puppy he'd been begging for. He walked around singing and smiling all day.

_____ 7. Some child stars reached the _____ of their careers at a very young age and later felt like failures because they couldn't stay at the top.

_____ 8. Last Friday night, my sister and I popped popcorn, put on our pajamas, and cried together over a silly, sentimental movie. Then we laughed at ourselves for being so _____.

_____ 9. Harry's relationship with his two sisters had always been poor, but he completely _____(e)d them when, without their knowledge, he took several of their mother's belongings from her home on the day their mother died.

_____ 10. Phyllis stole a tube of mascara just because she felt like it. She later discovered that her _____ act wasn't worth the humiliation and grief that resulted when she was caught.

SCORE: (Number correct) _____ × 10 = _____ %

Mastery Test: *Chapter 5 (A Get-Rich-Quick Scam)*

In the space provided, write the word from the box needed to complete each sentence. Then put the **letter** of that word in the column at the left. Use each word once.

A. **charlatan**	B. **corroborate**	C. **disseminate**	D. **diverge**	E. **dormant**
F. **hoist**	G. **illicit**	H. **irrevocable**	I. **precipitate**	J. **proliferation**

_____ 1. It's hard to believe that every little acorn contains the _____ seed of a great oak tree.

_____ 2. A small plane flying over the beach _____(e)d advertising flyers to the sunbathers below until beach police objected to the litter.

_____ 3. The real estate agent insisted that Ron's agreement to buy the house was _____. However, Ron's lawyer stated it was possible to cancel the deal.

_____ 4. "Your Social Security card isn't enough," said the clerk taking my check. "You'll have to _____ your identity with a driver's license and a major credit card."

_____ 5. I wonder how people who earn their money through _____ means can enjoy their wealth. For me, gaining money illegally would spoil much of its pleasure.

_____ 6. After earthquakes, special machinery is often brought in to _____ up the heavy walls of collapsed buildings.

_____ 7. It's not wise to hire people who don't have a business address. They are likely to be _____s whose only skill is taking your money.

_____ 8. Rachel knew that she wanted to leave her home town one day, but the sudden offer of a job in another state _____(e)d her departure sooner than she expected.

_____ 9. The firehouse was at the edge of town, where the two main roads _____(e)d. Firefighters were thus able to respond quickly to an alarm in either direction.

_____ 10. The _____ of flowers along the borders of country roads is partly due to people throwing their extra flower seeds out on the roadsides.

SCORE: (Number correct) _____ × 10 = _____ %

Mastery Test: *Chapter 7 (A Phony Friend)*

In the space provided, write the word from the box needed to complete each sentence. Then put the **letter** of that word in the column at the left. Use each word once.

A. **equivocate**	B. **fortuitous**	C. **impeccable**	D. **liaison**	E. **predisposed**
F. **propensity**	G. **reprehensible**	H. **sham**	I. **solace**	J. **solicitous**

_____ 1. Alice knows she has a(n) _____ to overspend on clothes, so she has put herself on a clothing budget.

_____ 2. Because my grandmother is _____ to pneumonia, I make sure she stays warm and healthy during the flu season.

_____ 3. Teenagers often _____ about their plans. When asked where they're going, they say "Out," and when asked what they'll be doing, they say "Nothing much."

_____ 4. Because Julie speaks both Vietnamese and English well, she acts as a(n) _____ between various Vietnamese immigrants and the telephone company, banks, and so on.

_____ 5. Children traveling alone on airplanes generally get very _____ attention from the flight attendants, who keep them well supplied with coloring books, snacks, and pillows.

_____ 6. Stealing money is bad enough, but stealing from a charity is really _____.

_____ 7. Bob and Tina's meeting was unusually _____: intending to visit someone else, Bob knocked on Tina's apartment door by mistake.

_____ 8. I used to envy my neighbor's _____ housekeeping until I realized how much time she spends cleaning. I live a messier but more balanced life.

_____ 9. Mrs. Walker has been lonely since all her children moved to other areas. Her children hope that their frequent e-mails and photographs provide her with some _____.

_____ 10. After Billy spent ten of his hard-earned dollars on an autographed picture of his baseball hero, he was heartbroken to learn that the player's signature was a(n) _____.

SCORE: (Number correct) _____ × 10 = _____ %

Name: _____

Mastery Test: *Chapter 8 (Coco the Gorilla)*

In the space provided, write the word from the box needed to complete each sentence. Then put the **letter** of that word in the column at the left. Use each word once.

A. **attrition**	B. **circumvent**	C. **cohesive**	D. **grievous**	E. **inundate**
F. **oblivious**	G. **reticent**	H. **robust**	I. **sanction**	J. **vociferous**

_____ 1. Our house was so _____(e)d by carpenter ants that we finally were forced to call an exterminator.

_____ 2. The baseball player's protest was _____—he stamped his feet and screamed at the umpire.

_____ 3. There are many possible explanations as to why some families fall apart and have little contact while others are so much more _____.

_____ 4. The rate of _____ in William's high school class was terrible. Of the 104 students who entered ninth grade with him, only 47 graduated.

_____ 5. After the car accident, Rodrigo wandered around in a daze, _____ to the blood that was running down his face and soaking his shirt.

_____ 6. The pilot _____(e)d the storm by flying above it.

_____ 7. Many actors are quite happy to talk about their film careers, but _____about their private lives.

_____ 8. The earthquake was especially _____ for those victims who lost friends and family as well as possessions.

_____ 9. The principal wouldn't _____ the use of the gym for an after-school dance club, even though one of the teachers agreed to be in charge of it.

_____ 10. It's hard to believe that Ana and Tomas's baby, who was so tiny and weak when she was born prematurely, has grown into such a _____ one-year-old.

SCORE: (Number correct) _____ × 10 = _____ %

Mastery Test: *Chapter 9 (Our Annual Garage Sale)*

In the space provided, write the word from the box needed to complete each sentence. Then put the **letter** of that word in the column at the left. Use each word once.

A. **bolster**	B. **depreciate**	C. **indiscriminate**	D. **inquisitive**	E. **nebulous**
F. **relegate**	G. **replete**	H. **sedentary**	I. **tenet**	J. **terse**

_____ 1. A flaw in a diamond will cause the gem's market value to _____.

_____ 2. Being accepted to two good schools _____(e)d Amy's confidence in her ability to do well in college.

_____ 3. If the tax laws sometimes seem _____ to IRS agents, how is the average person supposed to make sense of them?

_____ 4. My sister's_____ shopping has resulted in a closet full of clothes that don't go together and that she doesn't even especially like.

_____ 5. Scott was such a(n) _____ child that his father teased him by saying, "You ask so many questions that you'll probably be a game show host when you grow up."

_____ 6. One _____ of the Ben & Jerry's ice cream company is that a percentage of their profits will be donated to peace efforts.

_____ 7. Our car was too old and broken-down to trade in. It could only be _____(e)d to the junk pile.

_____ 8. Since Carla is a receptionist, her work is very _____. As a result, she makes a special effort to exercise every day.

_____ 9. One expensive kennel guarantees that your dog will be well cared for during your vacation. It offers cages _____ with such luxuries as air conditioning and pillows.

_____ 10. Writer Dorothy Parker was well-known for her brief, witty statements. She once suggested this _____ sentence for her own gravestone: "Excuse my dust."

SCORE: (Number correct) _____ × 10 = _____ %

Mastery Test: *Chapter 10 (A Debate on School Uniforms)*

In the space provided, write the word from the box needed to complete each sentence. Then put the **letter** of that word in the column at the left. Use each word once.

A. **autonomy**	B. **bureaucratic**	C. **mandate**	D. **ostracize**	E. **raucous**
F. **recourse**	G. **reiterate**	H. **tantamount**	I. **tenacious**	J. **utopia**

_____ 1. Greatly exaggerating the truth is _____ to lying.

_____ 2. When we ran out of gas, our only _____ was a four-mile walk to the nearest gas station.

_____ 3. The city system is so _____ that it takes up to a year just to get a building permit approved.

_____ 4. John Boles's opponent was totally against taxes, so by electing Boles mayor, the voters expressed a clear _____ : It is sometimes necessary to raise taxes.

_____ 5. Those at the back-yard graduation party didn't realize how _____ they had become until a neighbor called to complain about the noise.

_____ 6. Malaria is a(n) _____ disease. Its symptoms of chills and fever can keep reappearing for many years.

_____ 7. General MacArthur was known to _____ his instructions so many times that his men could repeat them word for word.

_____ 8. Todd felt that his classmates _____(e)d him for no reason, but the other children said they avoided him because he was a bully.

_____ 9. Many groups tried to create a(n) _____ where there is no crime or fighting, but most of these efforts eventually failed.

_____ 10. Donna believes in allowing her children total _____ in their decisions, but I think it's irresponsible to give children aged 5 and 8 that much independence.

SCORE: (Number correct) _____ × 10 = _____ %

Mastery Test: *Chapter 11 (My Large Family)*

In the space provided, write the word from the box needed to complete each sentence. Then put the **letter** of that word in the column at the left. Use each word once.

A. **clandestine**	B. **contingency**	C. **egocentric**	D. **exonerate**	E. **incongruous**
F. **indigenous**	G. **liability**	H. **prolific**	I. **reinstate**	J. **superfluous**

_____ 1. Mint is _____ to the town of North Judson, Indiana. Each summer, the town hosts a "Mint Festival" to celebrate its favorite native crop.

_____ 2. _____ people do not necessarily feel good about themselves. Sometimes people focus on themselves too much because of self-doubt and insecurity.

_____ 3. To prepare everyone for the _____ of a car accident, many states require drivers to buy accident insurance.

_____ 4. After spending 45 minutes cramming our belongings into the back of our station wagon, Dad said, "The next time we go camping, we take only the necessities. All this _____ junk stays home!"

_____ 5. Johann Sebastian Bach was _____ as both a composer and a parent. In addition to writing numerous pieces of music, he fathered twenty children.

_____ 6. People who oppose the death penalty point out that occasionally, a person who has been put to death has later been _____(e)d of the crime.

_____ 7. My little brother loves belonging to a "secret society." Only its members know where and when the society's _____ meetings are held.

_____ 8. My brother's shyness is a great _____. Whenever he meets someone who interests him, he's usually too embarrassed to speak.

_____ 9. Madeline's boss _____(e)d her in her old job as shop manager when she returned to work after maternity leave.

_____ 10. Hal and Lisa spent so much on their new house that they had almost no money left to furnish it. It seems _____ to have this lovely, expensive home filled with cast-off sofas and chairs from thrift shops and garage sales.

SCORE: (Number correct) _____ × 10 = _____ %

Mastery Test: *Chapter 13 (Ann's Love of Animals)*

In the space provided, write the word from the box needed to complete each sentence. Then put the **letter** of that word in the column at the left. Use each word once.

A. **advocate**	B. **antipathy**	C. **emancipate**	D. **idiosyncrasy**	E. **imminent**
F. **impede**	G. **inclusive**	H. **jurisdiction**	I. **precarious**	J. **preposterous**

_____ 1. Some of the people on the newspaper staff have odd habits. One reporter, for example, has the _____ of always wearing a bow tie.

_____ 2. That biography of Benjamin Franklin is all-_____; it covers all stages of his life, from birth to death.

_____ 3. My English teacher _____s students' doing a lot of personal reading in addition to their homework assignments. He feels that the more we read, the better we'll write.

_____ 4. The little girl's hearing loss had _____(e)d her speech development, so she couldn't speak as well as most other children her age.

_____ 5. Dogs seem to have a natural _____ for snakes. The first time my usually gentle collie saw a snake, she began snarling and showing her teeth.

_____ 6. The fleeing criminal headed for Mexico, where U.S. authorities had no _____.

_____ 7. Black clouds and rumbling thunder made it obvious that a storm was _____.

_____ 8. According to the Bible, Moses demanded that the Egyptian king _____ the slaves.

_____ 9. For elected officials, even the appearance of dishonesty can be _____, threatening the end of their careers.

_____ 10. Why in the world would a multi-millionaire shoplift a four-dollar bottle of aspirin? The act seems _____, but that's what police say happened.

SCORE: (Number correct) _____ × 10 = _____ %

Name: _____

Mastery Test: *Chapter 14 (A Costume Party)*

In the space provided, write the word from the box needed to complete each sentence. Then put the **letter** of that word in the column at the left. Use each word once.

A. **austere**	B. **esoteric**	C. **facsimile**	D. **grotesque**	E. **mesmerize**
F. **metamorphosis**	G. **notorious**	H. **perfunctory**	I. **provocative**	J. **travesty**

_____ 1. Hitler is so _____ that his name has come to represent evil to most people.

_____ 2. A native of Kansas, Randy was _____(e)d by the towering skyline of New York City.

_____ 3. My brother's major—nuclear physics—is so _____ that he finds it difficult to discuss it at length with most people.

_____ 4. Quaker meeting houses tend to be very _____ because the worshippers don't want to be distracted by a lot of decoration.

_____ 5. I spend a little more money by buying my clothes at Bloom's, but it's worth it. The salespeople there give me sincere personal attention, instead of the _____ treatment I've experienced at other stores.

_____ 6. Common ways to make ads _____ are the use of humor and famous singers.

_____ 7. Numerous bee stings caused Levi's face to swell in such a _____ manner that he was barely recognizable.

_____ 8. In the front window of a local French restaurant is a _____ of the Eiffel Tower— in miniature, of course.

_____ 9. With its violence and phony drama, most so-called "professional" wrestling is really a _____ of the sport.

_____ 10. Panicked by his wife's leaving him, Travis immediately promised to undergo a complete _____: from a cold workaholic to a warm person who makes time for his family. To do so, he's even willing to go into therapy.

SCORE: (Number correct) _____ × 10 = _____ %

Name: _____

Mastery Test: *Chapter 15 (The Missing Painting)*

In the space provided, write the word from the box needed to complete each sentence. Then put the **letter** of that word in the column at the left. Use each word once.

A. **connoisseur**	B. **conspiracy**	C. **contrite**	D. **distraught**	E. **germane**
F. **lucid**	G. **plight**	H. **superficially**	I. **symmetrical**	J. **verbose**

_____ 1. Someone who admires all things French—food, art, wine, and literature—is called a Francophile, while a _____ of everything English is called an Anglophile.

_____ 2. To argue fairly, stick to the topic. Don't bring up old sore points that aren't _____ to the issue at hand.

_____ 3. In Shakespeare's well-known tragedy *Julius Caesar*, a group of Roman senators join in a _____ to assassinate Caesar.

_____ 4. When the young mother first missed her little boy in the park, she wasn't too disturbed, but after ten minutes of searching without success, she became _____.

_____ 5. The day-care teacher was disturbed to see Emily's father's reaction to the birthday card Emily had so carefully made for him. He glanced at it only _____ and said, "That's nice. Now get in the car."

_____ 6. Wendy's financial _____ is severe. She's out of work and has barely enough money for the bus fare to interview for a new job.

_____ 7. Because humans are basically _____—their left and right sides are mirror images of each other—they have a well-balanced appearance.

_____ 8. When my dog is scolded for some misdeed, her drooping tail and saddened eyes make it seem that she's _____.

_____ 9. If your essay is _____, it doesn't necessarily mean you're naturally wordier than other students. You just haven't taken the time to edit out repetitions and unnecessary words.

_____ 10. Cheryl was so helpless with laughter that she couldn't provide a _____ explanation of what had happened. She could only gasp out fragments of sentences, such as "And then the chair. . . . But Thomas was trying. . . . And the *noise!*"

SCORE: (Number correct) _____ × 10 = _____ %

Mastery Test: *Chapter 16 (An Ohio Girl in New York)*

In the space provided, write the word from the box needed to complete each sentence. Then put the **letter** of that word in the column at the left. Use each word once.

A. **adept**	B. **encompass**	C. **entrepreneur**	D. **eradicate**	E. **homogeneous**
F. **presumptuous**	G. **sordid**	H. **standardize**	I. **stint**	J. **stringent**

_____ 1. The principal called a special meeting to address the _____ problem of drug use in the school system.

_____ 2. Nancy has tried to _____ the ants in her kitchen, but no matter how often she sprays, they soon reappear.

_____ 3. The two-week survival course _____(e)d all we would need to know, from starting a campfire to building a shelter to finding food in the wilderness.

_____ 4. Some people would like all countries to adopt the metric system in order to _____ the system of weights and measures worldwide.

_____ 5. When Helen needed a kidney transplant, several of her friends insisted she take one of theirs. They didn't realize there are _____ guidelines determining who can be a successful donor.

_____ 6. When we were young, our grandfather would tell us colorful stories about his _____ as a circus clown.

_____ 7. I was annoyed with Eileen yesterday. I felt it was _____ of her to try to sell me magazine subscriptions since I had invited her over for a social visit.

_____ 8. An excellent public speaker with a likable personality, Jim is _____ at getting others to see things from his point of view.

_____ 9. On hot summer days in our small town, you can see many young _____s operating their own lemonade or iced-tea stands.

_____ 10. When we decided to get rid of our chickens, I offered our three white hens to a neighboring egg farmer, but he refused them. He wanted to keep his all-brown flock _____.

SCORE: (Number correct) _____ × 10 = _____ %

Mastery Test: *Chapter 17 (How Neat Is Neat Enough?)*

In the space provided, write the word from the box needed to complete each sentence. Then put the **letter** of that word in the column at the left. Use each word once.

A. **exhort**	B. **flamboyant**	C. **foible**	D. **innocuous**	E. **magnanimous**
F. **masochist**	G. **meticulous**	H. **rancor**	I. **recrimination**	J. **repugnant**

_____ 1. Determined that the casting director would notice her, the would-be actress wore a _____ costume—featuring feathers, pearls, and spangles—to the audition.

_____ 2. Elizabeth is so kind and good-natured that her friends cheerfully overlook her _____ of talking too much.

_____ 3. The scratch on our car's fender seemed _____ at first, but it soon began to rust. We ended up paying $275 to have it fixed.

_____ 4. Because he'd had so much difficulty with his studies, Oscar's parents _____(e)d him to go to summer school.

_____ 5. It's amazing how _____ a formerly appetizing dish can become after it's spent a few weeks forgotten in the back of the refrigerator.

_____ 6. It certainly was _____ of Charlie to forgive Eric for losing Charlie's winning lottery ticket worth $500.

_____ 7. Karen's friends called her a _____ when they learned that she planned to run in two marathons in one weekend.

_____ 8. The home-team fans felt such _____ for the visiting team that they began booing and shouting insults before the game even began.

_____ 9. Henry is _____ about his car's upkeep. He washes the car by hand every Saturday, changes the oil four times a year, and won't allow anyone to eat in it.

_____ 10. The warring couple spent their first session with the marriage counselor trading _____s such as "You're never home at night!" and "Well, if you weren't so grouchy, I might stay home more!"

SCORE: (Number correct) _____ × 10 = _____ %

Mastery Test: *Chapter 19 (Halloween Troubles)*

In the space provided, write the word from the box needed to complete each sentence. Then put the **letter** of that word in the column at the left. Use each word once.

A. chide	B. coalition	C. commensurate	D. connotation	E. diabolic
F. dilapidated	G. integral	H. noxious	I. scenario	J. yen

_____   1. For most people, the word *home* has warmer _____s than the word *house* does.

_____   2. In our literature class, we had an interesting discussion about sexism in fairy tales. For instance, why do such stories often feature a _____ witch or queen who is cruel to the hero or heroine?

_____   3. NATO (the North Atlantic Treaty Organization) is a _____ of countries joined together by common concerns about defense.

_____   4. My uncle can't understand his wife's _____ for pickled herring, but then she can't comprehend his desire for fried pork rinds.

_____   5. Flo can't seem to find a job _____ with her abilities. Although she has a master's degree in physics, she is now working as a temporary secretary.

_____   6. Humor is _____ to Jamal's way of looking at life. He finds a way to laugh at even the most difficult situations.

_____   7. Although the abandoned shack was _____, its roof was still whole and offered welcome relief from the sudden downpour.

_____   8. I _____(e)d the kids for spraying each other with the hose, but it was so hot out that I couldn't bring myself to scold them very severely.

_____   9. Elsie's parents are such completely different types of people that it's hard to imagine a _____ in which they would meet and decide to marry.

_____   10. I don't admire beautiful, perfect lawns as much as I used to. Now I worry about what sort of _____ chemicals the homeowners use to control weeds and insects.

SCORE: (Number correct) _____ × 10 = _____ %

Name: _____

Mastery Test: *Chapter 20 (Thomas Dooley)*

In the space provided, write the word from the box needed to complete each sentence. Then put the **letter** of that word in the column at the left. Use each word once.

A. **atrophy**	B. **deplore**	C. **deprivation**	D. **exacerbate**	E. **imperative**
F. **mitigate**	G. **objective**	H. **panacea**	I. **unprecedented**	J. **utilitarian**

_____ 1. You can _____ the stress of preparing for finals by studying carefully throughout the semester.

_____ 2. David's mother left an urgent message on his answering machine: "It's _____ that you call me before Thursday!"

_____ 3. The doctors explained that Uncle Tim's muscles will gradually _____, making it increasingly more difficult for him to walk.

_____ 4. My brother's dorm room is strictly _____. The room is empty except for the necessities: a desk, chair, bed, dresser, and bookcase.

_____ 5. Marie wished her husband would be more _____ and consider the facts instead of always judging things by his own narrow point of view, without even thinking.

_____ 6. Karen believes that moving away from home would be a(n) _____ for her problems, but I think it will take more than that to cure all her difficulties.

_____ 7. People who suffer a(n) _____ of foods containing vitamin C develop a disease called scurvy.

_____ 8. Luis doesn't simply _____ the evils in the world; he tries to work to make the world better.

_____ 9. The high-school band has won the state competition for a(n) _____ six straight years. The previous record was five years in a row.

_____ 10. Bonnie thought ice water would cool the burning in her mouth from the Chinese mustard, but a drink did just the opposite—the water _____(e)d her discomfort.

SCORE: (Number correct) _____ × 10 = _____ %

Mastery Test: *Chapter 21 (Twelve Grown Men in a Bug)*

In the space provided, write the word from the box needed to complete each sentence. Then put the **letter** of that word in the column at the left. Use each word once.

A. **decorum**	B. **espouse**	C. **exhilaration**	D. **exorbitant**	E. **extricate**
F. **facilitate**	G. **orthodox**	H. **rejuvenate**	I. **synchronize**	J. **tenuous**

_____ 1. A man on the street corner handed out pamphlets that _____(e)d the cause of the homeless.

_____ 2. The injured deer carefully _____(e)d itself from the thorny brush by the side of the road.

_____ 3. The ski trip was worthwhile just to see the _____ on Joanne's face the first time she made it down the hill without falling.

_____ 4. People hired for the staff of the elegant new hotel must have a strong sense of _____. Guests there will expect to be treated with formal politeness.

_____ 5. Dawn's boyfriend sometimes shows poor judgment. Although he makes a very low salary, he spends a(n) _____ amount of money on fancy sneakers and leather jackets.

_____ 6. Uncle Richard loves his power tools because they _____ tasks he finds difficult because of his arthritis.

_____ 7. "A cup of warm cocoa will _____ you," said Mom. And sure enough, I soon felt as good as new.

_____ 8. My friendship with Debby is _____. If it were subjected to the least bit of conflict, I don't think it would survive.

_____ 9. The differing times on the clocks in the living room, kitchen, and bedroom drive me crazy. Before going to bed tonight, I'm going to _____ them.

_____ 10. _____ standards of dress vary from culture to culture. While men in the United States are expected to wear pants, men in other countries often wear long robes.

SCORE: (Number correct) _____ × 10 = _____ %

Mastery Test: *Chapter 22 (Adjusting to a Group Home)*

In the space provided, write the word from the box needed to complete each sentence. Then put the **letter** of that word in the column at the left. Use each word once.

A. **assimilate**	B. **belligerent**	C. **demeanor**	D. **denunciation**	E. **dissipate**
F. **indolent**	G. **inherent**	H. **nonchalant**	I. **unassuming**	J. **unilateral**

_____ 1. Will's moody _____ was a mystery to Mom, but I knew why his behavior was so strange.

_____ 2. To help new immigrants _____, the local college is offering evening and weekend classes in English as a Second Language.

_____ 3. In his _____ of my father's lifestyle, the doctor said, "If you don't stop smoking and start exercising, you'll get old before your time."

_____ 4. I was surprised to learn the Saudi Arabian girl in my economics class was a member of the royal family. She was so _____ that I never suspected there was anything special about her.

_____ 5. Once Bev and I agreed to talk about our differences, the tension between us _____(e)d, and we were able to discuss our points of view in a relaxed manner.

_____ 6. Most people believe that love is a(n) _____ human emotion, built into our very makeup.

_____ 7. Some dogs are as gentle as a butterfly, but others are _____ and should be kept on a leash.

_____ 8. Richie is so _____ that he will sometimes actually lie on the couch watching a program he dislikes because he's too lazy to use the remote control.

_____ 9. The boys were afraid Mr. Norton would lose his temper when he saw what their baseball had done to his fence, but, much to their relief, he was very _____ about it.

_____ 10. "I'm all for involving children in family decisions when possible," the counselor said, "but at times it's best for parents to make _____ decisions. After all, parents do have maturity and experience on their side."

SCORE: (Number correct) _____ × 10 = _____ %	

Mastery Test: *Chapter 23 (A Different Kind of Doctor)*

In the space provided, write the word from the box needed to complete each sentence. Then put the **letter** of that word in the column at the left. Use each word once.

A. **analogy**	B. **annihilate**	C. **criterion**	D. **emanate**	E. **holistic**
F. **placebo**	G. **proficient**	H. **staunch**	I. **subversive**	J. **vindicate**

_____ 1. To _____ himself, Joe produced evidence that he had been out of town the day that green paint was sprayed all over school.

_____ 2. One widely used _____ is the comparison of the pastor of a congregation to the shepherd of a flock of sheep.

_____ 3. A delicious aroma of baking bread _____(e)d from the kitchen.

_____ 4. It made me angry when my parents judged my boyfriends only by the _____ of the length of their hair.

_____ 5. I feel sorry for ants when they work so hard to construct an anthill, only to have a child come along and _____ it with one blow of his foot.

_____ 6. Dr. Wyatt is a _____ practitioner. She considers the health of the entire body when attempting to heal one of its parts.

_____ 7. The sports fans in our town are _____ supporters of the home team. They're loyal even during a losing season.

_____ 8. Zamil used to be a _____ secretary, but since she hadn't worked in a while, she decided to brush up on her office skills before going back to work.

_____ 9. The old movie was about a _____ plot that failed to overthrow a powerful, cruel dictator.

_____ 10. Carl was furious when he realized his doctor had been treating his headaches with _____s. He felt this treatment meant the doctor believed Carl was only imagining his headaches.

SCORE: (Number correct) _____ × 10 = _____ %

Mastery Test: *Chapter 25 (My Devilish Older Sister)*

In the space provided, write the word from the box needed to complete each sentence. Then put the **letter** of that word in the column at the left. Use each word once.

A. **disparity**	B. **forestall**	C. **insidious**	D. **insinuate**	E. **interrogate**
F. **obsequious**	G. **omnipotent**	H. **opportune**	I. **permeate**	J. **retribution**

_____ 1. To _____ any chance of the chicken salad spoiling, do not let it sit outside all afternoon at the picnic.

_____ 2. As _____ for starting a rebellion against the government, the leaders of the uprising were jailed.

_____ 3. Don't tell Jasmin that her new striped dress makes her look slender. She'll think you mean to _____ that she's overweight.

_____ 4. Lead poisoning may not be immediately apparent. It can be _____, eventually leading to effects as harmful as brain damage.

_____ 5. My grandfather believes his 22-year-old fiancée loves him, but the _____ in their ages makes it seem more likely that she loves his money.

_____ 6. In describing a(n) _____ coworker, Elizabeth explained, "If a superior says 'Jump like a frog!' her only response is 'How high?'"

_____ 7. Quicksand is formed when water _____s loose sand and makes its surface so soft that it cannot support weight.

_____ 8. In a democracy, no single person is _____. Even the President has to get approval from Congress in order to carry out his policies.

_____ 9. Since my parents were so pleased with my grades, I thought it was a(n) _____ time to ask if I could borrow the car.

_____ 10. When rumors began about steroids in the weight room, the principal kept all members of the weightlifting club after school to _____ them about drugs.

SCORE: (Number correct) _____ × 10 = _____ %

Mastery Test: *Chapter 26 (Harriet Tubman)*

In the space provided, write the word from the box needed to complete each sentence. Then put the **letter** of that word in the column at the left. Use each word once.

A. **complement**	B. **discreet**	C. **fastidious**	D. **flout**	E. **heinous**
F. **implement**	G. **impromptu**	H. **inference**	I. **intuition**	J. **obtrusive**

____ 1. Cynthia's all-white living room is a little dull. If it were my house, I'd _____ it with some colorful pillows and pictures.

____ 2. Bookkeepers and accountants must be _____. Overlooking even one little detail can cause problems in their work.

____ 3. The new people next door seem to actually want to create bad feelings with their neighbors. They _____ neighborhood standards by never cutting the grass, leaving an abandoned car in the yard, and dumping trash everywhere.

____ 4. When our school _____ s the reduced budget, there will no longer be money to support extracurricular activities.

____ 5. Politicians must be _____ about their personal lives because revealing sensitive information can give other candidates something to use against them in an election campaign.

____ 6. Leila's bright red dress was certainly _____ at the funeral.

____ 7. My parents haven't said what they think of my new boyfriend, but since they are silent, my _____ is that they dislike him.

____ 8. Obviously, some people enjoy reading about _____ crimes. Books about murders are often best-sellers, and the more gruesome the crime, the better the book sells.

____ 9. One group that had no time to rehearse a skit gave a(n) _____ performance so funny and lively that it may even have benefited from the lack of practice.

____ 10. I just knew Emil's business partner would let him down, but he wouldn't believe me until it happened. Now Emil says he should have trusted my "feminine _____."

> ***SCORE:*** (Number correct) _____ × 10 = _____ %

Mastery Test: *Chapter 27 (Tony's Rehabilitation)*

In the space provided, write the word from the box needed to complete each sentence. Then put the **letter** of that word in the column at the left. Use each word once.

| A. **auspicious** | B. **expedite** | C. **extenuating** | D. **fraudulent** | E. **innuendo** |
| F. **rebuke** | G. **redeem** | H. **subordinate** | I. **transgress** | J. **vehement** |

_____ 1. People who believe in astrology often plan important events for days that the stars "say" are

_____.

_____ 2. Any ad for a product that promises to help you lose weight without dieting or exercising must be

_____.

_____ 3. Needing his order soon, a customer spoke to the manager, who promised to _____
a rapid delivery.

_____ 4. I'll never forgive myself for gossiping so cruelly about our new neighbor. Now that I know and like

her, I've _____(e)d myself for my behavior a hundred times.

_____ 5. "It's true I lied to you about being out of town last weekend," Jan admitted to Brian, "but there were

_____ circumstances. I had promised your mother that I wouldn't see you

over the weekend so that you could concentrate on studying for Monday's exam."

_____ 6. Turning away from a life of crime, the robber _____(e)d himself by teaching
citizens how to protect themselves against theft.

_____ 7. Malik reports to his boss—the vice president of the company. She, in turn, is _____
to the executive vice president.

_____ 8. Joey's parents had laid down so many rules for him that it was impossible for the little boy not to

_____ once in a while.

_____ 9. My uncle is so _____ in his opinions on politics that it's impossible to have a
casual conversation with him on the topic. He gets too carried away by his passion.

_____ 10. Richard listened politely to the information about where to buy a hairpiece, but he resented the

_____ that his baldness made him unattractive.

| *SCORE:* (Number correct) _____ × 10 = _____ % |

Name: _____

Mastery Test: *Chapter 28 (Rumors)*

In the space provided, write the word from the box needed to complete each sentence. Then put the **letter** of that word in the column at the left. Use each word once.

A. **deride**	B. **derogatory**	C. **fabricate**	D. **impending**	E. **macabre**
F. **misconstrue**	G. **paramount**	H. **quandary**	I. **turbulent**	J. **validate**

_____   1. Children like to frighten each other at slumber parties by telling _____ stories about demons, ghosts, and vampires.

_____   2. Being with Fred can be depressing because of all his _____ remarks. Just once, I'd like to hear him say something good about someone else.

_____   3. When the staff heard that a huge snowstorm was on its way, everyone in the office left for home early, hoping to miss the _____ bad weather.

_____   4. You may get some laughs when you _____ someone's appearance, but some of us find your scornful remarks more in bad taste than amusing.

_____   5. Gina was so anxious to impress her college friends that she pretended to have a boyfriend at Harvard. The guy she _____(e)d was rich, intelligent, and spoke five foreign languages.

_____   6. My low opinion of Brian was _____(e)d when I learned he had faked an auto accident in order to file a dishonest insurance claim.

_____   7. I enjoy sailing when the water is calm, but if the lake becomes _____, I promptly become "seasick."

_____   8. Vicky always _____s my compliments, somehow finding an insult in every comment I intend to be encouraging.

_____   9. When your boss says a job is of _____ importance, you should consider it more important than any other project you're working on.

_____   10. Linda's adoptive parents were in a _____ about what to tell her regarding her birth. Should she be told the truth, or would it be too painful to know that she'd been left at the entrance of a hospital emergency room the day she was born?

SCORE: (Number correct) _____ × 10 = _____ %

Mastery Test: *Chapter 29 (The End of a Political Career)*

In the space provided, write the word from the box needed to complete each sentence. Then put the **letter** of that word in the column at the left. Use each word once.

A. **adroit**	B. **constituent**	C. **contention**	D. **irreparable**	E. **pinnacle**
F. **platitude**	G. **promiscuous**	H. **repudiate**	I. **spontaneous**	J. **stigma**

_____ 1. Our choir director claims that in the future, musicals will be considered as serious theater. Another _____ she makes is that jazz will be seen as classical music.

_____ 2. A former member of a white-supremacy group has _____(e)d his former beliefs and now lectures about the dangers of hate groups.

_____ 3. Not only was Aunt Minnie's antique Chinese vase _____ after Peter smashed it to bits, but his relationship with Aunt Minnie was also hopelessly ruined.

_____ 4. The family budget was tight, so Irene, _____ at using her garden for gifts, turned her vegetable crops into gourmet relishes and her flowers into dried wreaths.

_____ 5. For parents trying to teach their children to be faithful to one partner, it is maddening to hear athletes and other celebrities brag about being _____.

_____ 6. When the people at the beach realized that Tiger Woods was in the sailboat passing by, they burst into _____ applause.

_____ 7. Congresspeople who represent rural areas are likely to support farm relief measures that will help their _____s.

_____ 8. My grandmother had wanted to be an actress, but her parents would not allow that. They didn't want to deal with the _____ of letting their daughter go "on the stage."

_____ 9. Is the _____ of a career the time when a person makes the most money, has the most power, or knows the most?

_____ 10. Talking with Denise about my problem wasn't really very helpful. All she had to say were _____s like "I'm sure everything will work out" and "Someday you'll look back on this and laugh."

> **SCORE:** (Number correct) _____ × 10 = _____ %

Mastery Test: *Chapter 30 (Firing Our Boss)*

In the space provided, write the word from the box needed to complete each sentence. Then put the **letter** of that word in the column at the left. Use each word once.

A. **abrasive**	B. **admonish**	C. **antithesis**	D. **culmination**	E. **docile**
F. **emulate**	G. **hierarchy**	H. **incapacitate**	I. **prognosis**	J. **tumult**

_____ 1. Dee's parrot is so _____ that you can hand-feed it without fear of getting bitten.

_____ 2. Sandpaper comes in different degrees of roughness. The most _____ type has large pieces of sand.

_____ 3. When it comes to work, Marco is the _____ of Lee. Marco is ambitious and finds work challenging, while Lee tries to wriggle out of work whenever possible.

_____ 4. It's appropriate to _____ a worker who forgets to punch the timecard only once or twice, but a stronger reaction is needed for someone who forgets almost every day.

_____ 5. The Fourth of July show begins with a band concert. Next, there's a sing-along. The _____ of the evening is a fifteen-minute display of spectacular fireworks.

_____ 6. There's no way I'll be able to give a speech tomorrow. I've just begun to lose my voice, and the doctor's _____ is that it'll get even weaker for at least two more days.

_____ 7. What is the point of having a band play at that restaurant? The _____ from the diners is so great that you can't possibly appreciate the music.

_____ 8. My broken arm was beneficial in that it _____(e)d me for most household chores.

_____ 9. My brother quit smoking the day he saw his six-year-old pick up one of his cigarettes and put it in her own mouth. "I want my daughter to _____ my good behaviors, not my bad ones," he said.

_____ 10. If I ever entered the military service, I'd have to learn the _____ of ranks. I have no idea if a major is higher than a lieutenant or vice versa.

SCORE: (Number correct) _____ × 10 = _____ %

Answers to the Mastery Tests: ADVANCING VOCABULARY SKILLS

Chapter 1 (Apartment Problems)

1. I	6. A
2. E	7. B
3. H	8. F
4. D	9. G
5. J	10. C

Chapter 2 (Hardly a Loser)

1. E	6. C
2. I	7. A
3. B	8. D
4. J	9. F
5. H	10. G

Chapter 3 (Grandfather at the Art Museum)

1. D	6. G
2. C	7. J
3. H	8. I
4. F	9. E
5. B	10. A

Chapter 4 (My Brother's Mental Illness)

1. I	6. C
2. A	7. J
3. E	8. F
4. G	9. B
5. H	10. D

Chapter 5 (A Get-Rich-Quick-Scam)

1. E	6. F
2. C	7. A
3. H	8. I
4. B	9. D
5. G	10. J

Chapter 7 (A Phony Friend)

1. F	6. G
2. E	7. B
3. A	8. C
4. D	9. I
5. J	10. H

Chapter 8 (Coco the Gorilla)

1. E	6. B
2. J	7. G
3. C	8. D
4. A	9. I
5. F	10. H

Chapter 9 (Our Annual Garage Sale)

1. B	6. I
2. A	7. F
3. E	8. H
4. C	9. G
5. D	10. J

Chapter 10 (A Debate on School Uniforms)

1. H	6. I
2. F	7. G
3. B	8. D
4. C	9. J
5. E	10. A

Chapter 11 (My Large Family)

1. F	6. D
2. C	7. A
3. B	8. G
4. J	9. I
5. H	10. E

Chapter 13 (Ann's Love of Animals)

1. D	6. H
2. G	7. E
3. A	8. C
4. F	9. I
5. B	10. J

Chapter 14 (A Costume Party)

1. G	6. I
2. E	7. D
3. B	8. C
4. A	9. J
5. H	10. F

Chapter 15 (The Missing Painting)

1. A	6. G
2. E	7. I
3. B	8. C
4. D	9. J
5. H	10. F

Chapter 16 (An Ohio Girl in New York)

1. G
2. D
3. B
4. H
5. J

6. I
7. F
8. A
9. C
10. E

Chapter 17 (How Neat Is Neat Enough?)

1. B
2. C
3. D
4. A
5. J

6. E
7. F
8. H
9. G
10. I

Chapter 19 (Halloween Troubles)

1. D
2. E
3. B
4. J
5. C

6. G
7. F
8. A
9. I
10. H

Chapter 20 (Thomas Dooley)

1. F
2. E
3. A
4. J
5. G

6. H
7. C
8. B
9. I
10. D

Chapter 21 (Twelve Grown Men in a Bug)

1. B
2. E
3. C
4. A
5. D

6. F
7. H
8. J
9. I
10. G

Chapter 22 (Adjusting to a Group Home)

1. C
2. A
3. D
4. I
5. E

6. G
7. B
8. F
9. H
10. J

Chapter 23 (A Different Kind of Doctor)

1. J
2. A
3. D
4. C
5. B

6. E
7. H
8. G
9. I
10. F

Chapter 25 (My Devilish Older Sister)

1. B
2. J
3. D
4. C
5. A

6. F
7. I
8. G
9. H
10. E

Chapter 26 (Harriet Tubman)

1. A
2. C
3. D
4. F
5. B

6. J
7. H
8. E
9. G
10. I

Chapter 27 (Tony's Rehabilitation)

1. A
2. D
3. B
4. F
5. C

6. G
7. H
8. I
9. J
10. E

Chapter 28 (Rumors)

1. E
2. B
3. D
4. A
5. C

6. J
7. I
8. F
9. G
10. H

Chapter 29 (The End of a Political Career)

1. C
2. H
3. D
4. A
5. G

6. I
7. B
8. J
9. E
10. F

Chapter 30 (Firing Our Boss)

1. E
2. A
3. C
4. B
5. D

6. I
7. J
8. H
9. F
10. G

Mastery Test: *Unit One*

PART A
Complete each sentence in a way that clearly shows you understand the meaning of the **boldfaced** word. Take a minute to plan your answer before you write.

Example: I was being **facetious** when I said that _____ *my parrot can tell the future. In fact, he's always wrong* _____.

1. An **illicit** way to make a living is _____

   _____.

2. A common **detriment** to good health is _____

   _____.

3. Rhetta **frittered** away her money on _____

   _____.

4. A **zealot** in the environmental movement would never _____

   _____.

5. Being **gregarious**, Marisol wants to celebrate her birthday by _____

   _____.

6. I was **despondent** because _____

   _____.

7. An **inane** way to study for final exams is to _____

   _____.

8. At the mall, my **impetuous** friend _____

   _____.

9. The mayor **estranged** many voters when he _____

   _____.

10. In **retrospect**, I realized that _____

   _____.

(Continues on next page)

PART B

Use each of the following ten words in sentences of your own. Make it clear that you know the meaning of the word you use. Feel free to use the past tense or plural form of a word.

A. **ambiguous**	B. **charlatan**	C. **hoist**	D. **infallible**	E. **irrevocable**
F. **ostentatious**	G. **proliferation**	H. **scoff**	I. **scrupulous**	J. **ubiquitous**

11. _____

_____

12. _____

_____

13. _____

_____

14. _____

_____

15. _____

_____

16. _____

_____

17. _____

_____

18. _____

_____

19. _____

_____

20. _____

_____

SCORE: (Number correct) _____ × 5 = _____ %

Mastery Test: *Unit Two*

PART A
Complete each sentence in a way that clearly shows you understand the meaning of the **boldfaced** word. Take a minute to plan your answer before you write.

Example: On our picnic, we carried a basket **replete** with _____ *a complete meal and plenty of snacks* _____ .

1. A very **terse** answer to the question "Did you have fun at the dentist's office?" is "_____

    _____."

2. A loud voice would probably be a **liability** in _____

    _____.

3. One good way to **bolster** a friend's spirits is to _____

    _____.

4. Marcie has a tendency to be **vociferous**. When the waitress brought her the wrong food, for example, she

    _____

    _____.

5. Reverend Patterson's appearance is **incongruous** with my image of a minister. He wears _____

    _____.

6. When Barb's grandfather died, she found **solace** in _____

    _____.

7. Vanessa is so **egocentric** that _____

    _____.

8. I have a **propensity** to _____

    _____.

9. One way to **circumvent** rush-hour traffic is to _____

    _____.

10. My idea of a **utopia** is _____

    _____.

(Continues on next page)

PART B

Use each of the following ten words in sentences of your own. Make it clear that you know the meaning of the word you use. Feel free to use the past tense or plural form of a word.

A. **autonomy**	B. **clandestine**	C. **depreciate**	D. **exonerate**	E. **inquisitive**
F. **raucous**	G. **reiterate**	H. **relegate**	I. **sedentary**	J. **sham**

11. _____

_____

12. _____

_____

13. _____

_____

14. _____

_____

15. _____

_____

16. _____

_____

17. _____

_____

18. _____

_____

19. _____

_____

20. _____

_____

SCORE: (Number correct) _____ × 5 = _____ %

Mastery Test: *Unit Three*

PART A
Complete each sentence in a way that clearly shows you understand the meaning of the **boldfaced** word. Take a minute to plan your answer before you write.

Example: Kim must be an **adept** manager because _____ she was just promoted again _____ .

1. My parents often **exhort** me to _____

   _____ .

2. I was **distraught** when _____

   _____ .

3. My best friend has an odd **foible**: _____

   _____ .

4. The **magnanimous** boss _____

   _____ .

5. Two things I find **repugnant** are _____

   _____ .

6. The singer's **flamboyant** outfit consisted of _____

   _____ .

7. As a child, I was **contrite** after _____

   _____ .

8. Mr. Cowens has such **stringent** standards that _____

   _____ .

9. One **verbose** way of saying no is " _____

   _____ ."

10. At the party, Len told a **preposterous** story about _____

    _____

    _____ .

(Continues on next page)

PART B

Use each of the following ten words in sentences of your own. Make it clear that you know the meaning of the word you use. Feel free to use the past tense or plural form of a word.

A. **antipathy**	B. **eradicate**	C. **grotesque**	D. **idiosyncrasy**	E. **mesmerize**
F. **meticulous**	G. **plight**	H. **precarious**	I. **stint**	J. **superficially**

11. _____

_____

12. _____

_____

13. _____

_____

14. _____

_____

15. _____

_____

16. _____

_____

17. _____

_____

18. _____

_____

19. _____

_____

20. _____

_____

SCORE: (Number correct) _____ × 5 = _____ %

Mastery Test: *Unit Four*

PART A
Complete each sentence in a way that clearly shows you understand the meaning of the **boldfaced** word. Take a minute to plan your answer before you write.

Example: Because Joanne had a sudden **yen** for M&M's, she ___*ran to the convenience store to buy some*___.

1. Two **utilitarian** objects are _____

_____.

2. In a **belligerent** mood, my brother said, " _____

_____."

3. I realized just how **indolent** Teri is when she _____

_____.

4. To me, some **connotations** of the word *summer* are _____

_____.

5. An **integral** part of school is _____

_____.

6. A good way to **exacerbate** a sore throat is to _____

_____.

7. I **deplore** _____ because _____

_____.

8. Flo's boss **chided** her when _____

_____.

9. I am quite **proficient** at _____. For example, _____

_____.

10. **Emanating** from the kitchen was _____

_____.

(Continues on next page)

PART B

Use each of the following ten words in sentences of your own. Make it clear that you know the meaning of the word you use. Feel free to use the past tense or plural form of a word.

A. **analogy**	B. **assimilate**	C. **denunciation**	D. **dilapidated**	E. **exorbitant**
F. **imperative**	G. **nonchalant**	H. **panacea**	I. **rejuvenate**	J. **vindicate**

11. _____

_____

12. _____

_____

13. _____

_____

14. _____

_____

15. _____

_____

16. _____

_____

17. _____

_____

18. _____

_____

19. _____

_____

20. _____

_____

SCORE: (Number correct) _____ × 5 = _____ %

Name: _____

Mastery Test: *Unit Five*

PART A

Complete each sentence in a way that clearly shows you understand the meaning of the **boldfaced** word. Take a minute to plan your answer before you write.

Example: Jeff should be **discreet** about the party because _____ *it's meant to be a surprise* _____.

1. One extremely **macabre** movie is _____

   _____.

2. Ted **flouted** the traffic laws by _____

   _____.

3. There was a huge **tumult** when _____

   _____.

4. After the date, my parents **interrogated** me by _____

   _____.

5. Charles **misconstrued** my dinner invitation to be _____

   _____.

6. Maureen obviously had **fabricated** her excuse. She told the teacher, "_____

   _____."

7. To **implement** her vacation plans, Ruth started to _____

   _____.

8. After getting a D in chemistry, I tried to **redeem** myself by _____

   _____.

9. You can tell that my sister is **fastidious** by looking at her bedroom, where _____

   _____.

10. When Len said that his brother wouldn't even give him the time of day, he meant to **insinuate** that _____

    _____

    _____.

(Continues on next page)

PART B

Use each of the following ten words in sentences of your own. Make it clear that you know the meaning of the word you use. Feel free to use the past tense or plural form of a word.

A. **antithesis**	B. **complement**	C. **contention**	D. **emulate**	E. **intuition**
F. **irreparable**	G. **paramount**	H. **quandary**	I. **rebuke**	J. **spontaneous**

11. _____

_____

12. _____

_____

13. _____

_____

14. _____

_____

15. _____

_____

16. _____

_____

17. _____

_____

18. _____

_____

19. _____

_____

20. _____

_____

SCORE: (Number correct) _____ × 5 = _____ %

THE TOWNSEND PRESS

Vocabulary Placement Test

This test contains 100 items. You have 30 minutes to take the test. In the space provided, write the letter of the choice that is closest in meaning to the **boldfaced** word.

Important: Keep in mind that this test is for placement purposes only. **If you do not know a word, leave the space blank rather than guess at it.**

_____ 1. to **deceive**   **a)** prove   **b)** mislead   **c)** reach   **d)** get back

_____ 2. **earnest**   **a)** serious and sincere   **b)** illegal   **c)** wealthy   **d)** hidden

_____ 3. **inferior**   **a)** not proper   **b)** clear   **c)** poor in quality   **d)** inside

_____ 4. to **comprehend**   **a)** describe   **b)** understand   **c)** make use of   **d)** prepare

_____ 5. **unanimous**   **a)** alone   **b)** animal-like   **c)** unfriendly   **d)** in full agreement

_____ 6. the **vicinity**   **a)** area nearby   **b)** city   **c)** enemy   **d)** information

_____ 7. **current**   **a)** healthy   **b)** modern   **c)** well-known   **d)** necessary

_____ 8. **internal**   **a)** forever   **b)** inside   **c)** outside   **d)** brief

_____ 9. **maximum**   **a)** least   **b)** expensive   **c)** cheap   **d)** greatest

_____ 10. an **objective**   **a)** goal   **b)** puzzle   **c)** cause   **d)** supply

_____ 11. a **potential**   **a)** favorite   **b)** possibility   **c)** refusal   **d)** desire

_____ 12. to **detect**   **a)** discover   **b)** make   **c)** follow   **d)** commit a crime

_____ 13. to **establish**   **a)** receive   **b)** delay   **c)** set up   **d)** attract

_____ 14. to **pursue**   **a)** follow   **b)** run from   **c)** suggest   **d)** create

_____ 15. **vague**   **a)** missing   **b)** unclear   **c)** kind   **d)** necessary

_____ 16. **suitable**   **a)** simple   **b)** needed   **c)** profitable   **d)** proper

_____ 17. a **category**   **a)** kindness   **b)** horror   **c)** type   **d)** question

_____ 18. **reluctant**   **a)** unwilling   **b)** lost   **c)** unhappy   **d)** well-known

_____ 19. to **coincide**   **a)** pay   **b)** decide   **c)** get in the way   **d)** happen together

_____ 20. to **inhabit**   **a)** enter   **b)** live in   **c)** get used to   **d)** understand

_____ 21. **apparent**   **a)** together   **b)** obvious   **c)** motherly   **d)** welcome

_____ 22. **accustomed**   **a)** in the habit   **b)** specially made   **c)** necessary   **d)** extra

_____ 23. to **revise**   **a)** give advice   **b)** go back   **c)** change   **d)** awaken

_____ 24. a **contrast**   **a)** purpose   **b)** choice   **c)** agreement   **d)** difference

_____ 25. **awkward**   **a)** forward   **b)** boring   **c)** clumsy   **d)** clever

(Continues on next page)

_____ 26. **urban**   **a)** of a city   **b)** circular   **c)** not allowed   **d)** large

_____ 27. **lenient**   **a)** light   **b)** not strict   **c)** delayed   **d)** not biased

_____ 28. to **endorse**   **a)** suggest   **b)** stop   **c)** support   **d)** start

_____ 29. a **novice**   **a)** book   **b)** false impression   **c)** beginner   **d)** servant

_____ 30. to **deter**   **a)** prevent   **b)** make last longer   **c)** refuse   **d)** damage

_____ 31. to **verify**   **a)** imagine   **b)** prove   **c)** keep going   **d)** cancel

_____ 32. **moderate**   **a)** generous   **b)** not final   **c)** medium   **d)** bright

_____ 33. a **diversity**   **a)** separation   **b)** conclusion   **c)** enthusiasm   **d)** variety

_____ 34. **accessible**   **a)** easily reached   **b)** itchy   **c)** difficult   **d)** folded

_____ 35. **lethal**   **a)** sweet-smelling   **b)** ancient   **c)** deadly   **d)** healthy

_____ 36. **vivid**   **a)** brightly colored   **b)** local   **c)** large   **d)** very talkative

_____ 37. to **convey**   **a)** allow   **b)** communicate   **c)** invent   **d)** approve

_____ 38. **inevitable**   **a)** unavoidable   **b)** dangerous   **c)** spiteful   **d)** doubtful

_____ 39. a **ritual**   **a)** business deal   **b)** war   **c)** ceremony   **d)** show

_____ 40. **elaborate**   **a)** large   **b)** complex   **c)** expensive   **d)** boring

_____ 41. the **essence**   **a)** fundamental characteristic   **b)** tiny part   **c)** much later   **d)** rule

_____ 42. to **coerce**   **a)** attract   **b)** refuse   **c)** remove   **d)** force

_____ 43. **skeptical**   **a)** stubborn   **b)** forceful   **c)** generous   **d)** doubting

_____ 44. **vital**   **a)** weak   **b)** stiff   **c)** necessary   **d)** unimportant

_____ 45. **innate**   **a)** learned   **b)** underneath   **c)** inborn   **d)** clever

_____ 46. a **vocation**   **a)** hobby   **b)** trip   **c)** report   **d)** profession

_____ 47. to **defy**   **a)** send for   **b)** resist   **c)** improve   **d)** approve

_____ 48. **adverse**   **a)** strict   **b)** profitable   **c)** rhyming   **d)** harmful

_____ 49. **consecutive**   **a)** late   **b)** following one after another   **c)** able   **d)** at the same time

_____ 50. **audible**   **a)** able to be heard   **b)** believable   **c)** willing   **d)** nearby

(Continues on next page)

_____ 51. to **encounter**   **a)** come upon   **b)** count up   **c)** depart from   **d)** attack

_____ 52. **obsolete**   **a)** modern   **b)** difficult to believe   **c)** out-of-date   **d)** not sold

_____ 53. to **terminate**   **a)** stop   **b)** continue   **c)** begin   **d)** approach

_____ 54. **altruistic**   **a)** honest   **b)** lying   **c)** proud   **d)** unselfish

_____ 55. to **enhance**   **a)** reject   **b)** get   **c)** improve   **d)** free

_____ 56. **nocturnal**   **a)** supposed   **b)** not logical   **c)** complex   **d)** active at night

_____ 57. to **suffice**   **a)** think up   **b)** be good enough   **c)** allow   **d)** reject

_____ 58. to **retaliate**   **a)** repair   **b)** repeat   **c)** renew   **d)** pay back

_____ 59. to **incorporate**   **a)** combine   **b)** anger   **c)** separate   **d)** calm

_____ 60. an **incentive**   **a)** fear   **b)** pride   **c)** concern   **d)** encouragement

_____ 61. **covert**   **a)** distant   **b)** hidden   **c)** changed   **d)** adjusted

_____ 62. to **alleviate**   **a)** make anxious   **b)** depart   **c)** infect   **d)** relieve

_____ 63. to **aspire**   **a)** dislike   **b)** strongly desire   **c)** impress   **d)** respect

_____ 64. an **extrovert**   **a)** shy person   **b)** magnet   **c)** main point   **d)** outgoing person

_____ 65. **prone**   **a)** disliked   **b)** tending   **c)** active   **d)** rested

_____ 66. **ominous**   **a)** happy   **b)** threatening   **c)** depressed   **d)** friendly

_____ 67. **complacent**   **a)** workable   **b)** lazy   **c)** self-satisfied   **d)** healthy

_____ 68. a **consensus**   **a)** majority opinion   **b)** total   **c)** study   **d)** approval

_____ 69. to **condone**   **a)** forgive   **b)** represent   **c)** arrest   **d)** appoint

_____ 70. **deficient**   **a)** forgotten   **b)** lacking   **c)** complete   **d)** well-known

_____ 71. **fallible**   **a)** capable of error   **b)** complete   **c)** incomplete   **d)** simple

_____ 72. **pragmatic**   **a)** ordinary   **b)** slow   **c)** wise   **d)** practical

_____ 73. **avid**   **a)** bored   **b)** disliked   **c)** enthusiastic   **d)** plentiful

_____ 74. **explicit**   **a)** everyday   **b)** distant   **c)** permanent   **d)** stated exactly

_____ 75. **ambivalent**   **a)** unknown   **b)** having mixed feelings   **c)** temporary   **d)** able to be done

(Continues on next page)

_____	76. **vicarious**	a) experienced indirectly	b) lively	c) inactive	d) occasional

_____ 76. **vicarious**   a) experienced indirectly   b) lively   c) inactive   d) occasional

_____ 77. **rudimentary**   a) rude   b) planned   c) partial   d) elementary

_____ 78. to **collaborate**   a) respect   b) work hard   c) work together   d) search

_____ 79. to **venerate**   a) protect   b) create   c) make unfriendly   d) respect

_____ 80. **inadvertent**   a) unintentional   b) not for sale   c) distant   d) near

_____ 81. **predisposed**   a) against   b) unwilling to speak   c) undecided   d) tending beforehand

_____ 82. **robust**   a) extremely careful   b) healthy and strong   c) tall   d) loyal

_____ 83. **sedentary**   a) sitting   b) excessive   c) harmless   d) repeated

_____ 84. **clandestine**   a) well-lit   b) secret   c) noble   d) harmless

_____ 85. **austere**   a) wealthy   b) complex   c) plain   d) far

_____ 86. **notorious**   a) too bold   b) written   c) known widely but unfavorably   d) lacking skill

_____ 87. **lucid**   a) clear   b) generous in forgiving   c) careful   d) bold

_____ 88. to **encompass**   a) include   b) draw   c) separate   d) purchase

_____ 89. **meticulous**   a) broken-down   b) curious   c) careful and exact   d) irregular

_____ 90. **innocuous**   a) delightful   b) harmless   c) dangerous   d) disappointing

_____ 91. to **rejuvenate**   a) set free   b) grow   c) refresh   d) make easier

_____ 92. to **facilitate**   a) approve   b) make easier   c) serve   d) clear from blame

_____ 93. **proficient**   a) proud   b) wise   c) skilled   d) well-known

_____ 94. to **emanate**   a) go above   b) run through   c) go down   d) come forth

_____ 95. to **implement**   a) encourage   b) carry out   c) insult   d) prevent

_____ 96. to **fabricate**   a) misinterpret   b) put away   c) clothe   d) invent

_____ 97. to **emulate**   a) be tardy   b) misunderstand   c) imitate   d) prepare

_____ 98. a **prognosis**   a) hope   b) prediction   c) opposite   d) memory

_____ 99. a **tumult**   a) uproar   b) uncertainty   c) series   d) scolding

_____ 100. to **insinuate**   a) demand   b) state   c) deny   d) hint

STOP. This is the end of the test. If there is time remaining, you may go back and recheck your answers. When the time is up, hand in both your answer sheet and this test booklet to your instructor.

To the Instructor: Use these guidelines to match your students with the appropriate TP vocabulary book.						
Score	0–9	10–24	25–49	50–74	75–90	91–100
Recommended Book	_VB_	_GBV_	_BVS_	_IVS_	_AVS_	_AWP_

ANSWER SHEET

1. _____	26. _____	51. _____	76. _____
2. _____	27. _____	52. _____	77. _____
3. _____	28. _____	53. _____	78. _____
4. _____	29. _____	54. _____	79. _____
5. _____	30. _____	55. _____	80. _____
6. _____	31. _____	56. _____	81. _____
7. _____	32. _____	57. _____	82. _____
8. _____	33. _____	58. _____	83. _____
9. _____	34. _____	59. _____	84. _____
10. _____	35. _____	60. _____	85. _____
11. _____	36. _____	61. _____	86. _____
12. _____	37. _____	62. _____	87. _____
13. _____	38. _____	63. _____	88. _____
14. _____	39. _____	64. _____	89. _____
15. _____	40. _____	65. _____	90. _____
16. _____	41. _____	66. _____	91. _____
17. _____	42. _____	67. _____	92. _____
18. _____	43. _____	68. _____	93. _____
19. _____	44. _____	69. _____	94. _____
20. _____	45. _____	70. _____	95. _____
21. _____	46. _____	71. _____	96. _____
22. _____	47. _____	72. _____	97. _____
23. _____	48. _____	73. _____	98. _____
24. _____	49. _____	74. _____	99. _____
25. _____	50. _____	75. _____	100. _____

ANSWER KEY

1. b	26. a	51. a	76. a
2. a	27. b	52. c	77. d
3. c	28. c	53. a	78. c
4. b	29. c	54. d	79. d
5. d	30. a	55. c	80. a
6. a	31. b	56. d	81. d
7. b	32. c	57. b	82. b
8. b	33. d	58. d	83. a
9. d	34. a	59. a	84. b
10. a	35. c	60. d	85. c
11. b	36. a	61. b	86. c
12. a	37. b	62. d	87. a
13. c	38. a	63. b	88. a
14. a	39. c	64. d	89. c
15. b	40. b	65. b	90. b
16. d	41. a	66. b	91. c
17. c	42. a	67. c	92. b
18. a	43. d	68. a	93. c
19. d	44. c	69. a	94. d
20. b	45. c	70. b	95. b
21. b	46. d	71. a	96. d
22. a	47. b	72. d	97. c
23. c	48. d	73. c	98. b
24. d	49. b	74. d	99. a
25. c	50. a	75. b	100. d

To the Instructor: Use these guidelines to match your students with the appropriate TP vocabulary book.

Score	0–9	10–24	25–49	50–74	75–90	91–100
Recommended Book	VB	GBV	BVS	IVS	AVS	AWP

Words and Word Parts in BUILDING VOCABULARY SKILLS

List of the 260 Vocabulary Words

absurd	compile	drastic	indignant	perceptive	sedate
accelerate	comply	dubious	indulgent	persistent	sequence
accessible	concede	ecstatic	inept	pessimist	severity
acknowledge	conceive	elaborate	inevitable	phobia	shrewd
acute	concise	elapse	infer	plausible	simultaneous
adapt	confirm	elite	infinite	pretense	site
adhere	consecutive	emerge	inflict	prevail	skeptical
adverse	consequence	encounter	ingenious	procrastinate	sophisticated
advocate	conservative	endeavor	inhibit	profound	stereotype
affirm	conspicuous4	endorse	initiate	prolong	stimulate
affluent	contempt	equate	innate	prominent	strategy
agenda	contrary	erode	integrity	propaganda	submit
alienate	controversy	erratic	intervene	propel	subside
alleged	convey	essence	isolate	prospects	subtle
allude	data	evasive	lament	provoke	summon
alter	deceptive	evolve	legitimate	prudent	superficial
alternative	deduction	exempt	lenient	query	supplement
ample	defect	exile	lethal	radical	surpass
anecdote	defer	exotic	liable	rational	susceptible
anonymous	defy	extensive	liberal	recede	sustain
antidote	delete	fallacy	literally	recipient	tactic
apathy	delusion	fictitious	lure	reciprocate	tedious
apprehensive	denounce	finite	malicious	recur	tentative
appropriate	derive	fluent	mania	refrain	theoretical
arrogant	destiny	forfeit	mediocre	refuge	transaction
ascend	detain	fortify	menace	refute	transition
assess	deter	frugal	miserly	reinforce	transmit
audible	deteriorate	futile	moderate	relevant	treacherous
avert	devise	gesture	morale	reminisce	trivial
awe	dialog	gruesome	morbid	remorse	undermine
bestow	dimensions	gullible	naive	reprimand	unique
bland	diminish	harass	nostalgia	restrain	universal
blunt	disclose	hypocrite	notable	retain	urban
candid	discriminate	idealistic	novice	retort	valid
chronic	dismal	illuminate	obsession	retrieve	verify
chronological	dismay	illusion	obstacle	revert	versatile
cite	dispense	immunity	obstinate	revoke	vigorous
coerce	disperse	impact	optimist	ridicule	vital
coherent	distort	impair	option	ritual	vivid
comparable	diversity	impartial	ordeal	ruthless	vocation
compatible	doctrine	imply	overt	sadistic	
compel	dogmatic	impose	parallel	savor	
compensate	dominant	impulsive	passive	scapegoat	
competent	donor	indifferent	patron	seclusion	

List of the 40 Word Parts

-able	dis-	-less	multi-	script, scrib	trans-
anti-	em-, en-	-logy, -ology	ped	-ship	tri-
auto-	ex-	mal-	phon, phono	spect	un-
bi-	-ful	man	port	sub-	uni-
cent-, centi-	graph, gram	mem	post-	super-	vis, vid
con-	in-	micro-	pre-	tele-	
dict	inter-	mono-, mon-	re-	therm-, thermo-	

Words and Word Parts in IMPROVING VOCABULARY SKILLS

List of the 260 Vocabulary Words

absolve	congenial	eccentric	immaculate	muted	revulsion
abstain	consensus	elation	impasse	niche	rigor
acclaim	constitute	elicit	implausible	nocturnal	rupture
adamant	constrict	empathy	implication	nominal	sabotage
adjacent	contemplate	encounter	implicit	nullify	sanctuary
affiliate	contemporary	endow	implore	nurture	saturate
agnostic	contend	engross	improvise	obscure	scrutiny
alleviate	contrive	enhance	incentive	obsolete	secular
allusion	conventional	enigma	inclination	ominous	shun
aloof	conversely	epitome	incoherent	orient	sibling
altruistic	covert	escalate	incorporate	pacify	simulate
ambivalent	credible	esteem	indispensable	paradox	sinister
amiable	cryptic	euphemism	inequity	pathetic	smug
amoral	cursory	evoke	infamous	perception	sneer
animosity	curt	exemplify	infirmity	persevere	sparse
antagonist	curtail	exhaustive	infringe	plagiarism	speculate,
appease	cynic	explicit	infuriate	poignant	squander
arbitrary	decipher	exploit	inhibition	ponder	subjective
aspire	default	expulsion	innovation	pragmatic	subsequent
assail	deficient	extrovert	intercede	precedent	succinct
attest	deficit	facade	interim	predominant	succumb
attribute	degenerate	fallible	intermittent	prerequisite	suffice
augment	demise	falter	intimidate	pretentious	syndrome
averse	demoralize	feasible	intricate	prevalent	taint
avid	depict	feign	intrinsic	prompt	tangible
banal	deplete	fiscal	introvert	prone	terminate
benefactor	designate	flagrant	irate	proponent	transcend
benevolent	deter	flaunt	ironic	pseudonym	transient
benign	detract	flippant	jeopardize	punitive	traumatic
bizarre	detrimental	fluctuate	latent	qualm	turmoil
blase	devastate	formulate	legacy	quest	venture
blatant	deviate	frenzy	libel	rapport	viable
blight	devoid	furtive	longevity	rationale	vile
calamity	digress	gape	lucrative	recession	vindictive
charisma	dilemma	garble	magnitude	reconcile	virile
commemorate	diligent	gaunt	malign	redundant	vivacious
complacent	discern	genial	mandatory	rehabilitate	vulnerable
comprehensive	disdain	gist	mediate	relentless	waive
comprise	dispatch	glib	menial	render	wary
concurrent	dispel	gloat	mercenary	repertoire	zeal
condescend	dissent	habitat	methodical	reprisal	
condone	diversion	hamper	mobile	retaliate	
conducive	divulge	haughty	mortify	retort	
confiscate	dwindle	hypothetical	mundane	revitalize	

List of the 40 Word Parts

ann, enn	cor, cour	forc, fort	il-, im-	pater, patri-	quart, quadr-
aster-, astro-	cycl, cyclo-	-fy	-ish	path, -pathy	rect
-ate	di-, du-	-gamy	-ly	pend	semi-
audi, audio-	-dom	geo-	magni-, magn-	phob	the, theo-
bio-	-er, -or	-hood	mis-	pop	-ward
claim, clam	fin	hum	non-	pro-	
contra-	flex, flect	hyper-	omni-	psych-, psycho	

Words and Word Parts in ADVANCING VOCABULARY SKILLS

List of the 260 Vocabulary Words

abrasive	depreciate	fastidious	interrogate	precipitate	spontaneous
adept	deprivation	flamboyant	intuition	predisposed	sporadic
admonish	deride	flout	inundate	preposterous	squander
adroit	derogatory	foible	irreparable	presumptuous	squelch
advocate	despondent	forestall	irrevocable	proficient	standardize
ambiguous	detriment	fortuitous	jurisdiction	prognosis	staunch
analogy	dexterous	fraudulent	juxtapose	proliferation	stigma
annihilate	diabolic	germane	lethargy	prolific	stint
antipathy	dilapidated	gregarious	liability	promiscuous	stringent
antithesis	discreet	grievous	liaison	propensity	subordinate
assimilate	discretion	grotesque	lucid	provocative	subsidize
attrition	disparity	heinous	macabre	quandary	subversive
atrophy	disseminate	hierarchy	magnanimous	rancor	superfluous
auspicious	dissident	hoist	mandate	raucous	symmetrical
austere	dissipate	holistic	masochist	rebuke	synchronize
autonomy	distraught	homogeneous	maudlin	recourse	tantamount
belligerent	diverge	idiosyncrasy	mesmerize	recrimination	tenacious
berate	docile	illicit	metamorphosis	redeem	tenet
bolster	dormant	imminent	meticulous	regress	tenuous
bureaucratic	egocentric	impeccable	misconstrue	reinstate	terse
charlatan	emanate	impede	mitigate	reiterate	transgress
chide	emancipate	impending	nebulous	rejuvenate	travesty
circumvent	embellish	imperative	nonchalant	relegate	tumult
clandestine	emulate	impetuous	notorious	relinquish	turbulent
coalition	encompass	implement	noxious	replete	ubiquitous
cohesive	entrepreneur	implicit	objective	reprehensible	unassuming
collaborate	equivocate	impromptu	oblivious	repudiate	unilateral
commensurate	eradicate	inadvertent	obsequious	repugnant	unprecedented
complement	esoteric	inane	obtrusive	resilient	utilitarian
connoisseur	espouse	incapacitate	omnipotent	reticent	utopia
connotation	estrange	inclusive	opportune	retribution	validate
conspiracy	euphoric	incongruous	optimum	retrospect	vehement
constituent	exacerbate	indigenous	orthodox	robust	venerate
contend	exhilaration	indiscriminate	ostentatious	rudimentary	verbose
contingency	exhort	indolent	ostracize	sanction	vicarious
contrite	exonerate	infallible	panacea	scenario	vindicate
corroborate	exorbitant	inherent	paramount	scoff	vociferous
criterion	expedite	innocuous	perfunctory	scrupulous	yen
culmination	extenuating	innuendo	permeate	sedentary	zealot
cursory	extricate	inquisitive	pinnacle	sensory	zenith
decorum	fabricate	insidious	placebo	sham	
demeanor	facetious	insinuate	platitude	solace	
denunciation	facilitate	instigate	plight	solicitous	
deplore	facsimile	integral	precarious	sordid	

List of the 40 Word Parts

a-, an-	-cian, -ian	-en	-log, -logue	phil, -phile	ten
anima	-cide	extra-	miss, mit	poly-	ver
ante-, anti-	de	fid	mort	prim, prime	vit, viv
arch, -archy,	dec-	homo-	nov	rect	voc, vok
ben-, bene-	dorm	-ism	oct-, octo-	sur-	vol
bibl-, biblio-	duct, duc	ject	-ous	sym-, syn-	
chron, chrono-	-ee	liber, liver	pan-	tempo, tempor	